The Girl from Glengarry

(Ralph Connor)

CHAPTER I

The Ottawa, tawny and turbulent with spring freshets, rolled majestic, full bank to bank, and flooding the flats, marooning the great elms which stood guard over a little old solidly built log cabin. From across the river upon a curving line of hills the sunset fell in a glow of purple and gold. High upon a cut bank, jutting over the backwater of the overflow, a girl stood outlined against the purple of the hills, slender, lithe, exquisitely formed with soft girlish curves, yet firmly erect upon shapely legs, whose beautiful contours the playful wind clearly revealed. The sunlight turned the little curls of bobbed hair into a tangle of red gold, a striking foil to the transparent clarity of her skin. The face beautifully modelled into lines of strength and tenderness was gloriously lit up by eyes that seemed to catch the flying color from the bunch of blue wood violets at her breast, the same blue, with darker iris rims. A picture of rare loveliness she stood, strength, high courage in her pose, and in her eyes the lure and witchery that is supposed to make men mad.

"Good boy, Paddy! Stick to it old chap." The voice rang out clear and vibrant.

The girl was encouraging a yearling Irish setter pup in a struggle to land a branch of a tree from the river. Cheered on by his mistress the pup pulled and hauled, growling savagely the while, and finally landed the booty.

"Good old boy! Not afraid of water, eh? Fine! Time for home Paddy. Come along."

Paddy frisked and gambolled in a state of high triumph, and ended by leaping up at the girl with his paws on her frock.

"Down Paddy, you beast!" she cried, bringing her leash sharply down upon his nose. The answering howl brought swift penitence.

"Oh Paddy darling! So sorry!" Her arms went round Paddy now wriggling ecstatically his forgiveness. "You have made a mess of me, Paddy, but no matter. Come along! Away you go. I'll race you to the fence."

Like the wind Paddy was away, and like the wind his mistress was after him arriving at the fence in a dead heat.

The fence was an old-fashioned structure of cedar logs built end to end with a cap rail on top. A quick scramble and the girl was over, leaving the puppy behind.

"Ha ha! Fooled you there, Paddy. Come on! Find your own way out. Oh, you great baby!" she cried, taunting him as he began to whine. "Come along till you find a hole," she said setting off up the muddy road, while Paddy whimpering kept leaping at the fence in vain efforts to make exit from the field.

"Oh come on baby!" cried the girl, running along the road. "There are plenty of holes. Don't be a whining quitter." The square little chin carried high was sufficient indication that its owner was no quitter. At length a hole was found and the pup came dashing after his mistress.

Down the road meeting them came a flock of sheep in charge of a supernaturally wise and patient collie. Paddy dashed forward with a joyous bark.

"Paddy! heel sir!" The voice of the girl carried quite unmistakable authority.

Paddy paused, looked back at his mistress and again at the sheep now huddling and backing, held together only by the steady, resolute shepherding of the collie.

Paddy came back slowly and reluctantly.

"Bad dog! 'ware sheep!" said the girl. Catching him by the collar she began cuffing his ears, repeating with emphasis at each cuff, "No, No! 'ware sheep!"

Drawing him close to the fence she held the pup on the leash but loosely, controlling him by word only.

Shivering with excitement, the pup stood trembling as the sheep, with ears pricked forward, sidled past slowly and carefully at first, then at last with a rush. That rush proved altogether too alluring for Paddy's self-control. With a quick spring he dashed for the sheep. The leash was long in the line. Two long jumps the girl allowed him, but at the third and in mid air, with a sharp "No no! 'ware sheep," the girl threw her weight on the line. With a yelp the pup came back in a complete somersault, lay sprawling, then crawled to his mistress's feet.

"Bad dog!" she said sternly, "'ware sheep!" Again she cuffed his ears while he lay belly flat to the ground.

"Ay! Miss Sylvia. It may save him a hanging some day."

"Yes indeed. Besides he must learn obedience. I won't have a dog that doesn't obey me." Two red spots burned in her cheeks.

"It's a guid rule for dowgs, aye an' for men as weel, and indeed it might be for lassies as weel. Wha kens?"

The stern young face softened; the girl smiled a little strained smile.

"You have me there, Mr. Brodie, I guess. But all the same Paddy must obey me," she said looking down at the pup, who was still grovelling abjectly at her feet. "Look at your Heather Bell there, heeding us not a bit, but strictly attending to her duty."

"Aye, she's a canny lassie, but like all lassies she has her times," said Mr. Brodie, gravely shaking his head, "she needs patience."

"Lassies patience? What about the laddies?"

"Aye, they require patience as well, but with a difference. They are slower to learn but surer to bide."

"Surer to bide? You mean they are more dependable?"

"Na na--hardly that--na na not that exactly. Dependable? Na na the lassies are dependable. Yon collie now ye can trust till the deith. But in her there is a wee something incomprehensible. She has her moods and requires patience and understanding."

"Are we all like that? All girls?"

"Ye are as God made ye. An' na mere man can get tae the secret hairt o' ye. Na na, ye need patience and understanding."

"How did you train Heather Bell then? Didn't you have to punish her at times?"

"Aye, I did and sorely, till I maist ruined her entirely. I cam' near to breakin' her, the puir lassie. And a broken dowg is a useless dowg for the sheep."

"And how then did you train her?"

"I made her prood to serve me."

"And now she never fails to obey?"

"Hoots lassie! She has her moods, but less and less."

"And when in her moods?"

"I jist leave her be. I feed her a' the dainty bits, but I give her neither word nor look till she's like tae grieve the very hairt oot o' her."

"Oh Mr. Brodie! But what a terrible thing to do."

"Aye it is. And it's hardest on masel', but we both learn oor lesson by it."

"Did I jerk Paddy too hard?"

"It's no the jerk."

"What then?"

"It's the way ye dae it. It's the same wi' all admeenistration o' justice, human and divine."

"You are too deep for me, Mr. Brodie. I'm only an ignorant girl."

"No that ignorant, lassie, not you. But ye'll heed an auld man that has learnt his lesson by long and sair experience. Will ye forgive me? Justice is a terrible thing, a cold and terrible thing without passion--but maist terrible when administered by love. That's where our law makers and oor law administrators fail us. They rage at criminals. There is nae rage in justice, human or divine. It is inevitable as the march o' the seasons, but like the seasons it is administered by love."

"Poor Paddy," said the girl, stooping to pat the pup still crouching at her feet.

"Na na!" interrupted Mr. Brodie quickly. "Now ye've spoiled it 'a, let him dree his weird."

"What do you mean?"

"Let him suffer oot his punishment. He was wrong. But he would learn better if his punishment came with terrible coldness."

"Oh dear! I shall have to send him to you Mr. Brodie," said the girl in a voice of despair.

"Na na lassie. He's your dowg and your responsibility. An' dootless he'll teach ye as muckle as ye teach him. Guid nicht. It's a lang lang task, but it's worth while." He took off his hat, and with the bow of a great gentleman went his way.

The shadows were lengthening over the fields. The light was still clear in the west, but along the fences it had faded into a soft purple. The girl unsnapped the leash from her pup.

"Paddy dear," she said putting her arms suddenly round his neck, "I'm afraid I shall never be able to train you. It is indeed a terrible business. I love you too much--and yet--and yet--well not just now Paddy darlin'. We will just skip home."

The pup released from her embrace dashed madly about her, now grovelling at her feet, then leaping upon her in the ecstasy of his return to favor.

"Now for a race, Paddy," cried the girl and together they dashed up the road to meet the main Montreal-Ottawa highway, along which the flaming lights of racing motors could be seen.

"Now Paddy, we take no chances here boy. Come back Paddy!"

At that instant from a fence corner under Paddy's very nose jumped a tall Leghorn rooster, and dashed for the highway. The challenge was too direct to be borne. Away went Paddy hot foot on the Leghorn's trail, pointing fair across the highway.

"Paddy come back!" screamed the girl as she saw a north bound car bearing down upon the fleeing rooster. But both bird and dog unconscious of anything but escape and pursuit dashed out upon the road fair in the motor's track with Sylvia in frantic chase.

There was a wild cry, a screeching of brakes as the car came to a halt. A south bound car at high speed, however, suddenly appeared from nowhere. Again there was a wild cry, a screeching of brakes and an agonized yelp. The south bound car swervingly, swiftly went crashing through the paling on to a level sward and came to rest.

From this car a young man hurled himself headlong, scrambled to his feet and rushed on to the road toward the girl sitting there in the dust, dazed and shaken.

"Oh, my God! are you hurt?" cried the young man, lifting her bodily out of the dust and setting her on the grass.

"Oh no, no!" she cried brokenly. "My dog! my puppy!"

"Dog," said the boy. "Thank the good Lord, I thought I had got you!"

The girl staggered to her feet, gazed about her, then ran back up the road where in the dust lay a squirming, shuddering mass that once was her Paddy. Down in the bloody dust she flung herself with a moaning cry.

"Oh Paddy! Darling Paddy. Has he killed you? Oh my dear, my dear!"

The wounded pup lifted its head and turned to lick the girl's hand, whining the while, but not with pain.

"Let me look at him," said the young man. "I know about dogs."

He ran his hands over the limbs, up and down the spine and lifted the legs.

"Say, let me get him to a drug store," he said. He ran to his car and returned with a rug, beautiful and costly. Carefully he rolled the pup in the rug, carried him to the car, and laid him gently on the back seat.

"Get in!" he ordered.

Dazed and shattered in nerve she obeyed. In a few minutes he drew up at the red lamp of a drug store. Into the store he bore the moaning whimpering dog, and carried him straight through to the back shop.

"Hey, what's the game?" said the clerk.

"Here, get me chloroform, and keep the girl out. Get a move on!"

He had a way of getting his orders obeyed.

In a few minutes he called the clerk into the back room.

"Get something for the young lady--something to tone her up, two glasses. And say! Don't fuss--and get a move on. Your chief knows me. Bring the stuff here."

The clerk carried out his orders with swift efficiency.

The young man came out into the front shop carrying two glasses.

"Drink this," he ordered. "We both need it."

Without hesitation the girl obeyed, then turned her blue eyes upon him.

"Paddy?" she whispered.

"No more pain for Paddy," said the young man taking her hand in both of his.

"He is--"

"His back was broken, poor chap. He suffered not at all. Just slept off. Shall I-- do you want me to--"

"I want him taken home," she said quietly.

"Right oh. Will you get in please." He took her arm, led her to the car and placed her in the front seat. "Steady there now," he said. "Back in a minute or two."

"Some water, a towel and basin, and move lively."

The clerk impressed by his manner, his dress and by the magnificence of his car lost no time in question or remark.

With capable, swift moving hands the young man cleansed the beautiful golden hair of the setter from mud and blood, handed the clerk a five dollar bill, rolled the body in the rug and carried it out to the car.

"Which way?" he asked.

The girl without a word waved her hand to the right, and the car moved on in the direction indicated.

The driver glanced at her face. A little color was showing in the transparent cheeks. The blue eyes had lost their dazed stare.

"Say! You're a brick!" said the young man. "No use making excuses and lamentations just now. I feel pretty rotten of course about your puppy. Hope you give that full weight."

"Yes!" she whispered. "Oh yes! You didn't see! It was my fault. Should have had him on the leash. I was right after him, when he saw the bird--and--oh I couldn't get him!"

"My soul! I thought I had got you! Lord! what a moment! I shall see that whole business in my dreams! Thank the good Lord! If I had hurt you I should never have got over it! Never!"

"Up the hill to the right, the house among the trees there."

"Say, who is at home? Any man?"

"No. Only my aunt!"

"That's bad. Is she--I mean--How will she take it? Say! Let's drive round and talk about it. I mean, what shall I do with Paddy-- that's his name, eh?"

They drove on past the gate, round a block and again on to the highway. Soon they approached the entrance to the side road.

"Let us go down here," said the girl.

Promptly the young man swung the car into the narrow mud road and without a word they rolled smoothly down the slight incline toward the river. By this time the afterglow only was left in the western sky. Over the rolling river a faint haze of purple lay like a shimmering mantle, against the sky stood the elm trees and maples with their tender young leaves, and in stiff serried ranks the dark tall pines and the straight cone-shaped cedars.

As they neared the out-jutting cut bank the girl touched his arm.

"It was here we were--an hour ago," she said.

The car came to a stand. The young man sat looking quietly at the scene before him.

"Mighty fine, eh? You love this spot?"

"Yes, we come here in the summer. Can you see the cabin out there in the water under the elms? Father built that forty years ago."

"Forty years ago!"

"He was just a boy. He lumbered all these hills."

"Lumbered?"

"Yes, he brought mother here from Glengarry when I was a wee girl, so I am a Glengarry girl and very proud of it. Later he cleared the pine forest off--built the old mill--and later the factory."

"By Jove! How splendid! How magnificently splendid! And this was all forest?"

"Yes, all those hills across there--and on this side too. They floated the smaller logs down the river to the mill in booms."

"Booms? I'm a poor ignorant city bum!"

"Yes, the smaller logs they just enclosed in logs bound together with chains and floated them to the old mill. But the great logs were made into square lumber and there were built into great rafts and floated down to Quebec for the European market. Britain used to get her ship's timber from here."

"My soul and body, what a life! What a game! And they just let them go off down the river."

"No, no! They lived on the rafts for weeks. Sometimes built a little cabin on them."

"What a life! And you come here in summer?"

"Yes, we camp in that cabin there. It is quite comfortable."

"Comfortable? I should say! What a glorious camp! By Jove--I say! I mean what a time you must have! What do you do?"

"Oh, we are very lazy. Canoe, swim, the boys fish a bit--and play tennis!"

"The boys?"

"Yes, our working boys--and--and their friends."

"Lucky beggars!"

For some moments they sat silent, their eyes upon the darkening hills across the river.

Then the young man said quietly:

"Say! About Paddy?"

"Yes, we must--"

"I was thinking. Is this your place? This point I mean?"

"Yes all down to the river."

"Well--wouldn't this be a great place for Paddy?"

"I--I was thinking of the garden."

"The garden? Well--but--out here--under the trees--no digging and fussing with planting things--all by himself out here?"

The girl sat for a few minutes thinking.

"Yes, you are right," she said slowly. "I think this is the very spot. We can get the--a spade from Sandy Brodie. He lives just a mile down the road. Yes this is the very spot! And Paddy just adored coming here!" The tears were dropping quietly down her cheeks, but she made no sound of weeping.

On the side hill, in clean yellow sand, in the midst of the scents and sounds that once used to drive him frantic with delight, Sandy and the young man laid Paddy away.

"Ay, it's a couthie corner for a huntin' dowg with the wild things a' aboot him."

They took Sandy home and drove slowly up the road again along the river. As they reached the turn at the cut bank the girl caught the young man's arm with a quick little gasp.

"Look!"

Across the river and resting on the blue line of hills the moon, full orbed and golden, was appearing.

"I say! What a moon! Can't we wait a bit? I'm not strong on moons--but a moon like that on a mountain? Eh what?"

"Lovely, oh lovely," breathed the girl. "Yes it is very lovely.

"Never saw anything like this in my life," said the young man looking at her. "But we really can't see it in the car. Let's get out where we can--can see--I mean--all round you know--everything. Eh what?"

"But we can't stay, my aunt will--"

"Do you never stay out in the moonlight?"

"Oh yes often, I love it."

"Huh! Well, why not now?"

"But--why? I don't even know your name."

"That's easy. How would Jack do?"

"You look like Jack," she said with a little smile, her first that evening.

"Oh you are a brick--and you?"

"Sylvia is my name."

"Just right. Jove! Sylvia! Perfect--'Who is Sylvia?' Of course Sylvia it must be. And in the moonlight too."

"But we must go now--Jack--" she said gently.

"Do you want to go--Sylvia? I mean--just right away?"

"I think we must go. Yes--we must go."

"Right you are." He threw in the clutch. "Whatever you say is right. Will always be right." The car began to move slowly. "And that's the very place for Paddy too. What did the old boy--Sandy say? About a hunting dog, I mean?"

"'A couthie corner for a huntin' dowg with the wild things a' aboot him,'" quoted Sylvia softly.

"Say, isn't that perfect?"

"Yes--oh Paddy darling, I hate to leave you but it is just the place for you," the girl's voice broke.

"For me, Sylvia, I only say with all my heart and soul, thank the good God," said Jack, his voice husky with emotion.

"Why? what do you?--what are you saying?"

"Oh Sylvia! It might have been you. I just had a gleam of you. Just a fraction of a second! Oh, my God! What would have come to me?"

They drove on in silence.

"Yes! The angels sure were there!" said Jack as if to himself.

Ten minutes later they drew up at the house.

"I can't ask you in to meet my aunt, she is out to-night."

"I don't want to come in, not to-night. You don't want me--not to- night-- perhaps to-morrow eh? What?"

"Yes--oh yes, to-morrow--Jack."

Soundlessly the car moved off round the drive and out of the gate. The girl stood watching. A hand waved at her. An answering wave and he was gone.

"Oh! I don't even know his name! Well, I needn't tell Auntie to- night, poor dear, she would be full of questions."

CHAPTER II

Breakfast was over at Hilltop House. Miss Elizabeth was digesting slowly and with a disturbed face Sylvia's account of the passing of Paddy. The registration of grief was sufficient, but no more. There was, however, an understratum of keen interest and inquiry.

"And what was he like? I mean did he seem a gentleman?"

"A gentleman? He was very kind, and very capable. He knew just what to do. And he was very quick--and--he seemed very nice." Her niece finished rather lamely.

"Good looking?"

"Oh, I don't know. Of course I was thinking of Paddy--at first. Yes he was rather good looking--I think--I mean--His eyes were kind of twinkling--you know--and dark--and he had a strong face--a kind of hard face."

"Hard?"

"Yes, but kind too. He was awfully sorry for Paddy, and--of course it got kind of dark you know. He might be pretty stern--but his voice was kind."

"What did you say his name was?"

"Jack--I--I really was so excited and worried--"

"But my dear--you don't mean--you surely didn't call him Jack."

"Why of course I did."

"You know his last name, I hope."

"Well, I wasn't thinking about names. I was thinking about Paddy-- and--"

"And I suppose he was so occupied with Paddy that he called you Sylvia?"

"Why--of course--I told him--"

"You told him to call you by your first name? Well I must say--"

"No no! We never thought anything about names--we just--I mean--oh you know what I mean."

"Can't say I do exactly. Well--it is over and done with. Of course in these days young people are so very daring and--well, well--never mind. It is over. And he was very kind. Of course he might well be. He nearly killed you." Miss Elizabeth's lips were shut in a firm line.

"He took a chance of killing himself. He just skinned a tree, and he crashed through a fence."

"No need for any heat my dear. I am very very thankful. My dear I am thankful to God for your escape. When I think--" Miss Elizabeth's voice came to an abrupt stop. "We ought to thank God, my dear."

"I do--I do--and I thank Mr.--Jack too. He really was splendid about Paddy, I mean, and very, very sympathetic."

"Um! No doubt! If he had been driving a little more carefully. These young men race along through towns at a most reckless breakneck speed. I really think they ought to be punished. I would jail every one of them. Horribly selfish I call it."

"But Aunt Elizabeth you don't know if he was driving at a breakneck speed. It was my fault. I lost my head. I just dashed after poor Paddy past one motor and there I was in front of Jack's. I just had strength and sense enough to fling myself headlong to one side. I think his guard caught my skirt."

"Well, well my dear. Let's not talk about it. When I think--What is it Annette?"

"A gentleman in a motor asking for Miss Sylvia, miss!"

Sylvia leaped to her feet.

"Oh I wonder--I believe it's--"

"Sylvia! Sit down Sylvia. Annette will--" But Sylvia was gone.

"Oh hello! Are you--" It was a man's voice clear, strong, vibrant, suddenly subdued into softer tones.

"It is that man. Annette never mind the dishes. Show him into the morning room. Not in here."

Meantime Sylvia had run out to the front door. Had she known the lively eagerness in her face, she might have waited for Annette.

"Oh Jack--come in here." She ushered him quickly into the morning room. "And for Heaven's sake what is your name?"

"Name? Jack of course."

"No, no, your last name. Quick, she's coming."

"Didn't I tell you?"

"No, no, oh do hurry. Here she is."

Jack turned swiftly to Miss Elizabeth.

"Awfully sorry to disturb you so early. I'm Jack Tempest of Montreal. Last night--I had--"

"Oh Mr. Tempest, I've heard all about your kindness to my niece."

"My kindness! Great Scott, Miss Murray! I was awake half the night thinking-- well, no matter what--but--"

"We are all very thankful, Mr. Tempest--very thankful." Miss Elizabeth's voice was very grave and very gentle. "Those motors are very dangerous, and go at such a pace!"

"They do, but as a matter of fact I was going quite slowly-- otherwise--" He stopped suddenly, turned away and looked out of the window. "But I came to show you something, Miss Sylvia. May I run and get it?"

He dashed out of the house, and returning in a few moments carrying in his arms a six months' old puppy, set him on the floor.

"He's an Airedale," he said with a note of pride in his voice.

A silence fell on the room.

Miss Elizabeth gazed with eyes of disapproval upon the dog. She loathed all dogs. "You can't say he is beautiful anyway, Sylvia," she said.

The girl was looking with pale face and trembling lips at the puppy. Suddenly her hands went to her face: "Oh please forgive me," she sobbed. "I can't--I just can't!"

"What? Oh, I see! Great heavens! What an--an! What an infernal ass!" muttered Jack. "Please forgive me and forget all about it, Miss Sylvia." He caught up the puppy, ran out to his car, chucked it into the back seat, slipped to his wheel and drove away.

"Well, my dear! At least it was a very kind intention. I can't say I regret his taking the little creature away--but after all--"

"Oh Auntie, I could not bear any dog in Paddy's place. You don't understand!" The girl turned hurriedly away and then walked up slowly to her room.

"You are not going to the office this morning, my dear," called Aunt Elizabeth after her.

But in a few minutes Sylvia was down stairs again and dressed for the street.

"I am sorry dear," she said to her aunt. "It was stupid of me. I shall not be home for lunch."

"Oh, I wish you would just stay at home this morning after your shock and--and all."

"Oh, no, no, I would rather go down to the office. They are really very busy you know. Don't look at me like that. I am quite fit-- though I was a fool this morning."

"A fool? Well I wouldn't just say that, but he seems a very pleasant young man and--"

"Oh never mind him. He can take care of himself. And for that matter so can I."

"I'm not so sure," said her aunt as the door closed behind the girl. "I'm sure I don't know what the girls are coming to these days. 'Jack' and 'Sylvia' indeed! With half-an-hour's acquaintance. Well, well, it is beyond me." On this despairing note Aunt Elizabeth took up the daily burden of her household duties. Her dead sister's child was to her as the light of her eyes, and a dear and loving niece, obedient and careful in all things. But she was of the modern world. For instance, after graduating from a perfectly trustworthy Ladies' College in Ottawa, with a year in Edinburgh added, she had insisted upon a Business College training, and six months ago had gone into the office of what had been her father's business. Vainly her Aunt had insisted that this was quite unnecessary. If she really wanted something to occupy her she might take a select number of pupils in music.

"I'm sure your father would prefer this for you. He certainly spent enough money on your musical education, and your diploma sufficiently attests your ability as a teacher--either vocal or instrumental."

"Music teacher! I love music too well to make money out of it. Not that I don't love business. James is quite pleased with my office work too. He often says I could manage the whole works."

"But it is so--well--common--not to say vulgar. I mean for a young lady, that is of your family. Not that I have any foolish snobbery of course."

But Sylvia with all her sweet gentleness had a core of steel in her make-up, and an office girl she became and loved it. So that was that.

It was not that her aunt had any foolish notions that there was anything degrading in office work. Nothing of the sort. But one must be reasonable in these matters. Whom for instance, would she ever meet in the office of the Riverside Mills. Working men, commercial travellers, managers of other mills occasionally. But Sylvia only laughed at her aunt's notions.

"After two or three years I will take a big holiday, do the grand tour and find me a man."

This was her Aunt's supreme anxiety. The modern girl was so very difficult.

"Find a man indeed! What kind of man, with the world full of so many undesirables."

"Now I quite liked that young man this morning," said Miss Murray to herself. "And there she--well, she has just flung him out of the door."

Sylvia meanwhile was on her way to the office, weighted with a sense of depression and failure. The depression, she explained to herself was the natural result of the loss of her beloved companion in many a delightful ramble along the river side, and through the woods, which everywhere still fringed the back lots of the farms along the highway. The sense of failure, however, was something rather different.

"He will think me terribly ungrateful," she said to herself. "And really it was thoughtful of him to bring that puppy. And last night he was splendid. He must be rather fine in his mind for it was his idea that Paddy should be buried in the cut bank among all the wild things. Of course he will think me a silly little mutt."

Haunted by these musings she made her way down the street. Everyone that met her halted her to offer sympathy for her loss with congratulations for her escape and laudations of the heroic conduct of the mysterious young man who had befriended her in need. She knew his name and that he was very nice and kind, but that was not much on which to build the romance which all her friends were so set upon weaving round the incident. Her way led her past the drug store where the young man had so very effectually proved his resourcefulness. She felt she ought to run in and thank the clerk who had so very promptly dealt with an emergency. As she neared the store she was startled by a sharp and very insistent barking. A glance at a car standing in front of the store revealed the Airedale puppy standing with his paws upon the sash of the open window, indignantly demanding attention and release. A swift glance revealed no owner in sight.

"Oh you darling," she cried, running to the window. "You are all alone, what a shame!"

The puppy accepted her endearments, at first with sober reserve, but very soon with frantic demonstrations of delight.

"He's an impatient little beggar, rather. Hungry I guess."

She swiftly turned, a warm color lighting her face.

"Hungry? What a shame!"

"You see we left Montreal rather early."

"Montreal? Must be hours ago!"

"Well he broke his fast about eight, I guess."

"And that's three hours ago. And he has had all that long ride. Oh, I am so sorry. It is all my fault."

She ran round to the other side and sprang into the seat.

"What? Where are--I mean--what's the game?" asked Jack, astonished.

"Breakfast, of course. Come along. Please don't wait. The poor little chap is just starving. It's a shame to treat a puppy so. They ought to be fed every two hours. How would you like to miss a meal like that?" Her indignation rather abashed the young man.

"Well--of course--I rather expected--I mean--"

"Oh! certainly! Rub it in. It is my fault of course. What are you waiting for? Get in."

"Sure thing. Whatever you say of course. Any way in particular? I thought you were on your way to the office."

"Office? What do you know about the office? Who told you about the office? You have been discussing me with the general public, I suppose. Spreading the rumor of my silly inhospitality, if there is such a word! What are you waiting for? Why don't you move?"

"Move? Of course. Let's move. Certainly. Ottawa? Montreal? The highway to Toronto is still open." The car was moving swiftly through the traffic.

"Right!" ordered Sylvia.

"Yes, my lady!"

"Up the hill!"

"Yes, my lady! May I ask where your ladyship--"

"Breakfast of course. Do you want the puppy's digestion ruined. Regular feeding is absolutely necessary. All the books and vets say so. He is just frantic with hunger. Poor little darling. Was he just starved to death?" Her arm was round the wriggling Airedale. "Everybody breakfast but you, fat lazy things."

"Fat! Fat? Say, where do you get that? I resent the suggestion of avoirdupois tissue in connection with you. On the contrary I have been most carefully observing the lithe sinuosity of your adorable form."

"Sinuosity? You think I'm an Amazon. Well, you are wrong. I weigh just--"

"I know. I am a judge of weights. I remember estimating you, if I remember rightly, at--"

"Stop it! I won't have you estimating my weight." Her face was a rosy flame. "Anyway I don't think it is exactly a nice thing to take a mean advantage of me when I couldn't help myself. But oh, Jack it was very dear of you. And I have been a perfect brute this morning. But you understand. I just couldn't let any dog take Paddy's place."

"Tut, tut my dear. I was an ass. A stupid confounded and unmitigated ass."

"You were not. You were just--I mean."

"Oh, go on, why did you stop?"

"Oh, I can't say it. I can't tell you--last night I kept thinking how awfully understanding you were. Thinking of everything. Especially that dear spot for Paddy to lie. Oh, that was so lovely of you!" The blue eyes were slightly misty.

"Please don't. You know--I mean go right on. I love to hear you. But--well last night. I spent hours laying you out carefully in your coffin--flowers--mourners--and everything!"

"Stop it! You are quite silly. And besides, here we are. What will Aunt Elizabeth say? I don't care, the pup must have his breakfast."

"May I say just a word?" said Jack with anxious gravity as they stopped at the door.

"Well it's just this. I've come to the conclusion that you are a perfect darling, and I want--"

"Hush!" she hissed, her face in a soft glow. "Here's Aunt Elizabeth. I think she rather approves of you."

"And her niece?" said Jack in a low anxious tone.

"Held in retentis?"

"Where? Who?"

"So Mr. Matheson our minister says. Here we are Aunt Elizabeth. Do you know this poor little pup has had no breakfast? And he is just perishing."

The girl gathered up the frantic puppy in her arms murmuring sweet endearments, and ran off to relieve his famine.

"Some dogs have all the luck," grumbled Jack looking after her.

CHAPTER III

"Sy-y-l-via!"

"Yes, Aunt Elizabeth."

"Can you wait to take a letter?"

"Ten minutes--only--you know I can't be late."

"Give me five."

"By the way, Auntie, did you write Jack about dinner to-morrow night. You were to let him know, you remember."

"Of course, don't disturb me. I am writing the closing sentences, and they are important."

"All right dear."

The letter which was being concluded was as follows:

Hilltop House, Riverside, May 17th, 1928.

My dear Arabella,

This letter you must answer at once. I am in a swither. I told you about Sylvia's accident--Paddy and the young man. Well this is about the young man. John Tempest is his name. He is hanging about Sylvia--nice enough--indeed fascinating and all that--has a wonderful car, abundance of time and money-- and is now devoting himself to my little girl. She is a sharp, clever girl in some ways--in some ways a silly child. No sense about young men. She treats them like chums, as if she were one of themselves. She has no sense of sex. Don't be shocked. You know what I mean, if any one does. Nothing crude or vulgar, but just plain human. She plays about with young men, or old men, as I say, as if she were one of themselves. All very fine, and wholesome and innocent, but well--you know--Then she has no sense of social values. You know I am no snob, but all this stuff about the equality of men I consider nonsense. And so do you.

What I want you to do is to find out all about this John Tempest-- his family-- his character--his prospects. I have only one girl, not of my flesh, though she might have been, as you know, if I hadn't been a stubborn fool. And she is not going to throw herself away on any man who has a handsome face and a clever tongue, but nothing else--not if her Aunt Elizabeth can help it.

Sylvia has no sense as to breeding and social standing. You ought to hear her with the butcher boy--a red-faced creature. She smiles at him and chatters away to him till the boy doesn't know whether he is standing on his heels or his head. Then she comes in perfectly radiant and says: "Isn't he just sweet!" I lose patience with her. She treats my washerwoman as if she were the banker's wife, indeed very much better. She doesn't hesitate to throw her arms round Maggie's neck and kiss her. Of course Maggie is a very nice woman, quite respectable and very clean and all that, but after all one doesn't kiss one's washwoman. You know what I mean. Of course they all adore her. The butcher boy gets the best cuts for her, and Maggie must spend hours over her frocks. She would gladly give her fingers, one by one, if she thought Sylvia would be the better for them.

I can see she is attracted by this young man. I don't want any heart-break for my little girl. I think he is getting quite mad about her, if I am any judge of signs. I used to be anyway. And after all, the years don't change the hearts of humans.

She is very young for her years. Thank God they keep young longer than we did. She is just twenty-one. Fancy when her mother was her age she had a baby a year old, and you had two of them. I wonder at the cheek of you and the courage.

But young as she is she is very much on her feet, awfully efficient in her work. James MacDonald, our foreman, a Glengarry MacDonald, (the Bhan not the Dhu MacDonalds, we are Glengarry folk you remember), said the other day: "She has the best business head in the bunch of us. She ought to be manager." And sweet as she is she has her father's disposition. He was a stubborn man; and her mother's too--the Murrays--were not much better, if any--as indeed I know to my cost. Ah me! If I had only been a little less stubborn, and he too-- well, it is not Sylvia's aunt I would be to- day. Twenty-two years ago! Well I have paid my price, and drop by drop! Though no one but you knows it.

But I want my little girl to make no mistake. So write as I tell you. I am trusting you. Indeed I have no one else to advise me, unless indeed the new minister, Mr. Matheson from Glasgow, a learned man, and a fine preacher too and obviously a gentleman. But I can hardly discuss my niece's love affairs with him. He is about my own age, and a bachelor. Now be quiet! I can hear you giggle. All the old maids and widows in the congregation are getting quite fidgetty about him--silly old things!

Now write me, my dear, by to-morrow's post. I am depending on you.

Your old friend,

LIZZIE MURRAY

P.S. Montreal, with its mountain and river must be grand these days, but you ought to see our River, with its hill sides just beginning to burst with the glory of spring.

P.S.S. What a long letter, you know me.

L.M.

Miss Arabella Foster did not fail her friend. Her answering letter caught the very next post. After various reminiscent excursions and sage advices, especially in reference to the new minister, the letter proceeded to deal with the main issue.

Now as to Jack Tempest, let me say right away that I am not to be trusted. The young devil is a friend of mine, and indeed of the whole family, especially the girls. In fact, he is my Tom's best friend--which may not be much to his credit, for Tom is a thorough scamp.

Jack graduated in engineering, and would have got his medal but for his pranks. Do you remember that terrible Convocation night when the whole business was broken up in confusion by the weird electric signs that would flash on and off during the speeches:

'Time's up.'

'Silly old ass.'

'Speak up, don't mutter.'

These were some of them. What a row! Well, it was Jack Tempest who was largely responsible. Do you remember his indignant protests against this disreputable conduct, standing up there in the audience looking like a grave senator. It was hugely funny. But yet I like Jack. He is no saint. But he is honest and straight--a wee thocht wild. He is an engineer, can take his car apart and put it together. Has an uncanny gift for machinery. The General Electric offered him a big job, but his father wanted him in his office. The old man is in bonds and stocks, making heaps of money, organizing companies and floating all sorts of concerns. An old pirate. They are all afraid of him in "The market." So Jack is a bond seller and loathes it. But as he says he operates chiefly on the golf course, and in the clubs. Now don't get panicky about him. If he wanted one of my girls to-morrow I would let him have her. But then I would see to it that he would quit fooling.

So there you are, my dear. Your Sylvia has her head screwed on the right way. Let the children play their own game. What's God for anyway?

How is the minister? It would be a shame if Miss Euphemia Straith would pick the plum right under your nose.

Yours affectionately,

ARABELLA F.

P.S. I'm coming out to see you and may take Sylvia back with me for a week-end.

It can hardly be said that Miss Foster's letter brought much comfort to Miss Elizabeth's heart. She glanced at the letter. "He's wild--'making heaps of money--bonds and stocks'--not much good ever came from that. Well, Mr. Jack Tempest, you can't have my little girl, if you're going to be wild. You'd break her dear, honest, sweet little heart. No. You'll have to kill me first, or make me kill you."

Her face looked old and grey.

"'Let the children play their own game'--But it's no game. It's life--and death--and hell may be. Oh God--'What's God for anyway?' Yes, she's right enough there." She fell on her knees, put her hands up high: "God, do you hear me? God, do anything you like to me, but my little girl! God! God! Don't let him hurt her." Again and again she moaned out her cry, till she heard Sylvia's voice downstairs calling her.

"Where are you, Auntie? We're here, and hungry as hawks."

"Oh hello! dearie! Just run into the kitchen and see if Annette is quite right. I shall be down in five minutes." She dashed to the bath-room, dabbed her eyes, rubbed her face gently.

"What a wreck I am!"

A little touch of color--of powder--a quick brush to her hair--and with a gallant lift to her head she came down to meet Jack.

"I must be nice to him," she said to herself resolutely.

It was a small dinner party, and very select for Miss Elizabeth was in no mood to preside at any party calling for any undue exercise of her wonted dignity and grace. She had in her mind a very definite purpose. She would find out for herself just what sort of a young man this was. Hence she had enlisted the aid of her minister, not for any advice he might give her, but because she knew his quite remarkable gift of meaningless, but quite entertaining conversation.

"Mr. Matheson, will you take my niece, please. Mr. Tempest, you will perhaps, put up with me," said Miss Elizabeth.

"I am greatly honored," said Jack, with his very best bow.

The dinner was very simple, but such as might delight the heart and satisfy the desires of hungry men, and withal was served in perfect style by Annette, looking very smart in her uniform of black and white.

Mr. Matheson more than justified the hopes of his hostess. He was evidently a man of wide reading, he was thoroughly en rapport with the topics of the day, and he had besides the rare gift of instinctively discerning the special theme most congenial to each of the guests in turn, and of leading the conversation to that topic. Beginning with her music, he soon discovered that Sylvia had no desire to discuss her newest songs. She had so little time for practice that she was thoroughly disgusted with her singing. She had forgotten all her teacher's instruction in voice production and playing, she had really quite given up her exercises.

"Yes, indeed she is very naughty," said her Aunt, "she really has quite a good voice, but she will not give the time she should to her practice. The radio is killing our real love of music."

"It really does take time and energy as well," said Mr. Matheson. "One does not keep up the voice to form without work, hard work. And Miss Sylvia's days are quite filled with all her varied activities."

"Such as they are," murmured Sylvia, with an apologetic grin, at Jack.

"Oh indeed she is no idler," said Miss Murray. "She is one of the busiest young ladies in this town."

"Ah! Indeed!" ejaculated Jack.

"Yes, indeed, what with her office, from which she practically administers the Riverside Mills Company," said the minister.

"Oh, Mr. Matheson!" Sylvia's blushes made violent protest.

"The Riverside Mills Company," repeated the minister with emphasis, "and her reading club, and her dramatics among the employees, not to speak of her Church activities."

"Ha ha! Church activities!" laughed Jack as if the minister had uttered a pleasantry.

"Church activities, my dear sir," repeated Mr. Matheson very gravely. "Why, my dear sir--"

"Oh Mr. Matheson, you make me ashamed. I often think I ought to give up my classes and clubs."

"Miss Sylvia--not another word," implored Mr. Matheson, "when you give up I shall at once resign. She has a quite remarkable Boys' Club you know Mr. Tempest--"

"Please Mr. Matheson! They are really a lot of the darlingest kids-- and they do all the work--I only just show--"

"Yes, that's all you do--just show them how to stop being young devils, and be young gentlemen. You ought to see that club Mr. Tempest!"

"I must indeed! Will you?" Jack began eagerly.

"No," said Sylvia, with abrupt decision.

"You really should, Mr. Tempest. You are interested in boys' work?" asked Miss Elizabeth.

"Oh--ah--sure! Tremendously!"

"Fine," said Miss Elizabeth. "Do you have a club or anything--"

"Ah--well--a club? Yes--That is, not exactly a Boys' Club--you know."

"Oh, I see," said Mr. Matheson, genially coming to his aid. "You probably run to athletics and that sort of thing."

"Exactly--athletics--of course--" said Jack gratefully accepting the minister's aid.

"The Montreal Athletic Association and, you know, the sort of thing," he continued. "Awfully interesting. Clean sport you know-- manly exercises--and--and--" Jack faltered a bit as to details.

"Exactly! Most important. Indeed I do think that it is one of the most hopeful indications of the general ethical trend of to-day."

"Tremendous thing you know, sir. Really the interest in clean sport in the city is--a--quite keen--and all that."

"Quite indeed," agreed Mr. Matheson. "And in these days when business life is carried on at such high tension, you know, young men require--"

"Exactly!" said Jack warmly. "You see, the competition is something fierce--really--the market is well--you have no idea--I assure you!"

"I hear only rumors, of course," smiled Mr. Matheson. "But I can imagine."

"You are an engineer, Mr. Tempest, I understand," said Miss Elizabeth.

"Engineer! Not on your--" exclaimed Jack, "I mean--not at all-- nothing so relaxing, I assure you."

"Oh, I understood you had taken a degree in engineering," Miss Elizabeth's blush indicated a sudden confusion.

"A degree--oh--who? I mean--Yes I did--at McGill."

"Did I mention that to you Miss Elizabeth?" said Mr. Matheson gallantly hastening to her relief.

"Mr. Tempest is in bonds and stocks, Auntie," said Sylvia quietly. "Tempest, Boyle, Price & Company, you know."

"Ah--of course--so many young fellows now-a-days switch courses, especially in this new and amazing trend toward the economic activities of life," said Mr.

Matheson, obviously seeking to be helpful. "Your father's firm?"

"Yes. Matter of fact, my Dad was quite keen on my going into the business. I can't say I liked the idea."

"You prefer engines, eh?" said Mr. Matheson. "I don't wonder. Not that bonds and stocks haven't their place in the modern economic world, indeed in these days apparently a very large place."

"Why Mr. Matheson do you understand stocks and that sort of thing?" asked Jack. "I confess I know nothing whatever about the Stock Market! Well you know--I mean a great many people seem to think that--what I mean is--don't you know?"

"Exactly so," said Mr. Matheson brightly, "stock gambling and that sort of thing. Wall Street--eh--old Vanderbilt, Fisk, Field, Gould that lot! Ha ha! Great old pirates those old boys--good deal like Captain Kidd and Morgan of the Spanish Main days. Fascinating stories--remember reading about them. But those days are gone, I suppose."

"Gone? My dear sir, don't you believe it. The present Wall Street operators would make old Commodore Vanderbilt, Drew, Field, Fisk and that lot look like kids playing marbles on Sunday for keeps." And for some minutes Jack enlarged, with a varied wealth of detail upon the lurid characteristics and eccentricities of the modern stock broker, with illustrations from real life, till Miss Elizabeth's eyes grew wide with horror.

"But the Montreal market Mr. Tempest is quite different, I suppose," said Mr. Matheson.

"Don't you believe it, sir. If our boys had the command of the little iron men--"

"Iron men?" gasped Miss Elizabeth, a dazed look in her eyes.

"Jack--Mr. Tempest is just being funny, Auntie," said Sylvia. "St. James Street is not at all like Wall Street."

"St. James Street? Well now! Let me tell you there are just as many--"

"But Mr. Tempest," said Mr. Matheson, pleasantly cheerful, but speaking with impressive deliberation, "there is a legitimate and perfectly honest and honorable business carried on in St. James Street. I mean--you know--by quite honest and honorable people."

"Honest and honorable? Oh--yes--oh most certainly!" replied Jack, hurriedly, casting a swift glance at Sylvia's face. "Stock broking is a straight enough business and--"

"And an absolutely necessary business, I mean necessary to our modern methods of industrial development," suggested Mr. Matheson.

"Why, of course! Most certainly!" said Jack.

"I am very ignorant Miss Elizabeth of the modern methods in stock broking--that is no practical knowledge, and to me it appears something like this." And for the next fifteen minutes Mr. Matheson proceeded to give in lucid simple and convincing terminology, a most complete, if somewhat rosy picture of the operations of the Stock Market, which made bond and stock selling take on the aspect of a truly noble and patriotic enterprise and one entirely necessary to the industrial development of the country.

As the minister proceeded with his lucid smiling discourse the faces of his audience gradually cleared. Miss Elizabeth's face lost its disturbed appearance, Sylvia's look of distressed anxiety gave place to one of pleased, but puzzled amazement, and Jack gradually recovered his air of debonair complacency. Mr. Matheson had rendered the company a fine bit of service. They were all correspondingly grateful.

"Mr. Matheson, may I ask where did you operate chiefly?" enquired Jack.

"Operate?"

"Yes, where did you play the market? In the old country? London, I guess. They tell me that's where they get the really high polish. Those old country birds are the real eagles."

"Have you the very slightest idea what the young man is referring to?" enquired Mr. Matheson of his partner.

"He wants to know where you learned about stock broking, and that sort of thing," said Sylvia, giving him a dazzling smile.

"Stock broking? I? My dear boy, I would not recognize a stock if I saw it on the street. Not I--But the rather painful experience of some of my friends in 1924-25 set me studying the whole economic basis of stock operations in England, on the continent and to a less degree of stock operations in America. I came to the conclusion then that the whole business of Stock manipulation is one of the very important businesses in the world, and in the hands of honorable and capable men can be of the very highest service to humanity."

Jack gasped at him.

"You really mean it?"

"Most certainly. Of course I am using the term 'stock manipulation' in a very wide and somewhat academic sense to include the general financing of the industrial and commercial operations of the world. For instance, had it not been for the magnificent services of the great American and British financiers and their courageous and wise handling of the various markets in Europe, as witness for instance the Dawes plan in 1924, the whole world would have been in complete and chaotic financial collapse. Of course, the whole matter was largely political, but the salvation of Europe was secured when the financiers took the whole business over from the politicians.

"Mr. Matheson," said Jack in solemn amazement. "I am a babe in arms playing with my bottle. I haven't a ghost of an idea of what you are talking about."

"But surely you remember that when under the burden of Reparations, that hideous legacy of hate handed to Germany by Versailles, the whole scheme of payment had broken down, the United States Secretary of State, Hughes, made the proposal to lift the whole business out of politics and make it a business proposition, you remember that?"

"Not a thing!" confessed Jack.

"Oh yes Jack, you remember the Dawes Committee."

"Well, I've heard of the Dawes Committee of course, and that they did something to get Germany out of the hole--but what they did--I haven't an earthly."

"And you a bonds and stocks broker!" exclaimed Mr. Matheson.

The minister's bland smile took the steel out of his thrust.

"Not that kind I'm afraid. I just push the stuff at the boys and indicate the dotted line, you know."

"You are young yet, my dear boy--but yours is a noble calling and--"

"Really? A calling Mr. Matheson? Like the ministry?" Miss Elizabeth was plainly startled, if not shocked.

"'Calling'--Miss Murray, a noble calling indeed. What is nobler than the organizing of a whole people for cooperative service in the building up of a nation's industry? That is what they did for Germany. Organized all the German railways into one great stock company--twenty-six billion gold marks. I remember the figures well, eleven billions mortgage bonds, two billions preferred stock, thirteen billions common stock. The figures stuck in my mind because of the thirteens--unlucky number, eh? Oh, it was a wonderful achievement. It was the Americans mainly who did that for the world."

"And the British," said Sylvia, her blue eyes shining.

"And the British," replied the minister. "Yes, the British did their part for the rehabilitation of Germany. But the job is not yet finished."

"Things seem to be humming just now all right," said Jack cheerfully.

"SEEM to be? Yes SEEM to be!" Mr. Matheson shook his head dubiously.

"But business is booming--at least in the United States and Canada too," Jack insisted.

"BOOMING? Yes but--Well, I know nothing about this country or America either."

"I wouldn't say that, sir," said Jack with obvious respect. "I believe you know a whole lot more than most of the hot air artists on the radio these days. You are like my Dad. He has no use for this boom. But the boys at the tape side are all for it. And believe me, they are making money."

"Everybody is making money," said Sylvia, with a little laugh. "Even the Riverside Mills girls. But James MacDonald is shaking his head, like Mr. Matheson."

"And a great many others are shaking their heads, Miss Sylvia. A great many wise folks in the old country. But of course they are rather old-fashioned."

"But everyone says Germany too is booming," said Jack, "I heard Mr. Black say so no later than yesterday."

"Yes," said Mr. Matheson, "but my weekly TIMES is calling attention to the fact that Germany is living on borrowed gold. About £750,000,000 imported during the last four years, largely from America."

"Say, you'd better come in and talk to my Dad. He would agree with you. But the younger chaps are all against him." Jack appeared to be lost in admiration for the minister.

"I assure you I know nothing about the finances of this country or America. We old country folk may be old-fashioned--'but I hae my doots.'"

"They are all certainly out for big business. I can't get the papers out fast enough for the new companies, new mergers, new combines," said Jack.

"Yes, I know. They even want to merge poor little us," said Sylvia, smiling at Jack.

"What Riverside Mills? What merger is that? Don't let 'em. You just let me merge you, if you are going to merge. I'll see that you get the best possible terms. Don't look at 'em."

"I'm not," said Sylvia cheerfully.

"Hurray!" cried Jack.

"Sound lassie," said Mr. Matheson. "But Miss Elizabeth, I must awa' tae ma kirk session. Please don't rise."

"But we are all finished, Mr. Matheson. So sorry you must go. Can't you come in later? These young folk need some sound advice."

"I'll say so," said Jack heartily. "Some of us, anyway." But the minister could not promise.

"Oh do!" Sylvia's blue eyes made him hesitate.

"Now lassie, nane o' that wi' yon glintin e'en. Ye're takin' a mean advantage of an auld haverin' buddie. But perhaps--for a cup o' coffee and a pipe, if the session prove unco' dreich--guid nicht!"

CHAPTER IV

After the minister had gone and they had adjourned to the drawing- room, Jack burst out with emphatic gestures.

"That man is a walking fraud."

"Fraud?" Sylvia exclaimed. "Why Jack?"

"A fraud? Mr. Tempest," cried Miss Elizabeth plainly shocked.

"Fraud! The most complete--Look at that sweet innocent cherubic face. It simply invites you to pour forth all the bombastic and bally-ass ignorance you are capable of, with the sure conviction that you can get away with it. And then, with a smile he proceeds to disgorge his expert stuff that makes one feel the bally ass he is."

"Mr. Matheson is an excellent man," said Miss Elizabeth.

"Excellent! I should say! Why he told me more about stocks and bonds in fifteen minutes than I have learned in St. James Street in the last two years. And all behind that baby face of his!"

"I was glad, very glad indeed Mr. Tempest, to hear him speak of stock gambling as a noble calling," said Aunt Elizabeth.

"He? ah--not exactly--I mean you know not exactly stock gambling, Miss Murray."

"But he did say a noble calling, Sylvia, did he not?"

"Yes, Auntie, stock buying and selling--not stock gambling."

"Oh well, I shall certainly ask him about that," said Miss Elizabeth.

"But Auntie, he will be tired talking about stocks and bonds and things like that."

"Will he, then? We'll see," said Aunt Elizabeth.

"By Jove," muttered Jack, who with Sylvia was turning over a book of prints. I'm seeing ghosts and things! Say, that cherub had me scared cold."

"Oh, he is just a dear. Wouldn't hurt a fly."

"Fly? Perhaps not--but what about a mosquito or a cockroach, as some of us bonds and stocks men are."

"So bad?"

"Worse! I want to tell you there are stocks being pushed to-day and sold up into the thousands that are three parts wind."

"You don't sell those, Jack?" Sylvia's blue eyes were searching his face.

"Say, what about a little vocal exercise?" said Jack. "I hate to think of the dollars and dollars invested in your vocal chords bringing no return. It's a sinful waste!"

"Sing a little, Sylvia dear," said her Aunt.

Sylvia sang after much protestation some old songs, with Jack turning her music and making selection of his favorites. Sylvia's was no great voice, but her instructors had obviously been sound in taste and in technique, so that in her choice of songs, and in her style of singing, the result was altogether charming.

"Oh, here we are!" cried Jack. "This is a perfect gem. Will you do this?"

"Which one is that, Mr. Tempest?" enquired Miss Elizabeth, looking up from her solitaire.

"Oh this lovely old canzonet of Haydn's: 'My Mother Bids me Bind my Hair.'-- A really perfect song and just written for you."

"But I don't do the accompaniment," said Sylvia. "My teacher always played that for me."

"Couldn't I do it for you?" said Aunt Elizabeth, coming to the piano.

"Not without practice, darling," said Sylvia. "The accompaniment means so much and the voice and piano must go together quite perfectly."

"Quite right," said Jack with emphasis, "but I happen to know this-- used to play for a friend of mine. Try me out. You hum it while I run it over."

"I don't believe I could. You see it must be done exactly right, I mean--I--would likely spoil the rhythm and--"

But Jack was already at the piano, humming the air while from his fingers the exquisitely delicate accompaniment flowed like a rippling sunlit rivulet.

"Oh how lovely!" said Sylvia, humming with him.

"There, I'll try not to ruin it," said Jack.

"Oh, but you won't, I just feel we can do it," cried Sylvia, her lovely face eager with delight.

Not often is this exquisite, dainty creation of Haydn's rendered with the simplicity, the restraint, the perfect regard for rhythm which it demands. But such was the perfection of sympathetic harmony in expression, in rhythm between voice and piano, that when the song ended on its exquisitely delicate final notes "a-way," with the two pianissimo staccato concluding notes, Jack seized her hands in his and cried:

"Oh my dear! my dear! How lovely! How perfect!" And sat silent bending over the keys.

"And yet not quite perfect," he added. "I spoiled it a bit."

"No no, I never sang it so well!" insisted Sylvia.

"No! I really believe you can do it better. You know I dominated you. I was leading you. You see I didn't trust you utterly. I am afraid to ask you to do it again. And yet--and yet--I should love to try it. And let me suggest a touch or two, will you? See just here, on the words 'or creep' you must c-r-e-e-p a little more. But in the next verse, on the words, 'or dead', first time, a very short hold, second time longer--like this--" and he hummed over the phrases, "And those last broken, breathless words 'is--a-way--is a-way--' you understand. What do you think?"

"You are right, exactly right," cried Sylvia with enthusiasm. "Let me try--" She hummed the words.

"Perfect, oh just perfect!" said Jack. "Now listen to what I tell you," he added solemnly. "You forget all about me and my accompaniment. Put your heart into the girl's heart. Perhaps you don't want to try?"

"But I do! I want to!" cried the girl, her face pale, her eyes aglow.

"Well look at the words again. Think of, see, hear that lovely, lonely girl and her misunderstanding mother. And when you are ready let me know."

Sylvia took up the music and read slowly the quaint old-fashioned words, set the music quietly back upon the piano and stood waiting.

"Now for heaven's sake, forget the piano," Jack urged in a low voice.

"Go on," she said quietly, and from under his fingers the soft ripple of notes began to flow.

Jack's suggestions produced their full effect. The voice assumed command and held it throughout, the accompaniment sustaining, stressing, echoing but never dominating or intruding. The effect was altogether delightful. The gentle pathos, the poignantly sweet, heart-breaking appeal breathed, sobbed, whispered through the steady flowing stream of the girl's pure, clear tones, straight to the hearts of her hearers.

"Sylvia dear!" cried her Aunt coming to her. "What is it?"

The girl's eyes were full of unshed tears. She turned and looked at her aunt in dumb wonder.

"I--was--thinking--of the poor little girl," she said. Then after a moment of silence, "Oh I am just silly," she cried and turned away from the piano.

"Silly!" muttered Jack. "By Jove what art! Or is it art? And a voice too! What a voice! You'd draw blood from a stone! Oh, if they could only have heard you!"

"Who Jack?" asked the girl in surprise.

"Oh that gang of music butchers in the city, with their airs and their arts and graces. But could you do it again?"

"Perhaps, if you were playing, Jack," she replied simply. "And if I could see the poor little girl again."

"By Jove, I'd like to try it!" said Jack, as if to himself. "And yet I don't know. But I'll never forget this night. And now I'm away home."

"You will wait for coffee, Mr. Tempest," urged Aunt Elizabeth. "Mr. Matheson will be sure to be in very soon now."

"And more stocks and bonds. No, no, not for me--not to-night-- thank you, Miss Murray. Do please ask me again. I want to come."

"Oh, do come again," cried Sylvia in a quick warm voice.

Her Aunt cast a sharp glance at her niece's face and her lips drew close in a firm line.

"We are very simple people here, Mr. Tempest," she said with quiet dignity, "but we shall always be glad to see you. Of course, it is a long drive, and you must be--very fully occupied."

"Ask me," pleaded Jack. "Just ask me. But why could not Miss Sylvia--you and Miss Sylvia come to town some evening--say Saturday, and stay the week-end with us?" The young man's voice was seriously eager.

"What, Sunday?" exclaimed Miss Elizabeth.

"Not Sunday, Jack," said Sylvia. "You see I have my class."

"Your class?"

"Yes, my boys you know."

"Oh--oh yes--ah of course--they would certainly hate it I guess-- Well some other night."

"I'd love to," said Sylvia simply.

"Thank you Mr. Tempest. Some time--Yes--we--will see--later," said Miss Elizabeth, but only with careful enthusiasm.

Her niece looked at her in quick surprise. Something of the eager light died in her eyes, but she said no word. They accompanied their guest to the door and stood in the radiant glory of the May moon while he got his car going.

"And you won't forget that 'creep,' Miss Sylvia," he said leaning out through the window.

"Oh no no! never!" she cried, running out close to the car.

"Good night again," said Jack offering his hand. The girl took his hand in a warm firm grasp.

"Good-night, Jack!" she said softly.

"What a night!" he said looking up at the moon. "What a night!" he said again, looking into the lovely face so near him. "I shall never forget this night, Sylvia. Oh Sylvia, will you?"

Her hands went swiftly to her breast. "No--oh, no, no, Jack, I shall never forget," she whispered.

CHAPTER V

The office of the Riverside Mills, an old, log farm house, stood back from the main Montreal-Ottawa highway in what had once been an orchard. Only two or three old apple trees, now just breaking into bloom, remained flanking each side of the door. The approach had been laid out in a broad cement drive, with a border of flowers now peeping up through the black soil. The office stood on a slight rising ground which at the back sloped sharply down toward the noble, swiftly flowing Ottawa, at present tawny with the spring rains.

Up to the office door swept a quite impressive Cadillac from which stepped a big man, grandly arrayed in a spring suit of grey tweed, with a flower in his buttonhole, soft grey hat, tilted at quite a "Prince of Wales" angle over the left ear. A very fine gentleman indeed, and obviously conscious of his impressive appearance. His attire, the massive ring on his little finger and the very fragrant Corona in the corner of his mouth proclaimed a gentleman of luxurious, if not refined taste, and no common drummer.

Opening the door he was surprised, but not at all disconcerted, to find himself in an office that for all its smart and efficient equipment in desks, filing cabinets, safe, etc., still carried somehow in its furnishing a suggestion of almost feminine refinement. It was spotlessly free of dust, there were flowers about the room, in the windows, half-a-dozen prints on the cedar lined walls, curtains on the windows.

Sitting behind a desk at his right was a young lady, with quiet pale face, and with extraordinarily bright black eyes. Immediately she rose.

"Good morning," she said in a very calm voice.

"Oh, good morning, GOOD morning! Well, well! This IS a sweet little office, and a sweet little officer, too. Ha, ha! Rather neat that, eh?"

"You were wanting something?" The black eyes were very steady and very cold.

"Oh, a whole lot of things. Some of 'em right here, but not just at the present. Meantime, my dear, could you lead me to the secretary of this outfit?" he glanced at the card. "Mr. S. Rivers." He was leaning confidentially over the desk.

"Will you sit down, please?" said the girl, pointing to an armchair tinted blue and white.

"Oh, I'm all right here. And say little black eyes, I didn't quite catch your name, eh?"

"Will you please sit down?" The tone was imperiously polite.

"Well, little one, as I was saying, will you please tell your Secretary, Mr. S.-- Sam is it, or Solomon? Anyway, Mr. S. Rivers that I should like a few minutes with him."

"May I ask the nature of your business, and your name, please?"

"U-u-g-g-h!" The gentleman shivered. "Chilly weather! Eh? Ah, here you are." He handed his card to the young lady. "And if you would be so kind, would you please suggest to your chief that speed, despatch, time in short is of the essence of this interview. In fact, I am catching a director's meeting, eh?"

The young lady with quite unmoved countenance took the card, tapped at the door and passed into the inner office.

"Guess that'll hold Miss Icicle, eh? Ain't she chilly though? Say, you wouldn't be like that, not by the colour of your eyes. I prefer 'em blonde myself."

"Oh, I beg your pardon? You were saying." The blonde was excessively bright and cheery and spoke with a slight drawl.

"Oh, nothing at all, my dear. But I could say a whole lot. If you'd only give me a chance, what? Oh, hello! Here she is--"

"The Secretary is very sorry, Mr. Brady, your appointment was for one-thirty, I believe. Perhaps you would call then at one-thirty?"

"At one-thirty? My dear, does Mr. Rivers realize that my time is important. At one-thirty I am due at a director's meeting in Montreal. And I must have my report on these Riverside Mills ready for that meeting. You got my letter?"

"Yes, we have it here, Mr. Brady," said the young lady, pulling out a file. "You set the hour at one-thirty."

"Oh, come, you know! Say! let me see him just a minute."

Mr. Brady moved toward the inner office door. But black eyes was in his path with an OVER-MY-DEAD-BODY look on her face.

"Please sit down, Mr. Brady," she said pointing a very straight finger to the blue and white chair, "and I shall enquire." She passed through the door.

"Say, where am I? What's all the pressure? What's all the big celebration? Orders from Government for a refurnishing of the Parliament Buildings?"

"Oh, no sir. We haven't quite got round to that yet," said the blonde in a very brisk manner and with a most disarming smile.

"Say, sweetheart, you breathe a different atmosphere. You're human-- you give me--real--real--palps, you know."

"Yes, cardiac reactions," suggested blondie brightly.

"Car--what? Come again, cutie."

The office door opened suddenly and "black eyes" appeared.

"Will you please step in, Mr. Brady?" she said.

"Sure thing. Good bye." He winked at blondie, passed into the office and stood gaping. His hat came quickly from his head, his cigar fell from his fingers.

"I--I--beg your pardon, Miss--are you--?" Mr. Brady for once lost his perfect equipoise, which was his characteristic with ladies.

"Good morning, Mr. Brady," said Sylvia, in her sweetest voice. "Won't you please sit down?"

"But I--Holy Mike! You're not the secretary?" He pulled a card from his pocket and read, "S. Rivers, Secretary, Riverside Mills." "Say, they never told me. I want to apologize for buttin' in like this on a lady. Fact is I thought you was some stubborn old grey headed guy. I do hope--"

"Please don't mind. It is my own fault. But really, 'Sylvia Rivers, Secretary' looked rather silly. It is a charming day."

"Lovely. And you've got a lovely office--and them blossoms now--"

"Yes, aren't they lovely? This was my father's first home, an old log house, so I made it into an office. I am very fond of it," said the girl with sweet seriousness. "You want to speak of a--a-- kind of merger, I understand, a kind of--"

"Yes, Miss Rivers--a big thing--an amalgamation of all the principal lumber and furniture concerns in Central Canada, Ontario and Quebec, not including, of course, the big fellows in Hull. They are bucking this. The very kind of thing a young lady like you ought to be glad to get into. Here are the figures."

He laid his papers on the desk and in clear and lucid terms set before her the main outlines of the scheme. In fifteen minutes' talk the main structural outlines of the proposed Central Canada Lumber and Furniture Corporation stood clear before the eyes of the Secretary of the Riverside Mills.

"It's a big thing, Miss Rivers. This is the day of Big Business in Canada, you know."

"And the poor little things, Mr. Brady? Is there no place for them in Canada any longer?"

"Nary a place! They're gone phut! Can't stand up against the competition, mass production, high power salesmanship, low relative overhead and mechanization--that word in big caps, Miss Rivers. Now take your plant--by the way what is your capitalization, Miss Rivers?"

The Secretary had her figures ready.

"My father put over $75,000 into mill, factory and tannery. The tannery is of course idle. In those days materials were cheap, indeed, he made his own right here, you see, out of our own timber along the river. To-day it would cost a great deal more to replace the plant."

"But of course the plant is out of date now," suggested Mr. Brady.

"Not the factory. The tannery is not modern, though the vats, etc., are all there, but we won't count the tannery. The sawmill is fairly modern, and the factory not too bad."

"And what do you carry your whole plant at in your books?"

The girl hesitated.

"Should I tell you that? Well yes, I will. We have cut our capitalization to between $25,000 and $35,000."

Mr. Brady paused abruptly. This was a new experience for him. In preliminary negotiations, his first business was to get rid of the padding. This young girl in her simplicity had saved him all that trouble. "Say $30,000, Miss Rivers," he suggested and felt mean about it.

"Now, I'm prepared to make you a very attractive offer, Miss Rivers. The Corporation will take over your whole plant at say $50,000, $20,000 cash and $30,000 seven percent stock in the new company."

"But it isn't worth $50,000, Mr. Brady," said the girl, her blue eyes wide with surprise.

Mr. Brady gazed at her in amazement. This again was a completely new experience for him.

"Well, I mean, you see in the new Corporation each unit will become more valuable, oh, immensely more valuable. You see massed production, modern machinery, low relative overhead, no competition and all that."

"But how can you pay seven percent on $30,000 and also $20,000 in cash. That means a cash dividend of about $3,500. You can't do that, no business can."

"That's the Corporation's business. Don't you worry. This is Big Business, see?"

"No, I'm afraid I can't.'"

"But really you don't need to. I can show you that others are doing it right now. Never fear, we are in a new world, with new possibilities." Mr. Brady was in his well-beaten trail and very soon was making excellent time.

The Secretary was listening with puzzled and slightly anxious face.

"And you would really advise us to accept your offer, Mr. Brady?"

Once more Mr. Brady was conscious of a quite unusual qualm of uncertainty, which he at once ejected from his system.

"Well, see here. You have your $20,000 cash--nice little nest egg-- and you have your $30,000 stock in the big Corporation, a chance to make big money there, and you get rid of all this worry--no more work--"

"No more work!" Dismay appeared in the blue eyes.

"No more work!" said Brady firmly. "Aren't you dead sick of the grind?"

"I love it!" The blue eyes were shining.

"Love it? Say, you don't mean it?" Mr. Brady had another shock.

"Besides, what about my people?"

"Your people?"

"The workers here. We run from fifty to sixty. What would happen to them? You might close down this little plant."

"Eh?" Another shock for Mr. Brady. As a matter of fact the possibility suggested was more than probable. "Oh, they'd be absorbed, find jobs somewhere."

"But their homes are here. They were born here."

An idea suddenly came to Miss Sylvia.

"By the way, would you like to look through the factory?"

Mr. Brady, with never a glance at his watch made eager reply. "Would you, could you spare the time?"

"Why yes, Mr. Brady, I'd like to."

"Come on!" he said.

Miss Sylvia sprang to her feet. "Splendid! Just a moment, please." She rang a bell and black eyes appeared. "I am showing Mr. Brady through the factory, Frances. You might put these through, please. They are a bit fussy, but perhaps- -"

"Yes Miss Sylvia!" said Frances. "It won't be the least trouble."

"Thank you. Now Mr. Brady, we won't bother with the sawmill. It is pretty ordinary. We will just glance in at the engine room."

The engine room was like the front office for order and neatness. Everything that could shine was shining.

"Good morning, Mack. How is she running to-day?"

"Aweel, not that bad," said Mack with some hesitation.

"What's that hissing?" enquired Miss Sylvia.

"Ay, I micht hae kent ye'd catch that," replied Mack in disgust. "Yon's a leaky valve, Miss Sylvia."

"Oh," said Miss Sylvia lightly. "Nothing serious, I hope. I mean nothing wrong, Mack?"

"Na, na, Miss Sylvia, there's naething seriously wrang." Mack's tone was slightly reproachful. "Naething like that."

"Of course not, Mack, I might have known."

"I'll set her richt the nicht. She'll be singin' like a mavis the morn's morn. I canna bide that valve. I'll sort it, mind ye."

"Never fear, but what you will, Mack. How is the baby?"

"Improvin'. She'll mak' oot, I doot." Mack was constitutionally a pessimist.

"But you are not anxious about her, Mack?" Miss Sylvia's tone was troubled.

"Hoots, never fash yersel, Miss Sylvia. A wee pech an' a bit hoast. But she'll mak' through."

"You've had the doctor? I told you, Mack."

"Oh, doctor? Not him. The wife canna bide a doctor. A wee drap o' ile and a guid rub o' goose grease and she'll win through."

"I must run in and see her, the darling. You're not nearly careful enough, Mack."

"Ay, but ye're the lassie," said Mack as the door closed behind her. Then he turned and shook his fist savagely at the engine. "Dod blast ye! An' ye wad select this verra day for yer capers, ye hissin' deevil. I'll sort ye the nicht ere I sleep."

From the engine room Miss Sylvia led the way to a room a little apart. "Would you like to see our Agricultural Implement Department?"

"Agricultural Department?"

"Yes, we make fanning mills. My father was very proud of The Riverside Grain Purifier. The patents are all his. Are you interested in fanning mills, Mr. Brady?"

"Am I interested in fanning mills? You certainly said it. Why fanning mills is the two middle names of me. Made and sold 'em for years." Mr. Brady fairly threw himself upon the fanning mills, brushing aside Miss Sylvia's explanations.

"Hi! What's this?"

"Oh, that's something quite new. My very own pet device." She called a workman to her.

"Tom, show Mr. Brady how this works."

Mr. Brady was instantly absorbed. "Say, this patented? What, not yet? Look here Miss Rivers, before I leave this plant I'll dictate letters to Ottawa and Washington applying for patents."

Miss Sylvia's voice rang out in delighted laughter.

"But Mr. Brady, your meeting?" she said, with demure shyness.

"Meeting? What meeting? Oh, meeting be--I mean--I'll make that meeting all right. Now, what next?"

"Well, I really must not keep you from your meeting."

"Forget that meeting. I want to see this outfit."

From one department to another they made their way. Mr. Brady full of sympathetic and intelligent interrogatives, Miss Sylvia eager to show off her pet machines, and their attendants.

As they arrived at the third and top flat Miss Sylvia paused at a closed door and said:

"This room you will despise, but I am rather proud of it myself."

"Listen. Wait a bit!" said Mr. Brady staying her hand as she reached for the door knob. "Be the powers I know that one, 'The Rose of Tralee.' Twenty years ago I last heard it in Ballymena. A lovely girl she was too. My dear, she was a singin' bird. Wait, wait--" The coarse fat face of the Irishman seemed to grow finer as they stood listening.

"They always sing another along with that. Can you wait?"

"Can I wait, is it?"

Following "The Rose of Tralee" came the "Old Londonderry Air," with weird and it must be confessed rather "barber pole" harmonies.

"Hivens above, it's 'Danny Boy'!" said Mr. Brady. Softly, to the accompaniment of tapping hammers and the whirring of sewing machines, came the music. Mr. Brady waited till the very last harmony sighed into silence.

Miss Sylvia opened the door and disclosed a large, airy room, beautifully lighted, with flower-decked curtained windows, prints on the walls, and in one corner a small upright piano. Some twenty girls were busy at a variety of jobs, sewing and leather stamping machines, hand decorating kitchen and nursery furniture, window curtains, lamp shades, knitting and quilting frames, children's sleds and a host of other things for the home.

"The girls are on piece work with a minimum and maximum of stent and wage," explained the secretary.

A tall, pale girl with large dark eyes came up to Miss Sylvia.

"We are just looking round, Nell. Don't let us disturb you. Carry right on." Not a girl lifted her head from her work.

"This is our Club room too," said Miss Sylvia, in a voice of unmistakable pride. "We spend three nights a week here. One for fun, dancing, singing and two for dramatics, reading and debating. Oh, we have a grand time, I assure you, Mr. Brady."

Mr. Brady made no reply. Indeed after they returned to the office he was strangely silent, and so remained for some minutes while Miss Rivers told him about the varied activities carried on by the Riverside Girls' Club.

Suddenly he burst forth.

"See here, Miss Rivers. You've got me stalled sure enough. I've got a flat tire and I'm clear out of juice. Say! Tell me what you're going to do?" He was almost rough in his speech.

"About the Corporation, Mr. Brady?" said Miss Sylvia in her gentle voice.

"Listen! I offered you $50,000, $20,000 cash, the rest stock. I've got authority to make that $60,000, $25,000 and $35,000."

"And if I refuse?"

"They'll close you up dead. They're a bunch of soulless blood- sucking brutes. Individually, meet 'em at dinner, they are most chawming, I assuah yah. But as a Corporation, their innards are brass and iron. They'll close you up. Funny agent, I am eh?"

"And my people?" said Miss Sylvia, very gently.

"Them singin' birds, eh? 'The Rose of Tralee,' an' 'Danny Boy' and all an' all, eh?"

"You see, Mr. Brady, their fathers worked for my father. He built most of their houses, and they own them now. And they are all friends of one another and my friends."

"Stop it," said Mr. Brady savagely.

"What would you advise?" said Miss Sylvia with quiet insistence. "I really don't--"

"Stop it, I tell ye!" said Mr. Brady, slapping his hand on the desk. "If it's the Closing Agent of the Central Canada Lumber and Furniture Corporation ye're askin', my answer is 'Close the deal and pull out.'" Mr. Brady leaned over the desk and regarded the secretary with his blue Irish eyes, shining like points of light. "But if it's Tim Brady yer askin', that's got a home and wife and childer av his own, my answer is, tell them to go to hell, and shure the good Lord that loves angels and looks after fools and little childer will be good to ye. And it's a fool's advice I'm givin' ye, so it is."

Miss Sylvia rose from her chair, came slowly round the desk and offered her hand shyly.

"Mr. Brady, I am glad you came to see me to-day," she said, her face radiant with the smile of a child. "And thank you, oh, thank you!" Her voice grew slightly husky. "And I am sure Mr. Timothy Brady must be a good man." Mr. Brady laughed loudly.

"A good man? God bless yer lovely blue eyes! And what would the bhoys say to that from Kincardine to Quebec?"

"It would make no difference what they said, Mr. Brady," said Miss Sylvia in a firm voice. "I know." The blue eyes were soft and kind that looked into his.

Mr. Brady seized his hat suddenly, glanced at his watch, closed his brief case with a snap, but still lingered.

"If ye were only of the true faith now, I would send ye to your priest," he said earnestly. "But listen, I am not taking yer answer to-day, nor am I givin' ye advice to-day. Ye've put a witch on me. Look at the way ye've got me back to me ould mother's tongue. But my offer stands. $60,000, $25,000 cash and $35,000 stock. Take time, take time--and think of yourself."

"Really, Mr. Brady? Of myself only?" She smiled brightly into his face.

"The Saints save ye. It's the quare Closing Agent I am--"

He did not offer his hand, but with a low almost reverential bow he backed out of the door.

"My dear," he said to Frances at the outer desk in a confidential but very respectful tone, "you were right--quite right. Don't let every roughneck barge into your young lady in there."

"I won't," said the girl firmly.

"Say! She's--well, I guess you know the kind she is, all right."

"We do sir. Thank you, sir," said Frances throwing him a smile for the first time, so charming that Mr. Brady was startled.

"Hello! Not so frosty after all, eh?"

"Oh, no sir, not always," said Frances smiling again.

"Not when Sunny Jim comes round," said the typist at the other desk in her soft drawl.

"Eh? Not Jim this time--Tim. And say, when next I blow in here I'd like to blow you both to the best dinner the Royal can afford. Straight goods."

"Thank you, Mr. Brady," said Frances.

"Sure thing, Tim!" said blondie.

"Good-bye," said Mr. Brady winking slowly at her. He cocked his hat over his left ear, threw out his chest and marched gravely out to new fields of battle.

CHAPTER VI

Arabella Foster never appeared to better advantage than when dispensing hospitality in her own drawing-room. She was there at her grandest.

"A very grande dame indeed," murmured Jack in Sylvia's ear. "She terrifies me, or would if she hadn't cuffed me so often as a youngster for stealing her cookies."

"She really is splendid," said Sylvia. "And how beautifully dressed!"

"I'm all for a white frock tricked out with baby blue. It is baby blue?" said Jack, his eyes appraising the lovely lines of the girl's figure.

"Yes, but it's an old thing--done over--of course. I don't think Aunt Elizabeth knew we were to be so very grand. 'A little dinner,' she said."

"Well, this is a little dinner, only a dozen or so. And bound to be dull."

"Dull? In this room, and with that view and these charming people!"

"Dull as a directors' meeting and worse. You draw a fee at a directors' meeting."

"I know I'm going to have a lovely time," said Sylvia, her face and eyes aglow.

"That's just it. Of course, one can't kick too hard, but really you know. Old Tom is a good chap. He's your partner. Of course quite proper--eldest son and the guest of honour--stupid idea. I hinted delicately that I should like to take you in--old friends and all that, but--"

"Why I've known Tom for years. I mean, I knew him ten years ago. We used to play in the sand at Beauharnois. I don't think he liked me at all then--"

"But that was ten years ago. Now he will fall heavily for you, and the mater will smile on him. She's got you picked out for him already. Disgusting! He'll talk an elbow off you--golf and stocks-- possibly art--depends on his condition."

"But I'm awfully keen on golf, and I want to learn about stocks."

"That's right! I'm going to have a wonderful time!" Jack's face was a picture of gloom. "Well, here comes cheer. Antoine has a light touch on cocktails."

"Who is the young man with the long keen face?"

"That's Reggie Hale. Not so terribly young. A weird and wild Radical Economics professor in an American College--Cornell I think. But now he is doing research work here. He's a Bolshie and of course the darling of the 'gold bugs' here. They have already been reaching for that tawny scalp, but have just missed it so far. The McGill President befriended him, indeed said some strong words suited to their understanding, so they eased off a bit. They will probably get him yet."

"He looks awfully interesting," said Sylvia.

"Yes! Now that would have been the proper thing," grumbled Jack. "The distinguished guest should have been assigned to the most interesting and cultured man present. Besides Reggie never knows what a girl has on or hasn't. But he has CULTUAH in large gobs. Awfully interesting and entirely unamorous. Safe man, Reggie."

Sylvia's eyes followed Antoine's progress.

"Oh, but he's had one already!" she said to herself, noting Tom's second cocktail.

"I told you. Tom is working up brilliance. You will have a charming time. He'll talk art to you. Oh well! Will you look at me now and then?"

"Of course I will. You do look--fine--so--well--so all right. You know--as if you belonged with all this."

"I am most unhappy, and shall be worse. Reggie will jump on Cameron Ogilvie."

"Who is he? I have heard of him."

"Banker. President of the Empire Bank--big shot. Tells Canada where she gets off and on. The biggest of the big six. Learned his banking in Scotland-- Aberdeen likely--straight as a steel rail and as pliable. Look at him! No cocktail for him. He's like my Dad--despises the poison. Antoine will bring them each a Scotch in a minute."

"I think your Dad is the handsomest man here!" said Sylvia.

"Yes, isn't he? So thoroughbred eh?" Jack's eyes lingered on his father's face, caught his eye, waved at him.

"Come let's go and see him."

"Jack, I'm shy," whispered Sylvia, a quick little colour in her cheeks. "He is so distinguished looking--strong--fine."

"He is all that and a lot more--runs in the family. Come, he wants to meet you."

"Oh Jack!"

"Come along--no stops--come right through. They'll all want to block you."

Under Jack's resolute piloting Sylvia found herself almost immediately being introduced to Mr. Roger Tempest who was indeed all his son had said.

"Dad, this is Sylvia," said Jack, in a tone of proud proprietorship.

"Oh, this is Sylvia! My dear, I knew both your father and your mother well. They were from Glengarry, and so you are a Glengarry girl."

"Oh, I am glad. I always like people who say that," said Sylvia giving him her hand and obviously her heart at once.

"And where have you been these years that we have never seen you? Our fault I fear."

"Away at school a good deal. Edinburgh for three years. And at home for the last year and a half."

"Running the Riverside Mills," said Jack.

"Splendid! At work eh? It is what a Glengarry girl and your father's daughter would do. Nothing like something to do."

"But Dad she's a lot more than a business young woman. You wait till she sings Scottish songs for you. Dad is mad about them."

"Better and better. Sorry I haven't known you before, my dear. But we live very quietly, Jack and I--since--"

"But she is coming to see us, Dad."

Sylvia threw him a quick look of surprise.

"Oh, when Jack?"

"To-morrow, of course. You are coming to see Dad's pictures--and--"

"Ah, you know pictures?" said Mr. Tempest eagerly.

"No. Alas, I am very ignorant of all that--but I love them. I know the National Gallery and the Academy in Edinburgh, of course."

"Ah, some excellent pictures there. Raeburn and Noel Paton--very old fashioned now-a-days, but none the less worthwhile, my dear!"

"I know one great Raeburn," cried Sylvia, a quick eager light in her blue eyes. "In the Royal Archer's Hall."

"What! You know 'The Archer'? A gorgeous thing. I have never met a Canadian who knew that great picture."

"Yes, I knew the Chief Archer's wife, and used to spend Saturday afternoon often at that wonderful old Archer's Hall."

"My dear. I can see you are the right sort. Jack, we shall lunch at home to-morrow, and if Miss Sylvia will do us the honour, eh?"

"I don't know. Oh, I hope Aunt Arabella hasn't anything else on," cried Sylvia.

"I shall speak to Mrs. Foster," said Mr. Tempest.

"Oh, isn't he a dear?" whispered Sylvia as Jack carried her off. "Jack, you are a lucky boy!"

"I don't know yet," said Jack looking straight into her eyes. "As far as the pater is concerned, yes. But," Jack's face clouded over. "Ah, I can see that Aunt Arabella is opening out a campaign, and she is a great Field Marshal."

"What are you talking about?"

"Tom Foster," said Jack savagely. "Millions of money--and a good sort. Yes a good sort, Tom. A wizard in stocks--a coming man among the gold bugs and all that. But he isn't fit to be a door mat for your little feet." Jack wore a gloomy face.

"But Jack you are talking nonsense. Oh, what a view!" They were standing now in the doorway of the Conservatory, which from its lofty site on the mountain side overlooked the city and the noble sweep of the mighty St. Lawrence.

"Yes, it is a great view," grudgingly admitted Jack. "Dash it they've got everything. Home--this is an awfully fine house really-- magnificent lay-out-- and view--and they are really fine people. Look at Julia there, the pose of an empress, and a fine girl too-- and social position with millions for upkeep. Oh dash it to blazes! And here is Tom coming to take you in. I'd like to kill him in some quiet, painless but effective way."

"But Jack why? Poor Tom!"

"Why? He wants you! Can't you see it? I can. He wants you, but he won't get you if I have to kill him!"

The girl turned a startled face toward him and looked steadily into his eyes.

"Oh Jack!"

"Yes. He wants you. And--oh Sylvia darling, can't you see?"

The girl's face flushed hot and then went pale and very still, while the blue eyes held his steadily.

"Can't you see, Sylvia?" said Jack very quietly. "I want you, Sylvia. More than anything else in the world, I want you. Oh, this is no place and time. What a fool I am! Here's the brute."

"Well young lady! Fine view eh? But views are not considered filling. So since I am to have the distinguished honour, perhaps you will run away Jack and do your duty. And, young fella, you needn't hurry back. This young lady is under my charge for the evening."

"Sylvia, I am really sorry for you. He is a predatory beast. But he is heading for bitter disappointment. Cheer up!"

"Beat it, boy. My little kid sister Peggy's eyes are like large saucers looking for you, poor kid."

Without a word Sylvia took Tom's arm and moved away as in a dream, heeding not at all Tom's stream of small talk.

Jack made his way to the waiting Peggy, the sixteen year old daughter of the home.

"Oh Jack, I was just awfully terrified you weren't coming for me, and that--that horrid foxy-faced Mr. Jessop--he is just like a fox-- sharp nose and sharp little eyes and red hair--would get me. And you looked as if you wanted to go with Sylvia. And she is lovely isn't she? But Tom wanted her and of course the eldest son of the family, so mamma said, must take the young lady visitor. And I am awfully glad you didn't. For now I shall have all I want to eat. I needn't be polite with you, Jack. And besides you are good fun, you know."

Peggy was a half-formed youngster at the awkward age when hands and feet are always in the wrong place, and the body has not yet got itself into its alluring curves. Dark-skinned, not yet cleared up, dark brown bobbed hair, fine dark brown eyes that looked straight at one, firm chin, a good straight nose, and a heart full of warm red blood and romantic passions. She was desperately in love with Jack as her adoring eyes kept telling him every moment.

"Well Peggy, my dear, I shall see that you are properly fed, but you must promise me good manners. I can't stand a piggy lady, and no wine--no, not a drop--well a little sherry with your soup, but no more, on honour. And of course no silly cocktail!"

"Cross my heart!" said Peggy earnestly. "Anyway I don't like wine. Only it is rather mean of mamma to let everyone else swig away and treat me like a baby. Come along, Jack, I know our places. You're next Julia. She would have that. She can't bear Cameron Ogilvie. Of course he wants to marry her, but she won't take him so long as she--"

"He's a very decent fellow, Peggy, and money!" said Jack.

"I know, and such a lovely Rolls-Royce," said Peggy. "He takes me out now and then when Julia is away, and he always treats me to something."

"Pig," said Jack in disgust.

"Well, I know, but--he knows exactly what I like. Of course I much prefer your racer, Jack."

"But I don't treat you to a banana sundae every time."

"As if I cared. And I do love your racer. Isn't Professor Hale exactly like a terrier, except for his long hair?" said the girl.

"Exactly, and a terrier he is. He will be at the bull dog in a minute or two."

"You mean Mr. Cameron Ogilvie? Yes. He wants Julia, but--" sadly added the child, "she won't have him. She wants you."

"Nonsense, you little devil. You mustn't talk like that."

"It's true!" she sighed deeply. "I can see it quite well in her eyes."

"Shut up, you little idiot!" said Jack in a savage undertone.

"There he goes--the terrier," said the girl in delight. "I love to hear him, a bark, a snarl and then a leap at the other fellow's throat."

"Reggie dearly loves a scrap. What is he at now?" said Jack, leaning forward to get a better look at Mr. Cameron Ogilvie, who sat on Aunt Arabella's left.

"You are congratulating us on the prosperity of the country, Mr. Ogilvie," Professor Hale was saying. "You think this prosperity well founded?" he enquired in a voice of utmost respect.

"Yes, I do. I base it first upon the marked improvement in trade and commerce. Second, upon the magnificent harvest in the west, and upon the higher rates on our call loans in New York."

"Rare combination! Mr. Ogilvie!" The Professor's shrill voice hushed all the conversation to silence.

"Rare combination? I do not quite get you." Mr. Ogilvie's voice was calmly respectful. This was not his first experience of Reggie Hale.

"The Western farmer, the trader, the New York Stock market, the benevolent banker and Almighty God. All except the last mentioned, however, not entirely trustworthy."

Mrs. Foster turned a shocked and startled face toward Professor Hale.

"Really, Professor Hale!"

"I sympathize with you, Mrs. Foster," said Professor Hale. "These bankers really they do shock one at times. They are so very certain of the partnership of the Almighty."

At this point Dr. Strang, sitting at the Professor's left hand, broke in. "But Professor Hale, surely in all honest work we may expect the co-operation of Providence."

"Sure thing padre, but I was talking of the combination suggested by our friend Mr. Cameron Ogilvie here. You are speaking of honest work." The silence grew very thick. "What I mean is, so as to be offensive to no one present, you would hardly associate in co- operative work the Almighty and the New York stock boomer whose call loans swell the profits of Montreal bankers."

"You do not approve of the operations of the stock market, I take it Professor Hale," said Mr. Tempest.

"Ah, Mr. Tempest, you know me better than that. But I will say, and I shall wait for your applause, that the stock boomer who sells the innocent public stock at a price which he is convinced does not represent reality in value, present or prospective, is a swindler and a scoundrel and should be put in a safe place."

"Yes, Mr. Hale. I most heartily applaud that statement. But why single out the stock broker? Surely there are others, merchants, traders, manufacturers."

"Yes, the stock broker distinguishes himself above others in two particulars, the magnitude of his operations, and his utterly unscrupulous manipulation of the greed and ignorance of his clients. He is a vampire, a pest."

"Who has been doing you, Reggie?" enquired Tom.

"No, I am immune by reason of my poverty."

"But Professor Hale, you don't object to stock trading," said Aunt Arabella in amazement.

"Save only for the highly ethical. Myself I shouldn't dare go into the game. I'd become a buccaneer, a bloody, brutal, walk-the-plank pirate, like the rest. A friend of mine, a dear sweet soul bought International Copper a month or so ago, made twenty points. She prays every night for the blessing of God upon the stockbrokers and their noble work."

"Good buying still, Reggie," said Tom.

"Why should anyone buy International Copper today?" enquired Professor Hale wrathfully. "Has it productive reality value at the present price?"

"It's a good buy to-day and it will certainly go higher," said Tom. "And besides who can estimate production reality in any industrial stock? Can you Reggie?"

"Not always. But any stockbroker who has any right to be in the business ought to be able to indicate the line beyond which production reality vanishes. And at that point he declines to promote such stock."

"My dear sir," said Mr. Jessop, a stockbroker of the wealthy firm of Chamberlain, Jessop and Foster, in which Tom was the junior partner. "Your theory is entirely unpractical. It is outside the range of business trends. The ancient law of caveat emptor must govern here as in any and every business transaction. The man who proposes to deal in stocks must know that he is in a dangerous game. Hence he must have a broker whom he can trust, and upon whose expert advice he must rely."

"I don't like him. He looks like a fox," said Peggy nudging Jack.

"Hush, you little beggar, they'll hear you. Behave yourself."

"Look at the terrier!" said Peggy in glee.

Professor Hale was indeed on him like a terrier. "Very well Mr. Jessop. Now I am not an EMPTOR, I am a VENDOR. The market has responded to the usual manipulation influences, and has gone in International Copper say from 100 to let us say, 400 at which point his broker knows that the stock crosses the very ultimate of reality in value. It will never, can never earn any dividend at that price, but he also knows that under the madness of the market it will go to 500. What will my honest broker advise me, the vendor, to do? Sell, or wait till some sucker offers 500. That is, sell wind to the unwary fool to the extent of 100 or more on every share he buys?"

"Isn't he lovely? Regular snapper," said Peggy enjoying the professor hugely.

"Mr. Jessop, we shall at this point abandon the stock market," said Mrs. Foster. "Sylvia, I can see, is keen to go on, but it is a question in regard to which there will always be room for difference of opinion. So Professor Hale we shall talk about-- anything else you like."

"Banks," suggested Professor Hale. "I'm all for a complete reconstruction of our Banking system, which the whole world is patting on the back, but which--"

"Regular little devil," whispered Peggy. "I wish I could jump down his throat. Here's Sylvia at him."

"But Professor Hale surely the Canadian Banking system is one of the finest in the world?" Sylvia said earnestly.

"Much better than that of the United States I grant you, but--"

"Professor Hale, you are incorrigible," said Aunt Arabella. "You do love a fight. Now can't we find something upon which we agree?"

"But that is so dull," burst out Sylvia suddenly. "Oh, I'm sorry," she apologized.

"Of course you're quite right," said Tom. "It surely is intolerably dull to agree with every one."

"Perhaps Professor Hale will discuss another basic ground of prosperity, say the Western harvests," said Mr. Cameron Ogilvie, who had already made something of a reputation in wheat, and upon whose advice the government at Ottawa was supposed to be relying.

"Certainly!" exclaimed Hale leaping at the proposition. "About the wheat market I--" He paused abruptly arrested by Sylvia's shining eyes.

Peggy clapped her hands. "Oh, do go on!"

"Peggy! Tut, tut, child, you forget yourself," said her mother.

"But do let us hear about the wheat, Professor Hale," said Mr. Cameron Ogilvie, evidently sure of his ground. "The car loadings last year were three million. You can't juggle with that. This year the prospects are even better."

The Professor smiled at him. "Providence is certainly doing its part with the wheat. And the market is holding up owing to the Wheat Pool, backing it up with a purchase of eight million bushels. But can any living man say where the price of wheat will go during the next six months? Absolutely not. To-day's quotations are ominous."

"Wheat is all right. Absolutely all right. It may vary a few cents, but it is basically steady," said Mr. Price, speaking with the air of an expert.

Mr. Tempest shook his head.

Professor Hale noticed him.

"Mr. Tempest, you agree?" he cried.

"I wish I could," said Mr. Tempest, "but the whole European situation is extremely critical. But why get gloomy? Mrs. Foster will be for sending us all home."

"No, but we shall leave you now to yourselves," said that lady, rising from the table. "Only, Professor Hale, I am going to ban every kind of argument."

"Dear Mrs. Foster, let me come with you. We shall be awfully dull here."

"No, stay and be good," said Aunt Arabella shaking her finger at him.

"Reggie Hale, you are a very stimulating person," said Julia as she passed his chair. "Don't be long in joining us."

"You may be quite sure not," said Professor Hale, smiling up at her eagerly.

"Can I stay with you?" Peggy implored.

"Certainly not," said Jack. "Be off with you."

"Oh Jack, I hate women. They'll talk about clothes. I'm a nudist, like the Germans I was reading--"

"See here young lady, I'll take you outside and give you a demonstration--"

"Oh, do Jack! Good-bye darling."

"I say, Reggie, be human rather than pedagogical," said Tom, "and tell us what you really think of the situation in regard to this boom."

"What's the use? All the big financial kings, princes and barons in America are against me. See articles this month in various magazines. Mitchell, Mullen, even old Coolidge, all praising God and acclaiming the New Era. Frankly I am pessimistic."

"Mr. Hale," said Mr. Tempest earnestly, "not for argument's sake, but man to man, do you mind saying quietly, why?"

Professor Hale looked round upon the faces at the table. Roger Tempest, an old trusted Conservative stock broker; Ogilvie, the biggest banker in Canada and one of the biggest on the continent; Jessop, a stock broker of the newer school, with Tom Foster, his under study; Dr. Strang, Montreal's leading surgeon, a man with an immense capacity for silence; Jack Tempest, perhaps the keenest brain in the company, camouflaged under the exterior of a devotee of sport.

"Mr. Tempest, when you speak like that I remember I am only a young man and have little right to express a serious opinion to serious men. Of course when I was out merely for scalps--"

"To get a rise out of an old-fashioned banker," said Mr. Cameron Ogilvie, with a smile. "But seriously I also would like to hear your opinion."

"Go to it, Reggie, we likely won't believe you," said Tom easily.

"I am going to say only one thing. Take it for what it's worth. I am anxiously asking myself this one thing. I have been keeping close tab on old country opinion. Tell me, when almost every economist of any note in England or Scotland is agreed that things on the Continent are extremely critical, and when they all agree that the present prosperity in the United States is resting upon a very questionable basis, why should not Canadian leaders and makers of opinion seek to advise caution? I am not arguing, I am asking two or three of the most trusted men in Montreal for guidance."

It was the complete change in his tone and manner that brought a new look into the faces of the men about him. He was no longer the pugnacious little terrier, spoiling for a scrap. He was an earnest student of economics, asking advice. They all looked at Roger Tempest.

"Hale, I am asking myself every day that identical question," he said gravely. "What do you say, Ogilvie?"

"Quite privately I may tell you," said Ogilvie quietly, "we had a private meeting to-day, half-a-dozen of us bankers. We have agreed that we shall gradually, but firmly reduce our loans and raise our rates for all stock operations. And I may add that the Federal Reserve is going to do its utmost in the same direction. This is not for publication, but solely for useful action."

"At the same time, gentlemen, we must not ignore the fact," said Jessop, "that there is a very real and very sound advance in all prices, and a very remarkable expansion in all industrial lines."

"True enough," replied Hale politely, "but you know also that as stocks are soaring the prices of commodities are steadily falling. And if wheat should fail us where would we be in Canada, and in the United States as well?"

At this Roger Tempest seemed to command the thinking of the little company.

"Gentlemen, there seems to be only one thing before us. Remember what happened in pulp and paper. There is recovery there, but it cannot be permanent. We must at all costs check this mad boom in stocks. Shall we rejoin the ladies. There is music I understand waiting us as well."

"We are with you, Tempest," said Ogilvie. "You may depend upon the bankers."

As they moved toward the music room Jack fell into step with Jessop.

"What's your idea, Mr. Jessop?" he asked.

"This is no time for the leadership of old men," said Jessop with a cynical grin. "Me, I'm all for backing my luck."

"Right you are, old boy," said Tom, but a glance at his flushed face did not increase Jack's confidence in the leadership of the younger generation.

Jack walked for some moments at his father's side.

"About that stock booming business, sir," he said. "I believe you are dead right. All the same Jessop will try to make a killing and of course Tom Foster is with him."

"Thank you, boy. And I'm afraid you are right about Jessop. He is difficult to control. This continent has gone mad. We are going to see strange things. And the worst of it is we shall all willy nilly be dragged into it."

"You think so? Can't we keep out?"

"Not if we keep in business."

"What about Reggie Hale's buccaneer talk?"

"More truth than poetry, I fear. But honest men need not join the pirate crew."

"What then? Walk the plank?" His father looked at him quietly for a single instant.

"Very gallant men have walked the plank, my boy."

Jack held his eyes steady for an answering instant.

"And pirates often swing, sir," he said with a gay little laugh.

CHAPTER VII

Mrs. Foster's late husband had been recognized in the city as a patron of music. The music room in his new house was considered one of the best adapted to its purpose in the city. A Casavant pipe organ and a magnificent Steinway grand piano, were indications of his love for the art, and of his desire to promote its development. But though much money and labour had been spent on their musical education, it was a disappointment to their father that none of his children showed any more than a moderate aptitude in either vocal or instrumental performance. They could all play both organ and piano with considerable mechanical exactitude, but there it ended. Any indication of true artistic taste or feeling was not to be found in any member of the family.

Mrs. Foster, however, after her husband's death, conceived it to be her duty to assume all the obligations of a patron of the art, both for its own sake, and out of loyalty to the memory of her late husband, who had taken a leading part in developing the musical taste of the citizens of Montreal. Hence, during the season it was her practice to offer her house to certain musical organizations for the production of severely artistic programs of an educative character for the benefit of a carefully selected company of patrons of the art, at the nominal subscription of five dollars, with a concession of ten dollars for a family group of three. The invitation programs to these musicales made it quite clear that while the presentations would be mainly educative in their purpose, they would not fail to be artistically delightful as well.

But while anxious to promote the musical culture of those citizens of Montreal who might be expected to aspire to be classed among the patrons of music, Mrs. Foster was not unmindful of a large circle of her friends and acquaintances, who while not aspiring to be patrons, were enthusiastic devotees of the art. These were invited from time to time to spend the evening at her home, where an informal program of vocal and instrumental music would be presented. The program was usually a pleasing combination of professional and amateur performances, to which latter class members of her own family, to their own disgust more or less, and her friends, were expected to make their modest contributions.

Her son Tom possessed a voice of a deep sonorous quality, which he rather enjoyed displaying in jolly rollicking sea ballads and war songs, as well as in the better known operatic numbers.

Nothing, however, but her sense of duty and an unwillingness to hurt her mother's feelings kept her daughter, Julia, from utterly declining to take any part whatever in the program, either vocally-- she really had a fine contralto voice, though not invariably certain in its pitch--or with a piano number which she could render with very considerable technical skill. Peggy, the youngest member of the family was still laboriously struggling with the technical intricacies of the pipe organ, and not without success. Her "foot work" however, she was rather proud of, and was never unwilling to give an exhibition of her skill in this direction.

To Jack Tempest these "informal" musicales were rather an ordeal, not so much because he himself was expected to contribute "an exhibition of potent painless piano punching," as Peggy put it, but because as a rule, he loathed amateur performances. It was therefore with a vast relief that on entering Mrs. Foster's music room, he saw lined up behind the piano a quintet of men apparently preparing to open the program.

"Let's go and sit beside Sylvia," suggested Peggy. "See, she wants us."

"Noble thought, Peggy," said Jack. "Let's slide."

He placed himself between Sylvia and Peggy.

"Ah! The Laval Quintet," he whispered to Sylvia. "Now you will hear something worth while."

"Oh, they are perfectly divine!" breathed Peggy, ecstatically. "French Canadian songs, every kind. And so easy to look at too! Aren't they?"

"Huh! Lovely things!" said Jack, for which Peggy made a face at him.

Suddenly he sprang to his feet, ran across the room to Mrs. Foster.

"Aunt Arabella," he begged. "Can you give me just five minutes till I run over to get Nickie, I promised him, and he is just mad crazy about these Laval boys? Awfully sorry!"

"Why certainly," exclaimed Mrs. Foster. "Glad you thought of it, Jack. The dear little chap. He will enjoy it."

"I'm going too, Nickie will love it," cried Peggy darting after Jack. "Let Tom sing, Mummy, till we come back," she shouted over her shoulder. A suppressed smile rippled over the faces of the company.

"Peggy! Come back!" commanded her mother. But Peggy was out of reach, if not of earshot. "What a child! She is quite mad about Nickie, poor boy. Tom, perhaps you would sing something in the meantime."

"Oh certainly, I'm the 'am in the sandwich. Come along, Julia, we'll do our bit."

Before Tom had graciously acceded to the demands for an encore Jack, with Peggy in triumphal attendance, had appeared with his young brother at the door, and in the slight confusion of the applause accorded Tom's encore, had assisted him to a chair, relieved him of his crutches, handed him his violin, and had gone to the place vacated by Tom at Sylvia's side.

"What a lovely boy! Oh wonderful!" breathed Sylvia.

"Better not say 'lovely' to him," said Jack. "The young devil would probably brain you with one of his crutches."

"Nonsense! I want to sit beside him. Can't you arrange it?"

"Impossible. First he would object, and second I would object."

"Why?" asked Sylvia simply.

"He hates attention, loathes petting, actual or metaphorical."

"Do you think I would? How little you know me!" Sylvia was gently indignant.

"And then, I haven't had a dozen words with you this whole ghastly evening," continued Jack. "Are you aware what that means to me?"

"Let us be sensible, Jack," said Sylvia.

"Sensible? Good heavens! Don't you realize I am half through a proposal to you? And that the agony of uncertainty is as a fire within my veins? Don't you?"

"Now Jack, don't be silly. Especially here with all these people about. Oh, the Quintet is going to sing. Tell me about them."

But Jack had slipped over to his young brother's side and was talking eagerly to him, obviously explaining what the coming number was to be. The boy's very pale face, with its deep, dark, lustrous eyes was all aglow with eager expectation. Suddenly he turned to his big brother with an imperious demand. Jack shook his head. The boy's long thin fingers appeared to bite into Jack's forearm, his face suddenly seemed to be alight with a pale flame of passion, as he repeated his demand. Finally Jack appeared to surrender, and hurried over to

Sylvia.

"Come and sit beside the little devil. He wants you quick."

In an instant Sylvia was beside the boy just as the Quintet began their first number.

"Hush!" said the boy very softly, his fingers resting upon Sylvia's arm.

It was an ancient chorale of the seventeenth century, marvellously harmonized by their leader, and rendered with fine reverential restraint. The number was received in perfect silence, a tribute equally to the good taste of the audience and the artistic perfection of the rendering.

"How lovely! How perfectly lovely!" said Sylvia to the boy beside her.

"Wait. They are going on again," he said, his dark eyes luminous with a deep inner light. He was right. The Quintet almost immediately gave a second number. This time a simple old French Canadian chanson, but exquisitely harmonized, and exquisitely rendered. During the applause which followed, the boy caught her arm.

"Go and tell Monsieur Franck, the leader, I want 'A la claire Fontaine.' Quick please. They know me."

Immediately, forgetting to be shy, Sylvia moved to the piano to the leader and made her request, pointing to the boy.

"Ah! Le petit Nickie?" he replied, with a delighted smile and wave of his hand to the boy. "Tell him, with great pleasure." Once more the Laval Quintet charmed the audience with that best known and best loved of all the old chansons of the French-Canadian people, "A la claire Fontaine." During the interlude of conversation people began to move about.

"You are Sylvia," said the boy, his eyes searching her face with a grave, curiously ardent gaze.

"Yes," said Sylvia, "do you like me?"

"Jack told me about Paddy. He said you were lovely. And you are too. You are like a flower--a sweet pea."

"Oh Nickie, what a lovely thing to say."

"Yes, you are. I like you."

"Do you, Nickie," said Sylvia, a little flush on her cheek. "I'm glad you do. I think we are going to be good friends."

"Jack told me how you sing 'My Mother bids me,'" continued Nickie. "Are you going to sing that to-night?"

"Oh, no no! Nickie! Not to-night. Some time when you come to see me."

"Jack said you would sing it to-night." His grave voice expressed disappointment.

"But I am not a great artist--like the people here," said Sylvia.

"The people here!" Nickie's voice was full of scorn. "I can play that song, I play it with Jack. I was going to play it with you to- night."

"Were you, Nickie? Well--perhaps--Yes, since you want it, if they ask me--I'll try--with you."

The boy's face flushed with a quick glow.

"I knew it! You are a sport."

"I'm not much of a sport. But--since you are going to play it--you see."

"Yes, you are a sport. Oh, we will do it well."

"I am not so sure. You have your violin here?"

"Yes! I always take it wherever I go. They like to hear me. And I like to play to people that like to hear me play. The Laval boys always like to hear me. My violin is just out there."

"Let me get it," said Sylvia.

"You understand, don't you? You are quick to understand."

He opened the case, took out his violin, ran his hands lovingly over it, touched the strings, frowned a little.

"It's out a bit."

"Shall I get the A for you?"

"No no! I don't need it. I carry the A in my head. There that's it! The piano is not quite in tune--but it is as good as most of them. They're always out of tune. A piano is always like that. You always sing in tune. I can tell."

"Oh, Nickie. I'm no great singer."

"No, you're not a great singer, but you are a lovely singer. And you would never sing off pitch."

"How do you know, Nickie? You've never heard me sing. Did Jack tell--?"

"No, no!" said the boy impatiently. "I can tell by your face and by your voice. You could sing 'Young love lies sleeping.' Do you know it? Sommerville's you know. He is modern but quite good, in that song anyway."

"Yes, I sing that--at least I used to but--"

"You will sing that to-night--" Nickie announced.

"But Nickie, I'm afraid, I'm shy!"

"Shy? No, I don't think so. If you love music you won't be shy. Shy people are silly. They are thinking of themselves. If they were thinking of their music they wouldn't be shy, they couldn't. I'm going to do a little Brahms tonight. Do you like Brahms? And a little Mozart. Ah, he is the boy! There is no one like Mozart! Shy?" Nickie's voice was full of contempt. "Think how silly to be shy when you are doing Mozart."

"But I am shy, Nickie. I am silly, I suppose, but I am."

"If you would do Mozart with me, you won't be shy. I wouldn't let you. I wouldn't let you." The masterful tone of the boy was amazing. "It would be worse than silly. It would be terrible. A shame! Think Mozart!"

At this Jack came over to them.

"When do we come on Jack? She's going to sing 'Young love'--you know--Sommerville."

"Oh Nickie, I'm afraid," cried Sylvia in a panic. "I--Jack, how can I? I've never even tried it over with you. I don't know your tricks, Nickie, or anything."

"Oh pshaw! Don't be silly. We will go over it twice--Jack and I and then you will get it."

"Hold up, old chap! None of that! I know you. You'll want Sylvia to play second to you. And that won't do. You're a great conductor. Oh, I know him. He makes us all play second to him. He is a perfect bully. And I'm not going to have Sylvia bullied."

Nickie's face grew dark.

"Besides, it would be terribly bad art," said Jack.

"Come out here!" ordered the boy. "Take my violin!" he picked up his crutches and flung himself out into the next room.

"He is a frightfully spoiled little bully. Better come along."

"Now, will you hum it over. This is the key," said the boy.

He ran over a few bars. It never occurred to Sylvia to demur, not even to hesitate. The boy was heart and soul intent on the music. Personalities were nothing to him.

He played the few bars of introduction, gave her a note and she was away, the violin following pianissimo, but yet with full suggestion of stress and shading.

"Good! good!" said the boy. "But you must let yourself go here when you sing this phrase--right up, all your heart. No shouting, but all your heart. Listen!" In sweet, soft, tenuous whispering notes the violin sang the air.

"Now here!" In full throbbing tones the song swelled up in a magnificent crescendo. "Let your heart into it--and here--linger a bit--a lovely phrase--here--linger a bit--no dragging--but just a suggestion that you hate to let it go. See!" Again he ran over the phrase.

"Oh lovely," said Sylvia. "Yes I see--Oh, that is so right! Let me do it again."

Once more they ran over the song, both of them so completely wrapt up in their work as to be entirely oblivious of their environment.

"Say boy, that's great!" said Jack, "but don't bully her!"

"Bully her!" echoed the boy in scorn. "If she sings like that-- lets her heart into it, they'll never hear me or you either, if you do your stuff right. There's only one thing can beat the violin-- only one--the voice, oh! If I could only make it speak, sing like the voice! Now let's do, 'My Mother bids me.' This is quite different--very, very smooth--no bulges--no mountain tops."

The boy ran over the air--gave a nod and Sylvia began. A dozen bars and Nickie stopped dead, disgust in his face.

"Say! What are you thinking about?" he asked wrathfully. "Yourself? That crowd out there?"

Sylvia looked at him in surprise.

"Did you think once of Lubin? Lubin! He's the only one that matters. Lubin! And he's away. Your heart is broken."

Once more he played the introduction and again Sylvia sang, the violin sighing, throbbing its heart-breaking accompaniment.

"Oh Jack! She is lovely!" cried Nickie when she had finished, his dark eyes shining.

"Poor thing, poor thing. Lubin gone for ever--" said Jack. "Yes yes, sing like that, Sylvia, and you'll pulverize that crowd."

"The crowd! The crowd! Rot! Forget them! Only Lubin matters," said Nickie angrily. "Jack, you make me sick! Mind you don't spoil this."

Jack grinned at Sylvia.

"But Jack, he is right. If only I can think of Lubin, I won't be a bit shy. Oh Nickie, I wish you would come out to Riverside to my girls' club, and show my girls how to sing."

"Girls' club? Girls? Not me! I despise them, and I am terrified."

"What Nickie? Terrified. What about Handel and Mozart and Brahms and all the rest?"

"I don't like girls," he said gloomily.

"Well, let's slide in," said Jack.

"Jack, we'll come in after the Laval boys. You fix that--they make me feel like it. Eh?"

"All right, boy. I guess you're a good deal like the rest of us, eh?"

The musical evening moved along smoothly, pleasantly, under Mrs. Foster's kindly direction, the amateurs being made to feel that they were really conferring a distinct honour and pleasure upon the company in venturing to appear side by side with the professionals, the latter being delighted to be received for the time into the genial circle of family friendship and privilege.

The most distinguished among this class was the famous pianist Monsieur Armand La Marche, who had just returned from Paris where he had had the rare privilege of studying under the personal supervision of the great Satre himself, of whose work he was par excellence the expositeur on this continent. He usually presented only the great master's work, but to-night, as a special concession to the more professional character of the program, and as a favour to the friends of his dear friend and patroness, Mrs. Foster, he would render selections from Poulenc, and indeed he might even present something from Debussy.

When the great Armand, whose bushy hair and pointed beard sufficiently proclaimed his Parisian breeding--his home, by the way was in the neighbouring hamlet of St. Eustache--made his appearance, silence subdued the audience into a fixed rigidity of attention. The ecstatic and prolonged applause that followed the Satre number, attested at once the perfection of the performance technical and interpretative, the highly artistic nature of the composer's work, and very especially the discriminating taste of the audience.

Nickie alone sat with unmoved, puzzled, almost sullen face.

"What are you clapping for?" he asked Sylvia crossly.

"Well--I think he is wonderfully clever. He has wonderful fingers."

"Fingers! Not half so clever as an electric piano!"

"Besides, he did his best, you know," added Sylvia.

"What's eating you, boy?" asked Jack.

"Jack, tell me, is that music? I don't know what he is trying to do."

"Nor me," said Jack cheerfully, still applauding, "but he was trying something and apparently he got it. Must give him credit for that."

But Nickie was only enraged chiefly, it must be acknowledged, at his own inability to get even an inkling of what the great Satre was after.

With the Poulenc number it was the same. The Debussy presentation however, stirred the boy to enthusiasm. "Wonderful finger work!" he said "but--after all-- for music, for real music--" He shook his head.

"Cut it out, Nickie, you are a frightful snob!" said Jack laughing at him. "They can't all be like Mozart, you know."

"Mozart! No! not one of them. For music that gets you here," touching his head, "and especially here," touching his breast, "you must get Mozart. Jack I'm going home. I'm tired! I'm sick of this! I hate it!"

"But Nickie, what about Sylvia's songs?" said Jack in dismay.

"I don't care. I hate it! That Frenchman makes me sick! I can't! I won't play."

His face was convulsed with rage and disgust, his voice rose, high and shrill.

"Shut up!" said Jack sharply.

"Don't Jack!" said Sylvia. "I know just how he feels. I am exactly the same way. I couldn't begin to sing Haydn to-night."

The boy turned to her, caught her hand and held it to his cheek, the tears welling up in his eyes.

"Yes, you know! Of course you would understand," he said brokenly.

"Oh very well. Let's get out of this," said Jack handing the boy his crutches, and carrying out his violin into the next room. "We will have some refreshment anyway."

Having seen Nickie comfortably settled down before some cool drinks, flanked by ice cream and cake, with Sylvia to look after him, Jack made his way back to the music room and got into touch with the leader of the Laval Quintet. To him he explained the situation.

"He's a temperamental little beggar. Those Satre numbers he couldn't get on to- -And so he is all out of key."

"Certainement! Who can be anything but out of key? No? I am flappergast!"

"Go and talk to him and tell him that, and by the way, have you anything of Mozart that you can do?"

"Mozart? Ah--no--But yes! The very thing--Ah! Sublime, a petite pastorale. I will tell heem--Yes! He must not desert me. C'est impossible! Leave it with me, m'sieu Jacques."

The intermission for refreshments the leader of the Laval Quintet spent with Nickie and Sylvia. He knew exactly how to handle the lad. He loathed Satre, he adored Mozart. Especially that little sonatina that Nickie played sometimes. "You will play that to- night. And we are singing a lovely old Mozart canticle. Ah! You will love it. And Mademoiselle is to sing for us a little Haydn, not? With the violin obbligato--Ah!" Monsieur Franck rolled his eyes. "So delicate! So parfait! Yes, you will sing them Mademoiselle--wit' the violin obbligato-- then the Satre nombre--but we will skeep out like--like--dat beas'--what you call?--he's dere-- you put your finger dere--he's not dere."

"Flea," cried Nickie in great spirits.

"Oui! Flea," said M. Franck. "So we are not here! N'est ce pas?"

It all turned out as Monsieur Franck had arranged. There was no more word of going home with Nickie. The Laval Quintet did their Mozart canticle with beautiful expression, following which Nickie came with his Mozart sonatina.

Then came Sylvia's songs, first the Sommerville and then the Haydn, with Jack at the piano and Nickie with his violin supporting, sustaining, suggesting like one inspired. The startling loveliness of the girl, the utter absence of all self-consciousness, the exquisite purity of her voice, the unspoiled charming simplicity of her style, all this with the haunting vibrant obbligato from Nickie's violin, swept the audience into a perfect rapture of applause. Again and yet again the encore was demanded, the great Monsieur Armand La Marche leading. Jack was for a repetition, Sylvia was not unwilling, but with the instinct of the true artist, Nickie refused. M. Franck supported him.

"No no! You mus' do better to do as well," he said. "And you can't do better. No."

"I am going home," said Nickie.

"By Jove, you are right boy," said Jack. "Come along."

"I shall be back in a few minutes, Sylvia. Wait for me."

"Good-night, Nickie. And thank you for the obbligato. But I am afraid we tired you to death."

"Sylvia," replied the boy, his dark eyes warm with adoring gratitude. "It was a great night. That Sommerville was right, just right. Sylvia, I'm coming to play for your club."

"Nickie, you are a dear. That is just splendid."

"Kiss him good-night, Sylvia," suggested Jack wickedly.

The boy's face went red, a furious red.

"Aw, get out! I--I--don't kiss girls," he stammered.

"Quite right too!" agreed Jack heartily.

"Oh you! Huh, I've seen--" But Jack clapped his hand over his mouth.

"Now then young fellow. You look out--Remember! There are things I could tell."

"Aw! Go on--" muttered Nickie. But no more revelations were made.

"Come along," said Peggy. "I have your violin. We'll be right back, Julia. Hush, not a word to mother. Quick, here she comes." And Peggy dashed out toward the hall.

"It's quite all right, Julia. Tell your mother we'll be right back," said Jack.

"Good-night," said Julia in a doubtful tone. "You're a wild lot of kids. Thanks, Nickie, dear," she stooped down and kissed the pale cheek.

"Ah Nickie!" cried Sylvia, reproach in her voice.

"Pshaw! It's just Julia!" said Nickie with cool nonchalance.

"And Julia doesn't count," said Julia in exaggerated grief.

"You do! You know you do," protested the boy angrily.

"Oh, all right, Nickie, dear. We understand," said Julia kindly patting the boy's cheek.

"Huh, huh of course," he said smiling swiftly at her.

"We'll be back in twenty minutes, Julia. I've got to see him to bed you know," said Jack.

"All right Jack, old chap. Don't rush Nickie through his prayers," replied Julia.

"Isn't he a dear?" exclaimed Sylvia.

"Yes, Jack's a fine chap!" replied Julia.

"Oh! I meant Nickie," replied Sylvia hurriedly.

"Ah? Yes, he is a darling. Poor little chap! He hates going to bed alone-- especially these last two years. His father or Jack always puts him to bed."

"Oh Julia!" quick tears rushed to Sylvia's eyes. "Poor little soul!"

"Yes, a queer, difficult, lonely, little soul." Julia's voice was deep and tender with the mother note in it. "It is a lonely house since the mother died. Come dear. Perhaps you will help with the refreshments." She put her arms about the girl and drew her close.

"Oh Julia!" whispered the girl, clinging to her for a moment. "You are a dear."

"And so are you, darling," replied Julia kissing her.

The heart knoweth its own bitterness.

CHAPTER VIII

After the guests had departed Tom proposed a turn for Sylvia at the Ritz supper dance. His mother demurred.

"But Sylvia has never been at a supper dance in her life, she says," pleaded Tom.

"And none the worse for that, Tom. Besides she is tired out. Look at her, Julia."

"She looks very gay, if you ask me, and fit for anything," replied Julia. "Better let her go. She can sleep late to-morrow."

Her mother critically considered her son. Tom's face was flushed and his manner unduly expansive.

"Why, let the child have a little fling. Let her see the Ritz in all its glory. It is rather special to-night. I happen to know. Max Moreau's orchestra and--and that kind of thing."

His mother relented. "Oh, very well. But remember, Tom, take good care of her. No nonsense, and not too late."

"Sure thing, my dear mother. You can trust me," replied her son solemnly.

"Run along then, Sylvia, get your wrap," said Aunt Arabella doubtfully.

They had not been gone more than half an hour when Jack Tempest and Peggy made their appearance.

"Awfully sorry, Aunt Arabella. Nickie was rather more difficult than usual. He was all worked up over the show. La Marche seems to have stirred up something quite devilish in him. He was awfully worked up. And over Sylvia too. By the way where is Sylvia?" he asked, glancing about the room. "Off to bed? Tired I guess. Say, that girl was great to-night. Nickie certainly released some unsuspected powers in her. She never sang like that before. How is she? Used up?"

"Used up? Not at all, the monkey. She's off to the Ritz."

"The Ritz?" Jack looked at his watch. "Oh, well, it's early yet. Eleven-thirty."

"Yes, Tom insisted and--"

"Oh, Tom took her?" Jack flashed a look at Julia. She shook her head slightly.

"Well, I'll take a run round myself. What about it Peggy, eh?"

"Oh Mother!" said Peggy.

"Peggy, not a foot of you. Off to bed!"

"But to-morrow is Saturday, Mother. And I've never seen the Ritz at night. Just for an hour, Mother."

"Let her go, Mother. Jack will look after her."

"What about you, Julia?" asked Jack.

"You can go, Julia," said her mother.

"Not me, I loathe a supper dance, as you know. But let the child go."

Peggy stood looking at her mother in silence, but with imploring eyes.

"Well! Just a look in Jack and then bring them all home. Remember Jack, just an hour and bring the others with you."

"Thank you, Aunt Arabella. Come along, Peggy," said Jack.

"Thank you, darling," cried Peggy, rushing at her mother.

The supper room at the Ritz was crowded to overflowing with late comers from the movies and the theatres. With some difficulty Jack found a table in a corner remote from the dancing floor. All the tables were crowded with parties, large and small, all more or less noisy, and some quite hilarious.

"Oh, Jack, isn't it great," said Peggy in an ecstatic undertone. "Do you know all the people?"

"Not I, thank God. Where did this gang come from? What is the Ritz coming to? Oh yes! It's the races of course. I quite forgot, or I shouldn't have brought you here, young lady."

"Are there really a lot of bad people? I mean really? To-night?" asked Peggy hugely delighted. "But Jack, their dresses are grand! Look at that lady! Look right there!"

"Well don't point, Peggy. You will excite them quite too much. That creation in the green and gold sheathing is carrying quite all she can at the moment."

"And don't they dance wonderfully?"

"Very!"

"I don't see Sylvia, Jack. I wonder how she dances."

"I wonder! In this mob!" said Jack a grim look in his face. "Do you want to dance, Peggy?"

"Oh, Jack, do you think I could with all those grand dancers?"

"Grand dancers? Like that, eh? Or that? Come on Peggy, you can't be worse than the worst and you will be as good as the best."

"Jack, you won't be ashamed of my frock?" said Peggy shyly.

"Peggy, at least you are dressed--front and back. You are perfectly all right. Lord save us! Look at that kid! Ought to be spanked, or her fool mother? Come on Peggy, and show them a good time, eh?"

Peggy was a prize performer at school, and adored dancing. She had the poise, balance and sense of rhythm that go to make a girl a delight to her partner.

"You are all right, Peggy. No one on the floor can beat you, and few can equal you," said Jack, himself one of the best dancers in the city.

"Oh, Jack, you are just lovely," she breathed as they finished the second encore to the fox-trot. "You could make an elephant dance!"

"Peggy, you are a dandy dancer. You are quick in your guessing. What about an ice?"

"Oh, yummy, Jack!"

"What's your best bet. Banana sundae, if I remember right."

"Jack, the very thing I want most. But they are terribly expensive."

"Oh, let's go the limit!" said Jack. "What about a double one?"

"But not at once, Jack."

"Well all right. One at a time. Eh?" said the understanding Jack giving the waiter an order.

"I wonder where Sylvia is? I don't see her anywhere."

"Nor I," said Jack crossly.

"Oh, Jack, I hope Tom--Tom was pretty--I mean--" Peggy paused abruptly.

"Tut tut, child. What are you talking about?"

"Oh, I know all right. I could see quite well at dinner--"

"Shut up, child. You don't know anything about it."

"He was--I know well enough--" Peggy's face was full of shamed anxiety.

At this moment a rather noisy party came in to the supper room.

"Jack!" said Peggy, gripping his arm. "There they are now."

"Hush Peggy! Don't look," said Jack.

With face stern and set his eyes followed the party as they made their way toward a distant table.

After some considerable noisy confusion and protestation on Tom's part, the party found their table and sat down.

"That's Harry Hillyard," whispered Peggy. "He is horrid. I don't like him a bit. Don't let him ask me, Jack."

"Don't you worry, Peggy. He won't bother you," said Jack. "Never look at the little beast. He has seen us, and so has Tom. Here he comes, confound the fool," he muttered angrily.

"Hello, you people! Why Peggy, what's happened to you?"

Tom's voice boomed out above the noise. "Come on over to our table. We'll make room for you."

"Tom, you're making too much noise. And what the devil do you mean by allowing Sylvia to get mixed up with that gang?"

"Why, what's the matter with--" began Tom.

"Tom, you listen to me," Jack's voice was deadly quiet. "We are not going to your table. And you are going to get Sylvia right away from that crowd. Harry Hillyard! And as usual half shot! Haven't you any sense of decency. Now Tom, you know me. I simply won't have Sylvia sit there. You bring her right over here. Tell them she has a prior engagement with us, or anything you like. Your sister is here and though I hate to have you too, I'll stand that. But you bring Sylvia right here or so help me, I'll walk over there and take her from you, if I have to knock out every man in your party, and you with them."

Jack's face was set and white, his voice low, trembling with passion, his eyes spitting fire.

"Well, I'll be--"

"Tom, speak low and smile. I would hate to have that girl mixed up in any disgraceful scene in the Ritz before all this crowd. But as God lives, I will not have her stay with that gang. Make up your mind and quick. You know me--" Suddenly Jack rose to his feet. "Great Heavens above!" he said in a terrible voice. "I'll have to kill that brute!" He started from his chair.

"Wait Jack! Don't go. I'll do what you say. Don't go. Sit down I'll get her--"

"No no, sit down here Tom. Don't move! I'll handle this myself by gad. Look at the beast!"

At the other table, Harry Hillyard was half dragging to her feet Sylvia, who with pale and frightened face was trying to break from his grasp.

With easy swift-moving steps Jack crossed the room and coming upon Hillyard from behind, gripped his arm with fingers that reached the bone.

"Here! What the--" began the young man.

"Hello Harry! Good evening ladies! So here you are at last Sylvia. We've been waiting for you--" With smiling face Jack bowed to the company. "Come along, Sylvia! We are waiting for you. Good-night!" Again and still with a smiling face he bowed low to the company, gave Sylvia his arm, and chatting cheerily led her over to his own table, gave her his chair and stood smiling pleasantly at Tom.

"See here, Jack, you can't--" began Tom.

"Smile Tom, you big idiot! Go over to your gang and tell them just what you want to. If you don't like it I'll tell you what you can do. You have three men there, ask them to go out into the next room. I'll meet you there, and I'll lick blazes out of you, one by one. You know I can do it, and you know I will. Now smile everybody." He ended with a cheery hearty laugh, but his eyes were deadly cold, cold as death. With a mighty effort Tom responded with a loud guffaw. Peggy too, laughed bravely. Sylvia turned toward her late companion and threw him a dazzling smile.

"Well played, by Jove! You two are the stuff I like. Hurry up, Tom. Meantime Sylvia, what about a turn?"

Immediately though trembling so that she could hardly stand but with a face radiantly smiling, she lifted her arms to Jack and swung away into a fox-trot.

"Better sit down, Tom, and smile at me," said Peggy gaily. "Be a sport if you can."

With an oath, Tom sat down, his back toward his late companions. While Peggy, still gaily laughing in his face kept up a patter of bright talk.

"Oh, shut off your confounded chatter," he growled. "I'd like to smash his face. Cursed bully that he is."

"Oh, but you couldn't, Tom. You know you couldn't," laughed Peggy as if she were having quite a jolly time. "You remember quite well he held Belanger himself for six rounds. Me! I would love to see him hand that horrid little Hillyard one, just one would be enough. And one apiece would do for the rest. Ha! Ha! Ha!" Peggy's laugh rang out so pleasantly as she glanced over in the direction of the other table that she set them all laughing in response.

"Jolly kid, eh?" said Harry Hillyard. "Tom's kid sister, eh? Don't understand what--I'll just go over and see." He made his way across the room.

"Good evening," he said. "What's all the joke? Can't you spare us a bit?"

"Oh, I have been telling Tom something funny I just remembered. You tell him Tom." Her hands were trembling, her lips were dry, but her laugh rang out like a peal of bells.

"You're a crazy nit," growled Tom.

"What about a little fox-trot, eh?" Hillyard meant his smile to be full of lure.

"Oh, I'm engaged to Tom for the next, and besides--there, it's over and here's Jack."

"Come on out of this," said Tom sullenly, rising and turning to go with Hillyard.

"We will be going in a few minutes now, Tom," said Jack, as he came up. "We won't wait for you. I'll take Sylvia home."

"All right," grunted Tom. "I'll stick round a bit."

"Good-night, ladies. Good-night, Jack," said Harry Hillyard. The ladies bowed with their best grace. Jack looked at him as if he were one of the pillars about them.

"Have an ice, eh?" said Jack as they were alone.

"No, no--oh let us go away," said Sylvia.

"What about a banana sundae, Peggy?"

"Oh Jack, if Sylvia would only."

"Sure, we'll all have 'em." He summoned the waiter. "Two banana sundaes, and for me a highball." His face was still pale and set like carved granite.

"Jack you'd better smile," said Peggy. "They are all looking."

"Good girl. What were you laughing at?"

Peggy told him.

"Peggy, you are one gay old sport," said Jack with a laugh that rang out full of genuine humor. "I'll remember you. I'll give you a real supper dance sometime soon."

As they took their refreshments they all kept up a steady flow of light chatter, Peggy's wild laugh ringing out above all.

"Jack," said Sylvia, in low tones as she finished her sundae. "Can't you get Tom to come home with us?"

"I have lost all interest in Tom," replied Jack coolly.

"But Jack, he came with me. His mother would like him to come home with me, and I would too." Her voice was very quiet and very earnest.

"You would?"

"Yes Jack. Don't you see he must come with us. You can see that."

"Can I? You surprise me Sylvia."

"Jack, what will his mother say? Besides--oh Jack, you must see that he must come with us. Do get him for my sake, Jack." Her voice was tremulous, her lips quivering.

"For your sake!" replied Jack speaking quietly. "Then I'll get him. Excuse me."

He sauntered over to the other group who were just finishing their drinks, accepted a chair and a drink, chatted gaily with them for a few minutes. Then putting his hand on Tom's shoulder said, "Well, we must be going, I guess Tom. My young lady should have been in bed long ago. I begged her off from her mother, and Sylvia has had rather an exhausting evening. She is dead tired. She is waiting for you, Tom. Good-night all. Time you were all in your nighties or pygies, isn't it?"

Without demur Tom made his farewells and came away with him.

As they were putting on their wraps Sylvia said: "Peggy dear, do you mind if I ride home in Jack's car?"

"What? Of course I do!" She glanced at Sylvia's face. "Oh well-- all right--but-- oh darn it all! I suppose I must give him up to you anyway." Peggy was frankly hostile.

"No. It's not that Peggy, but I must speak to him. I caused him-- all of you, a lot of trouble to-night--and I must--oh I must speak to him, Peggy." The look of distress in the lovely face, the pain in the blue eyes swept away Peggy's feeling of hostility.

"Oh, you poor thing," she said with a quick rush of sympathy. "Go on home with him. Anyway it was you that brought Tom home. Mother will love you for that. Oh yes, she knows Tom. We all know him." Peggy's voice was very bitter. "You did a fine bit of work there."

"But you won't say a word to your mother, Peggy!"

"Oh, won't I?"

"Promise me, Peggy. That would spoil it all, don't you see."

"But--oh well--I suppose so. Say, how is it you make me do things. You make everybody do things."

"No. It is your own good heart, Peggy. You are a real brick. Some day, perhaps, I can help you."

"No, no. You can't do that," said the girl tragically.

"Some day, Peggy. Come along, old girl."

As they came out under the porte-cochère Peggy ran to Tom's car and climbed in. "Good-bye, Jack," she cried. "Thanks for a perfectly splendiferous evening and the sundaes!"

"Here!" said Tom wrathfully. "What do you mean coming in here?"

"Oh, drive on, Tom. Do you think she wants to come with you? After to-night?"

"What's the matter with you," snapped Tom. "Who are you talking to, kid?"

"Yes, that's it--that's just it. I'm talking to my own brother." Her voice broke suddenly. Tom could feel her body shaking with her sobbing.

"Oh darn it all, kiddy, don't cry," said Tom in sudden penitence. "I did make a fool of myself. I guess I had a cocktail or so too many."

"Yes, and I was so ashamed. Oh, I could have died. Before that rotten little drunken beast Harry Hillyard too, and--and all his horrid gang. You made me ashamed--the first time in my life I was out with you!" Her voice was broken now with agonized sobbing. "And you made Sylvia ashamed--And mother! I never knew what it was that makes mother look like she does sometimes."

"Hush, hush up kiddy. I'm awfully sorry."

"And now--I can--never go--out with you--when I--grow up." Peggy's sobs broke out with renewed violence. "And that's why Julia doesn't like to go with you. I never could understand. I do now-- oh--I do now!" The girl was becoming hysterical.

"For God's sake, Peggy, stop! I feel badly enough without all that. I guess I've lost to-night, the loveliest girl I ever met in my life." Tom's voice was full of bitterness.

Peggy's sobbing ceased at once.

"No Tom, you never had a chance with Sylvia. That was settled before you ever saw her."

"How do you know?"

"Shucks, any girl knows. I could tell by her eyes. When a girl gets that look in her eyes it's all over except the orange blossoms," said the worldly wise Peggy.

When Sylvia slipped in beside Jack he turned a stony face toward her, and with dry sarcasm remarked:

"Coming to smooth down my heckles, eh?"

"No Jack," she said slipping her hand under his arm. "Only to tell you how proud I am of you, and to tell you--to tell you--oh Jack-- won't you--finish what you began in the conservatory?"

"Sylvia! oh Sylvia!" cried Jack in a sudden ecstasy. "Oh dash it, why does this come on when I have only one arm free?"

"Let them go on, Jack, and a little further on there is a lovely view. Oh, what a terrible bold girl I am. You will just despise me."

"Just wait three minutes," said Jack. "I'll show you how much I despise and loathe you. I know an excellent spot."

"With a view, Jack?"

"Nary a view--darn all views--there's only one view I want." For five more minutes the car raced and twisted up the mountain side and came to rest in a little shady angle.

"But Jack, isn't this dangerous?" whispered Sylvia.

"Sure! Life is one long series of hazards. I'm taking my life in my hands now-- oh Sylvia, darling!"

"Oh Jack, Jack! my Jack! my very own boy!" she whispered, clinging to him, when her lips were free. "Oh, I never thought it would be like this. Oh I am perfectly shameless. Oh darling, you won't ever let me go?"

"Not till I lose my mind, or till I'm dead!"

"Oh!" she laughed gaily. "I was afraid for just a minute to-night. But then I remembered--and I knew."

"Remembered?"

"Yes, Jack. How you looked! Poor Jack! I knew--I knew and my heart jumped up in my throat and choked me. I was sorry for you!"

"Sorry for me?"

"Yes, sorry for you, that you loved me--a little girl like me--no money--no style--no--anything--"

"No sense! Not a darn shred of sense. You poor little fool. Do you know there isn't a man in Montreal wouldn't think himself a king if he could feel your arms round him, as I feel them, feel your heart beat as I feel it, feel your lips as I feel them now?"

CHAPTER IX

"No, Miss Sylvia, I'm telling you the story right. You go into this merger and you're safe. You'll have no responsibility. You're in with a big concern with strong financial backing. You've got a free hand in management, your people are safe. Stay out and you're alone. More than that you're up against a killing competition. And believe me they're out to kill. They don't know the meaning of mercy nor of justice either. They'll squeeze your life out just like that." And Mr. Brady's big hand rolled up and crushed into a misshapen bulk a sheet of paper and flung it into the wastebasket.

"Mind you, they're offering you better terms than to any of the others. I put up a fight for you. They want you in, and they sure don't want you out--not your father's daughter. Some of the big ones knew him. See here! You have a firm agreement appointing you secretary for two years--that will test out the thing-- You have practical control of all employees--hiring and firing. That's a wonderful concession. I had to pull hair for that. But I told them how it was with you and your people, and you've got a good price and a good interest in the Corporation, which may run up to ten, fifteen, twenty per cent. It may turn out a big thing, a mighty big thing."

"And your advice, Mr. Brady, is that I close with the offer?" The girl's blue eyes rested trustfully on Mr. Brady's big broad face. Mr. Brady gave her back look for look.

"Didn't ye hear me tellin' you?" he said lapsing in his excitement into his native Doric. "An' do you think I could be lookin' into thim lovely blue eyes of yours and lie till ye? I may be all wet, but that's me best to you, an' so it is, Miss Sylvia."

"I believe you, Mr. Brady. I believe you are a good man." Mr. Brady's loud and cynical laugh interrupted her.

"Good man is it? Well, well. Don't mention it outside the office."

"But I do, and I'm going to trust you. You are giving me till to- morrow."

"It's the last minute, Miss Sylvia. Be wise now. It's my heart will be broke for ye, if you give thim fellas a chance at your lovely throat. Good-bye thin. An' the saints be good till ye."

Mr. Brady held her hand for a few minutes. "My dear," he said kindly, "it's a man of your own you need to guide you. But the man good enough for you is hard to find. They're not hangin' on the bushes, so they're not."

"Thank you again, Mr. Brady. Good-bye," she said, a faint flush on her cheek.

Mr. Brady paused in the outer office at Frances' desk and cocked his hat over his left ear.

"Now then, young ladies," he said resuming his best business accent and manner, "what about a nice little dinner at the Royal to-night. And a little dance to follow?"

"Sorry, Mr. Brady," began Frances.

"Oh Mr. Brady, how sudden," drawled Sally. "Of course she'll come. She's young and shy. I'll make her come."

"Shall I call for you in my car, say 6.30? A little glide up the river for an appetizer eh? Cool breezes? What?"

"Oh how lovely--But Mr. Brady, right out in the open? In broad daylight?" Sally's blue eyes looked up at him through shrouding lashes.

"Say, Miss Frances, you've simply got to come along," said Mr. Brady anxiously. "There's things I'm afraid of after dark. All right 6.30 then." He took down Frances' number, lifted his hat, winked at the typist, a long slow wink, threw out his chest and sauntered out with a truly Napoleonic air.

Meantime Sylvia was on the phone. "Jack, I want you for dinner to- night."

"Yes Jack, it is important. In fact, a matter of life and death. Oh! But this is a big deal, too. What? A hundred thousand? No, mine does not quite reach that amount, but it's all I have. Oh, can you? That's very nice of you. Yes, I'll get him too. Yes, indeed he is very nice. Goodbye, Jack. I'm busy--Good-bye. Oh, by the way, do get Professor Hale. He's so very clever--what? Oh yes, he knows Mr. Matheson too. They belong to the same club. Yes, he's been out here once or twice. What? Well three times at least. No, no, nothing like that. Just economics. Yes sure! All right, you'll bring him. Good-bye--what? But Jack think of the charges! I must really ring off now--no! Good-bye."

Again Sylvia was on the phone.

"Auntie darling, Jack and Professor Hale will be out for dinner. I know it is short notice, dear. But I must decide to-night. It is really very important--what?

nonsense! Nothing like that--no, pure business--Big Business--Capital B. And Auntie, get Mr. Matheson too--what? But if you ask him he will--sure he will. Yes, really I want his advice. He is very wise. Huh huh--and so nice!" The telephone clicked sharply as Sylvia's laugh rang out.

As Sylvia turned from the telephone her face settled into an expression of grave concern, if not of anxiety. Within twenty-four hours she would be called upon to make a decision that would directly and indirectly affect the lives of two hundred and fifty people, for whom she felt responsible, and her own life as well. At present she was her own mistress. She was secretary of her little company, and also she controlled the stock. Her decision would determine whether the business associated for half a century with her father's name would pass into the hands of a corporation which would be governed by one sole consideration--that of profits. The whole country had gone mad for mergers. Big business both in the United States and in Canada was in the saddle and pressing hard.

That evening there gathered about the dinner table at Hilltop House a group of men whose main bond of fellowship was their common interest in the affairs of Sylvia Rivers. The first to arrive was Jack Tempest. There had been no announcement of an engagement between Sylvia and himself. Jack was desperately anxious for an immediate marriage. He hated the agony of a long engagement. With Sylvia, however, there were the two very important questions, of Aunt Elizabeth and the Riverside Mills.

"I want to be married, Jack, right away, of course, but I must consider what will happen to Aunt Elizabeth."

"Sylvia, it will be the very devil for her," said Jack solemnly. "But--then you will be quite near her, and--"

"Then too, there is the business here. I can't just abandon all these people of mine, with all their people--there must be at least two hundred and fifty of them."

"Sell out! You have your chance!" cried Jack.

"Jack, your advice I would value really very highly, but darling, I am not really sure that it would be quite disinterested. You know you are biassed."

"Frightfully, more than you can imagine."

"Oh, I wouldn't say that, Jack. I am fearfully biassed too. But I really want to do the right thing by them."

"Don't I know? You are leaning over backwards, you are so fearfully right. But there's me. Of course I'm not an Aunt or a business, I am a mere man, whose days and nights are one long consuming agony. I found a grey hair to-day."

"Jack, we must not begin by thinking only of ourselves. That would be horrible."

"Well, dear, don't look like that. Let's cerebrate on the problem a little longer. I shall try to-night at the conference to be coldly, passionately, disinterested. Self shall be wholly and ruthlessly immolated upon the altar of altruism. I shall think only of your Aunt Elizabeth. She is a perfect brick--and of the two hundred and fifty family retainers. You shall see! But my darling we may perhaps allow one little thought of self to interject itself now and then? You, I mean and me."

"That is why I asked Professor Hale," said Sylvia hurriedly. "He is very cool and clever and disinterested and--"

"Hold on just there--clever? Yes, as the very old Harry. Cool? Yes, as an active volcano--and disinterested? Well--" Jack's face became quite overcast, "if you really want from him an unbiassed opinion, he is as unbiassed as a starving wolf in the presence of a juicy lamb."

"Nonsense, Jack."

"Well, I give you this bit of data. He used to be ready for a discussion on economics any hour of the day or night. Now, whenever I meet him he becomes dreamy and asks when I last saw Miss Rivers. Frankly I don't like it."

"Do be sensible, Jack."

"That's it. I am far too sensible of his danger. First thing we know that young man will go nutty and lose his job, and I shall have to support him."

"You? And why you?"

"Quite obvious. While I refuse to acknowledge that I am the cause of his MENTAL collapse, I am quite certain I am the OCCASION. If you will brush up your logic."

"The occasion?"

"The occasion," replied Jack firmly. "With a positively wolfish appetite he hungers after you. His dewlaps fairly drip."

"Disgusting and silly, Jack."

"Exactly, but he can't see me. In his path I stand a veritable Verdun: 'He shall not pass.' So there you are. No, he is clever, but unbiassed? No! Firmly no! That young man is growing nutty and I don't blame him."

"Well, there is Mr. Matheson."

"Well, I can hardly pass him. He is a clever guy, but--unbiassed? Of course we can hardly expect him to become lyric in his support of the proposition that we deprive him of his leading soprano, his head push in the various clubs, guilds, circles and groups that have to do with the young life in his congregation. His is the disinterestedness of the O.C. who finds himself about to be deprived of his adjutant and sergeant major in one fell swoop."

"Oh dear, it really is very difficult."

"Then, there is your aunt. You would not suggest--"

"Oh, please don't Jack. It is really impossible to think clearly and--"

"Quite so. The only possible thing, quite obviously, is that you and I form a very definite two-power pact against all these thoroughly and quite naturally selfish forces in order to preserve anything like a decent equilibrium in the situation."

"You really don't help very much. And I must decide to-night."

"Well, my dear, I have one immediate and pressing duty to perform. I can not, in my own interest, allow my property to be threatened."

"Your property?"

"My property. Upon your face I see what might become a disfiguring frown. I must immediately attend to it."

"Oh Jack, you are silly. Do hurry, Aunt Elizabeth may be in any minute."

"Exactly, I shall waste no time, but the thing is not to be hurried. It will take time."

It did.

The little company that gathered about the dinner table in the Hilltop House reflected pretty fairly the financial atmosphere of the city.

"Great days, eh Jack?" began Reggie Hale, after the soup plates had been removed.

"Grand and glorious," replied Jack grinning at his friends.

"What are your winnings to-day, if one may ask?"

"One may ask, of course, but in the best circles one does not answer, unless with a definite and distinct taurential purpose."

"Torrential purpose? Why torrential purpose?"

"Ah, my dear sir, in deference to the limitations of your purely economic education, and with apologies to the classicists among us, may I be permitted to explain, that the word taurential is derived from the word 'Taurus' and not from the word 'torrent,' which would give a quite opposite meaning."

"Ah Taurus--eh--bullish in other words?"

"Exactly, with profound apologies to the ladies."

"Oh indeed, I know that quite well," exclaimed Aunt Elizabeth. "I remember the signs of the Zodiac--'Taurus a bull, Libra a pound, Scorpio a scorpion--and the rest.'"

"Again my apologies, dear Miss Murray."

"Oh, don't give in to him, Miss Murray," said Professor Hale. "He is trying to dodge the question. He is ashamed to let the extent of his piracies be known."

"Thank God for every sign of grace," murmured Mr. Matheson.

"Come on Jack, we won't tell anybody," said the Professor. "Out with it."

"Well, the market was rather slow, showing a gain of only twelve points in certain stocks," said Jack.

"Which on one hundred shares would be twelve hundred dollars exactly, and on a thousand shares would be twelve thousand."

"Quite right."

"And on ten thousand shares, not an unusual operation these days, that would mean one hundred and twenty thousand dollars. How much wind?"

"Wind? No wind. All wood and water."

"Wood and water?" enquired Sylvia in a puzzled voice.

"Yes 'pulp' you see," said Jack gravely.

"Pulp? Oh yes, I see--wood and water." Sylvia made a face at him.

"Don't mind him. He is quite too cocky to-night. No wonder with all that boodle in his belt," said Reggie in high disdain. "It is only another indication of the depths to which he has fallen. Truly facilis decensus Averno, if my classics may be pardoned."

"And what does that mean exactly?" enquired Aunt Elizabeth innocently.

"Reggie ought to be ashamed," said Jack in a shocked voice.

"Nonsense, Auntie," cried Sylvia, "it means--"

"It means, Miss Murray," interrupted Jack, "I regret to say: 'Greased are the skids to hell.' A somewhat free translation, I admit."

"Now Jack, we are not going to allow you to hold the stage any longer," said Sylvia.

"Me? Hold the stage? Why I have simply been answering questions fired at me from every side.'

"Well, anyway, I want you all to solemnly consider my merger. I must give an answer to-morrow. You all know the terms: twenty thousand dollars cash, thirty thousand stock in the new concern. Mr. Brady adds today a two years' contract for me as secretary, and power of hiring and firing. These are the main points."

There was silence for some time. The gravity of the moment weighed upon their minds.

Professor Hale was the first to respond.

"What is your inventory value of your plant as it stands?"

"It is so difficult to say. We have had three separate estimates and they vary from twenty thousand to fifty thousand dollars. As a going concern, I should say that twenty-five thousand would be a fairly low figure, and thirty-five thousand would be a fairly good figure. Of course put up for sale it would not bring that."

"No no, we are not talking sale prices. Twenty-five thousand to thirty thousand would be a low price for the plant from a production value point of view."

"I think so," said Sylvia. "There is quite a marked improvement during the last three months. That of course may be temporary."

"The trouble is that we can't get at real value in this case," said the Professor. "The merger is already formed. That organization is out for all it can get. But its main purpose at this juncture is to get all these concerns into its grip, therefore, any concern holding out has a certain 'nuisance' value."

"Nuisance value?" said Aunt Elizabeth indignantly.

"Exactly! Horrible thought!" said Jack. "The greater nuisance you become the greater value you have."

"Unless you become too much of a nuisance, and then they wipe you out," said Reggie.

"Regular poker game, you see, Miss Murray," suggested Jack.

"No, I do not see. I know nothing about poker. Never played poker in my life. Poker indeed!"

"Sorry, Miss Murray--awfully sorry--of course--I didn't mean to suggest--"

"Now Jack, please be sensible and let us get on with this," said Sylvia. "You know I must settle it to-night."

Again there was silence.

Then Mr. Matheson gravely said: "The main questions to be considered appear to me to be two: First, what will happen to Miss Sylvia if she goes in, and the merger is a failure? And second, what will happen to her if she stays out, and the merger is a success?"

"Excellently put, sir," said Professor Hale, "for if the merger is a success and she is in, nothing very serious can come to her and--"

"That is, if they don't interfere with our people," said Sylvia.

"That possibility appears to be taken care of for two years at least," said Reggie. "While if you are out and the merger fails you can't be injured very much. First, then let us consider these eventualities."

For two hours they sat in the drawing-room after dinner, discussing the issues involved from every possible point of view. "Except the point of view of our two-power pact," Jack found opportunity to whisper to Sylvia, who shook her head quite severely at him.

"If I could be quite sure they would let us carry on as we are," said Sylvia, in a distressed voice. "Mr. Brady says they will not interfere with the working of the plant. But who can tell?"

Professor Hale suddenly sprang to his feet, pushed up his fingers through his bushy, tangled locks, and exclaimed:

"Frankly, I am opposed to these mergers. They involve every evil in co-operative movements, and they eliminate every good feature. They place the lives and fate of workers in the hands of a small group of men, who are out to exploit everyone in their power. They are utterly irresponsible to any other authority than themselves, they can choke off all smaller competitors. They can exploit the consuming public, they can deprive their workers of anything like an equitable share of the profits from the business."

"But none of these things are necessarily concomitants of their scheme. And besides the question for us is, what is the alternative?" said Mr. Matheson, with just a shade of impatience in his pleasant and gentle voice.

His tone seemed to stir the Professor's wrath.

"That's just the curse of it all," he exclaimed. "Under our present system we are helpless." He seemed to check himself with a violent effort. "After all, I am really off the rails a bit. But I can't help feeling that this country, this whole continent, is on the eve of an appalling collapse.

"Of course, I am unpopular. A Cassandra never is popular. But Jack, will you tell me why is it that commodities are beginning to slide? Why is it that the Federal Reserve is issuing grave warnings against this stock booming? Why is it that every British economist of any standing is denouncing this whole speculative movement as dangerous?"

"Well, Reggie, you know those old country boys are fearfully conservative."

"Conservative? Perhaps so--but they know the European situation as no one on this continent knows it. And after all, surely their experience as world traders and financiers for the last hundred years, is worth something. No, no! I am terribly anxious. Jack, if you are plunging heavily in stocks for Heaven's sake sell. Sell to-morrow! Don't wait! To-morrow!" Reggie's voice rose almost to the point of hysteria.

Jack laughed at him: "I guess most stocks are good for ten points, any way."

"Ten points? Yes, twenty! a hundred! But the higher, the farther above the point of reality, the greater the fraud, the more disastrous the fall. But I've said my say."

"Then you are opposed to my merger?" said Sylvia in a distressed voice.

"My dear Miss Sylvia, if you were a stock manipulator without heart or conscience--"

"Like me," interposed Jack sotto voce.

"Yes, like Tempest, you could make a killing out of your merger. But you won't sell, not even on a rising market. You will hold on and lose out."

"She can't lose her twenty-five thousand cash," said Jack.

"No," said Reggie. "She won't lose that--but--well--that's all from me."

"No, no, Mr. Hale," pleaded Sylvia.

"Mr. Hale, you are not quite on the point, if I may say so," Mr. Matheson broke in. "Miss Sylvia is not deciding the question of the ethical implications of the present economic system. Suppose we grant, for the sake of argument that it is ethically indefensible. The main question with Miss Sylvia is how can she best protect her people's interests in any case, success or failure, by going in or by keeping out?"

"That is so," said Reggie gloomily. "Rotten choice either way."

"To my mind the answer is very obvious. Her vantage ground from which to serve the interests of her people appears to be definitely stronger within than without the merger."

"You are right," said Professor Hale, still gloomily. "You are unquestionably right."

The company decided for the merger, not without many misgivings on the part of Sylvia, to whom it seemed only the less of two evils, Jack however, laughed at her fears. "The padre has the word. It is your only choice, and it suits me well."

CHAPTER X

The merger being duly consummated and Riverside Mills being firmly established under its former management with James MacDonald as superintendent and Miss Sylvia as secretary, with managerial powers, things began to move at a rapid pace.

First of all the old sawmill was thoroughly overhauled, new saws put in place, a new engine installed of much greater horse power; for the Central Canada Company had planned that some old lumber limits, chiefly hardwood, long forgotten, belonging to the Riverside Mills should forthwith be converted into merchantable lumber suitable for the manufacture of furniture, especially for veneers. Already throughout the summer months gangs of lumbermen with modern equipment had been busy cutting roads, building camps, preparatory to active work when the snow began to fly.

"I am not satisfied with the reports from the camps," said Sylvia. "Indeed I am uneasy about the work up there, James."

"Why, I haven't noticed anything," said James MacDonald.

"No, perhaps not, but you don't see all the correspondence, James. The reports are too vague, too indefinite. Mr. Hample will not give me the particulars I ask for. You must go up yourself and look into things."

"But how can I possibly get away with all this new machinery being installed, and Headquarters insisting on daily reports? Of course, it is all a lot of nonsensical red-tape, but apparently that General Secretary demands them. I suppose he must show something for his $10,000 salary."

Miss Sylvia sighed with deeply furrowed brow.

"Huh! I'd like to step into his office some day and see them all at work, that gang of clerks," growled James MacDonald. "I can't help wondering what the average golf score is for the gang."

"Well we are not responsible for that office, but I am for this. And I am not happy about those camps up there. And Mr. Hample is so dreadfully vague. I wish I could just see the thing going for myself."

"Why not, Miss Sylvia? You know you will never be quite satisfied till you do." James MacDonald caught Miss Sylvia glancing at him suspiciously. "No, I am really in earnest. You know you are never quite satisfied with second-hand information. Too much Glengarry blood in you."

"Well James, you know I have no knowledge of things that men are working at in spite of my Glengarry blood. I must see things actually."

"Huh!" grunted James.

"I have no imagination."

"Huh!" grunted James again. "Well then, make up a little party and go up. It is only about a hundred miles. Motor for that first seventy and ride the rest of the way. You are good for that."

"Oh, I could do it. But what could I do with that foreman. Evidently the Corporation thinks him a wonder; certainly he carried marvellous testimonials."

"A little too marvellous, 'The King that carries a trumpeter needs one,' as my father used to say in the Gaelic."

"Well something must be done. I am not satisfied in my own mind."

"I will order the horses to be ready for you at the end of the motor road," said James MacDonald.

"Oh, James, I would be afraid of all those men," said Miss Sylvia, her blue eyes wide with dismay at the bare prospect of facing some sixty or seventy men in the heart of a great forest.

"Afraid?" said James. "Not you!"

"About the new machinery, James, you should have help. You can't be everywhere at once. I must see about that."

"Are you not satisfied with my work?" he asked sharply.

"I am not satisfied to see you overworking, James," replied Sylvia. "It is not fair to you."

"Nor to the work," James was evidently on edge, scenting criticism. "I am doing my utmost, whatever."

A shadow fell across the serenity of the lovely face turned toward him. "You need not tell me that, James. But--well--if you will arrange for four horses, I might manage the trip."

"Let me know a day ahead, Miss Sylvia. And--and--Miss Sylvia, I have a devil of a temper," said James as he flung out of the office.

That evening Sylvia discussed the trip to the camps about the dinner table, with her Aunt Elizabeth and Mr. Matheson, who had dropped in, and Jack Tempest.

Aunt Elizabeth was horrified at the idea.

"A slip of a girl like you among a lot of ruffians."

"Ruffians? I am quite sure they are as good as any other working men--and better too. James MacDonald got a lot of them from Glengarry, grandsons of the old Glengarry lumbermen, my father's friends."

"Yes, and how many Frenchmen from the Hull Lumber yards?"

"There wouldn't be any trouble from the men. Sylvia would be as safe with them as in this dining-room," said Jack. "I'm thinking of possible accidents en route. Bad roads, half broken bronchos, storms and that sort of thing. No, I don't like it, not a little bit. I only wish I could go. But three days! And just now! Utterly impossible."

"Jack, you should go. You need a change. You are looking ghastly. Isn't he Mr. Matheson?" said Aunt Elizabeth.

"He is not looking his best, that is true," said Mr. Matheson, who had developed a great liking for Jack. "It would do him a great good to escape from that Babylon even for three days."

Jack grinned at him. "Babylon in the hey-day must have been something to see, eh? Hanging gardens, silks and gems, gold, not to mention ivories and peacocks. What?"

"But never so frantically mad as our modern Babylon. I was in the Stock Exchange this week. I drop in now and then."

"For pointers?"

"To try and read signs of the times. Bedlam! If ever men were mad, those men are mad."

"My dear man, you should see New York. I spent a day there last week."

"Terrible!"

"Terrible? Not a bit. Regular circus! Great game! Tossing millions about hilariously like a volley ball. Tremendous sport! Everybody jolly, wildly jolly. Jove! I should like to go right into that game. If it were not for Dad." The boy's eyes were aflame, his face hard, thin, keen.

"A game for them, but what of the masses who are paying for their fun?"

"Well! Whose fault is it? No one asks them in. It is no game for children or weaklings."

"No. For bulls and bears. For beasts with horns and claws. The old Roman Amphitheatre was a Kindergarten to this. Vae victis! Paganism! Rank, stark paganism, very devils' game."

Jack laughed excitedly. "I grant you it is no place for Boy Scouts. But by Jove, it is a great men's game."

"But Jack," said Sylvia. "What of those who get trampled to death?"

"Let them keep out."

"Paganism, vandalism, Jack," said Mr. Matheson. "I am getting the repercussions in my work. A lot of my young men, yes and girls are turning in the savings of years, buying on margin."

"And making money too!" said Jack.

"Many of them, more's the pity," said Mr. Matheson, sadly. "If they would only LOSE their money at first."

"Yes, look at young Frank Scovil," said Aunt Elizabeth. "His father is nearly crazy. He had to leave the bank."

"Where is he now?" asked Jack.

"Oh doing fine! Selling bonds with that firm Harrington, Meredith and Sharp. Drives a car! One of the coming men!" The smile in the minister's round cheery face was not entirely joyous. "I saw him last week."

"Oh, did you?" asked Sylvia anxiously.

"Yes, he was very nice to me. I could see he was full of pity for me."

"A lot of my girls are buying on margin, Jack," said Sylvia. "They pity me too. Some of them have already made in three months more than their year's salary."

"Well, you can hardly expect them to put much heart into it. It is really rather dull."

"Your friend Tim Brady I see about a good deal, Miss Sylvia," said the minister. "He has a wonderful car."

"Yes, I know."

"And he gives wonderful parties."

"Yes, I like Mr. Brady--but--but I wish he would go away. You see he is terribly interested in our company. He regards it as his own pet child. He is fearfully thrilled at our success. But I wish he would go away. He is very kind to our girls."

"Kind? He has opened an office here and has young Albert Bingle in it as his head man. Now we all know what a fine laddie Bertie Bingle is. He was one of my bright boys. Brains and all that."

"He has a car too," said Sylvia. "I wish they wouldn't all get cars," she added mournfully.

Jack laughed at her.

"Well--you know a young man with a car--is a very real attraction."

"True! a terrible combination!" said Jack grinning at her. "But what about the camp expedition?"

"You couldn't come, Jack."

"Now then young lady turn those eyes away from me when you speak like that. Our office needs me most desperately. And my own investments these days-- Why in a single hour anything might happen!"

"Oh, Jack how terrible to be so involved!"

"Terrible is the word. Aunt Elizabeth, why don't you go? I have it! Magnificent scheme! Why didn't I think of it before! Why didn't we all think of it?"

They all sat waiting.

"Sylvia, Aunt Elizabeth and the padre here!"

"Silly boy!" said Aunt Elizabeth smiling pleasantly at him.

"I am serious. Quite serious. Can you ride, Aunt Elizabeth?"

"Can she? You ought to see her," cried Sylvia.

"And you padre?"

"Well, I have ridden at home--I mean--"

"Hurray," cried Jack. "What a brain I have!"

"But," continued Mr. Matheson, "only very soberly and sedately upon a farmer's cob."

"Hurray once more!" cried Jack. "My only regret is I can not be with you to see you."

"To see us? Well! you won't see me, nor will any one else," Aunt Elizabeth's tone was finality itself.

"But seriously, my dear Miss Murray, why not? You all can ride. September is the loveliest month for the woods. No heat, no flies. Sylvia needs the change. Look at her! Well--of course she is flushed now with the excitement of this glorious little holiday. Mr. Matheson would be the better for an outing. What day will you start? The sooner the better. I can run you up to the motor road's end. The horses can meet you there."

"James MacDonald will have the horses ready," said Sylvia innocently.

Jack shouted.

"What a head! Say, you ought to be in the Stock game. You have the gambler's gift--always one step ahead."

In spite of the joint protestations of Aunt Elizabeth and Mr. Matheson, the details of the camp expedition were worked out by Jack with masterly ability.

"Very well, I will agree, if you allow me to find a substitute in case duty prevents me at the last moment," said Mr. Matheson, with the air of a man making a supreme concession.

"A substitute?" cried all three.

"I was thinking of Professor Hale."

"Reggie Hale?" said Jack. "Isn't he returning to his job almost immediately?"

"No, as a matter of fact he was talking to me about a walking tour," replied Mr. Matheson. "But of course if he would not be acceptable to any of you--?"

"Nonsense! Acceptable?" exclaimed Miss Murray. "I'm sure he is a charming young man!"

"Can he ride?" asked Jack. "Does he know which end of a horse goes first? I mean in an emergency would he--"

"I know he rides," Sylvia suggested. "In fact he told me he has ridden on the Western ranches."

"Oh, all right," Jack's tone somehow lacked enthusiasm. "Why of course, that would be splendid. But why not four? The very thing!" Jack's enthusiasm took fire. "Four are much better than three--three is an awkward number riding. Sure thing! I'll see Reggie to-morrow."

"Well, if you think he will go," said Aunt Elizabeth. "And if you really mean this mad folly."

"Go? Oh, he'll go all right," said Jack with conviction.

Sylvia's face showed a distinct flush as she began hurriedly to discuss certain details with the minister.

"What day will you start?" asked Jack. "This is Thursday. Monday is rather a bad day for me, a lot of mopping up and planning to do. Tuesday, eh? That gives the padre time to get back and prepare for Sunday."

"What about Professor Hale?" asked Aunt Elizabeth.

"Reggie? Don't worry about Reggie! I'll guarantee him for any hour of any day next week." Jack's tone was emphatic.

Again a faint flush touched Sylvia's face.

"Then we shall say Tuesday," she hurried to say. "Auntie can be trusted to make up a hamper. I shall look after the horses."

"And I'll look after Reggie," said Jack, privately making a face at her. "What about clothes? All got riding breeches?"

"Breeches? Young man you may attend to your own affairs and leave us."

"I was thinking of the padre, Aunt Elizabeth," replied Jack innocently. "Of course, I could lend--"

"Thank you!" said the minister, while even Aunt Elizabeth joined in the general giggle. "But I am afraid--"

"Your father's, Jack," suggested Sylvia.

"As usual! On the spot--one step ahead. Now I must away. A hard day to-morrow. What about a turn round the block, for all of us, eh? Lovely night!" This had come to be a ritual with Jack. Both the minister and Miss Elizabeth declined the invitation.

"Don't be long, Sylvia," warned her Aunt.

"No darling, just a few minutes," cried Sylvia waving gaily at her.

"Poor things! They have very little time with one another," sighed Aunt Elizabeth. "They are both so very busy. I am sure I wonder how Sylvia gets through her day."

"Don't I know?" said the minister. "It is the talk, not only of the plant, but of the whole town. What with the new installation at the sawmill, the reorganization of the furniture factory--they are even making enquiries about the old tannery-- I can't see how she keeps up. But she does. Indeed as Jack says, she is always one step ahead, and were it not for her anxiety about those girls of hers,--you know they are really all going mad over this stock gambling, but only for that she would be happy as a lark."

"Oh yes, she loves her work--and--and--oh yes, she is very, very happy," said Miss Elizabeth, with a little sigh.

"Yes, it is a wonderful thing! It is the great thing! The greatest thing!" said the minister with emphasis. "He is the lucky man!"

"Yes, and he is a good man. She will be happy." Again came the little sigh.

"Yes, I know you will miss her," replied the minister answering her sigh, "but--"

"Nonsense! I am a foolish and selfish old woman! I am really very happy about it."

"Yes, yes of course! Still--"

"Tut tut, Mr. Matheson, you are becoming sentimental. It is the moonlight! But--"

"Well, why not? I insist on being sentimental if I feel like it. As to-night for instance. Who could look out upon these trees picked out by the moonlight, who could listen to the breathing of the night--"

"My dear Mr. Matheson, you alarm me. Besides you will surely get cold, and be unfit for your work on the Sabbath day."

"In other words, 'ye're an auld dodderin' buddie who should be in yer bed,'" said the minister with a gay laugh. "I am away off to my bed. It is safer there."

"Don't be mean now, Mr. Matheson. You know that you are neither 'auld' nor 'dodderin'. And everybody knows it. And your people are all just--well--they are all crazy about you."

"I think I shall go now. You are a great comfort to an old man. Good night, my dear Miss Murray."

"Nonsense! You are just fishing and I'm not biting, so good night. And mind you be ready for Tuesday."

"If it is within my power you may rely upon me to be on hand."

"Good night, Mr. Matheson," said Miss Murray softly, "and pleasant dreams."

"Dreams?" said the minister. "Ah! Good night."

CHAPTER XI

"And James," Miss Sylvia hesitated just a little, "there is no need that any one should know just where I have gone. I am away on business."

"It is not my custom to discuss your affairs with anybody, Miss Sylvia." James' back was like a ramrod, his tone had the buzz of a band-saw.

Miss Sylvia ignored his back and his tone.

"And I shall be back on Thursday night. Good-bye, James."

"Good-bye." James did not see the hand stretched out to him.

"Good-bye, James," repeated Miss Sylvia, still holding out her hand. "I'm going away for three days."

"Good-bye!" said James soberly, taking her hand. Suddenly the girl smiled at him, a smile so bewitchingly radiant that James' icy gloom melted quite away. "And a good journey to you and safe home, and we will be all glad to see you."

"I know you will. And be good to the girls, James."

"The girls! Oh, I'll be good to the girls," James said with a tightening of his lips.

"Now James be sure!" cried Sylvia waving and laughing at him.

"My God!" groaned James, and turned back into the office, a heavy shadow upon his handsome dark face.

Long before the Riverside folk were awake and about their work the Tempest Rolls-Royce slipped quietly out of town and along the highway toward Ottawa, heavily laden with passengers and camping gear. It was one of those golden days that rejoices the hearts of Canadians about mid-September. Bright sun and air with a tang in it quickened the heart beat, like champagne. In the tonneau rode the Professor, the minister and Aunt Elizabeth; in front Sylvia and Jack, the latter exuding gloom, till Sylvia was fain to remonstrate.

"Why so blue, Jack, this glorious day and with me beside you here?"

"Only an hour's run," grumbled Jack.

"But we don't need to do it in an hour, Jack."

"Why certainly not! I always drive this car at about sixty, but I will creep along at thirty," said Jack slowing down to the desired rate.

"I wish you were coming all the way, Jack. We have so little time together these days. You seem so driven."

"I know. There is a lot of work of the firm's which Dad likes me to supervise, and then there is a lot of my own."

"Everybody says you are a plunger, Jack." Sylvia's voice carried anxiety.

"No one that knows," said Jack impatiently.

"But you are buying on margin, Jack."

"Not much. I am sticking to the tradition of the firm. Dad never buys on margin--at least as a rule. I am buying only certain stocks on margin. But one of these days I am going to astonish some of those old boys who are trying to keep me out of their ring. Give me three months more and I'll show them something."

"Jack, everybody says you are the keenest stock man on the Exchange, and that you are making millions." Pride and fear were both in Sylvia's voice.

"Who is everybody?"

"Well Timothy Brady and--"

"Tim Brady!" exclaimed Jack. "That is a confession, for Tim Brady is a shrewd old wolf, and his people are after me a bit."

"But why should Cameron, Maclennan and Borland be after you?"

"Oh, they don't like Dad's attitude in some things, and two or three times I made them take my dust recently. Who else is talking to you?"

"Oh, I hear the girls talking. They think you are a young Napoleon. Naturally they admire you tremendously."

"Of course, dear things!"

"And James MacDonald, he disapproves. He thinks you ought to stick at engineering. Ever since you showed that expert where he was wrong in setting up the new engine, he thinks you are a wonder with machines. And you are, Jack. I wish you were in that business, Jack, and Reggie agrees--"

"Oh, does Reggie call me a plunger?"

"No, he does not. He thinks you are the most dangerous man in Montreal. He says you know better than to plunge. But oh Jack, all this buying and selling unrealities. I hate it. It is really robbery."

"Not the way I do it. I don't deal with suckers. I don't do like Tim Brady and Bertie Bingle. I go after the fellows who are in the game to make a killing."

"I don't like to hear you talk like that, Jack. Tom Foster talks the same way."

"Oh Tom! Tom's an ass, and they will get his ears some day. And his partner is worse, Jessop, I mean. He is no ass but--well let him go. Oh, let us forget the whole rotten game. Fascinating, tremendously, but fundamentally, as Reggie says, rotten."

"I wish you were in engineering."

"Sometimes I wish I were; I'd like to specialize as an Engine doctor. I really think I have a gift that way. You know I can step into a factory and can tell by the sound if the thing is running properly. But what a glorious light on those hills! I wish I could go off with you, Sylvia, away into the woods for a couple of weeks."

Sylvia squeezed his arm.

"Some day, Jackie, eh?" she said her voice all atremble.

"Just you and I, Sylvia, and a canoe. Away from all this stuff. Listen to Reggie booming economics behind there! And the padre backing him up! I say, Aunt Elizabeth, don't let those two Bolshies corrupt your sound and wholesome bourgeois economics."

"Oh, but they are not, and I quite agree with them. I'm quite sure that all these millionaires with their gambling and drinking and-- and all the rest of it are bad for the country. They set such a bad example."

"But not because they are millionaires. But let us forget the whole wretched business."

"Hear, hear! For Heaven's sake," cried Reggie, "look at that noble river, and that line of hills beyond and this glorious light upon it all. I hate to think that in another month I shall be away from it all, and from you all."

They all protested their dismay.

"Yes, my leave of absence is over. My work done, or at least as well done as I can do it just now."

"We shall miss you dreadfully," said Aunt Elizabeth.

"Sure thing! We shall all miss you!" cried Jack his arm pressing hard on Sylvia's clinging hand. "I fear I shall go quite off the straight road, Reggie."

"Go off? My dear chap. But we said no economics. Let us talk of beauty." And for the next ten miles the Professor talked enchantingly of beauty in the world about them, in art and in the soul of man, while Sylvia whispered to Jack.

"Isn't he wonderful?"

"Wonderful? A whale! A darned old animated encyclopedia and art gallery. But the sooner he is off to his own blessed university chair the happier I shall be."

"Nonsense Jack, don't be silly," whispered Sylvia vehemently.

"He's positively dangerous!" insisted Jack with a scowl.

It was still early morning when the car turned off from the Montreal-Ottawa highway, and indeed still early morning when the car left the smooth country road, and for another mile followed with infinite care the devious winding of a waggon track which ended in a burnt over clearing, a brule, in the midst of which stood a tumble down cabin.

"Where is Mr. Hambly, I wonder?" asked Sylvia, opening her bag and drawing forth a letter from which she read aloud, "Shall meet you at the cabin at seven A. M. Tuesday."

"Hello, here is something," called out Jack, who had gone to explore the cabin, and had found a chit pinned to the door, "Listen all."

"Very sorry. Can't possibly arrive with the horses till 8 A. M. etc. etc."

"Jack, we shall bring the stuff into the cabin and let you off. You will be late," said Sylvia.

"Not till your man appears. Suppose he doesn't turn up at all. No, we will wait, confound him!"

"He may have some good reason," said Sylvia. "Meantime what shall we do?"

"A cup of coffee would be good," suggested Aunt Elizabeth. "This air is extraordinarily stimulating. What do you think, Mr. Matheson?"

"Miss Murray, you are a seer. Does the cabin have a stove, Miss Sylvia?"

"Stove? In that dirty cabin? We'll make our fire here. I am a great camper," said Sylvia. "Besides, I'm a Glengarry girl."

"Allow me," said Jack, and within ten minutes he had a stone fireplace built, and a fire of pine chips going, and the coffee pot on to boil.

About the fire, for there was a nip in the air, they sat, the men smoking. There was little talk; the beauty of the morning held them silent. Their camping ground was on the edge of a ragged clearing from which the larger trees had been cut long ago, leaving stumps and the rough debris of a slashing.

"Shame to cut down a noble forest of clean pine trees and leave this mess. You lumber people are vandals," said Jack looking at Sylvia.

"But it is becoming lovely again. Look at the yellow of those young poplars and the maples," said the girl, a soft and tender light in her eyes. "They are doing their best to cover up the ugliness we make. Look at that flame of bramble."

"Those gorgeous crimson trees, Miss Sylvia, what are they?" asked Reggie.

"Those are maples, our glorious soft maples," replied Sylvia. "Don't you know them?"

"I don't know trees. I am a city bird. Never lived in the country, except one summer on the Western prairies. To me this is heavenly. And you are right, Miss Sylvia. Nature hates ugliness and is eager to cover up the mess we make. Look at those bushes and those young trees. Already they have covered from sight the ugliness man has made. Hello, padre, what do you think you are doing?"

"I am playing myself. It is an old Scottish bairns' game. We called it 'duck on the rock.' See, on this rock I place a stone-- my duck. You stand at a base, some fifteen feet away, and try to knock off my duck, and retrieve your own duck before my duck is in place again--you see--When my duck is in place on the rock you may not touch yours. Once my duck is knocked off, everyone may grab his duck and make for the base. If, however, I can replace my duck and touch the runner he becomes the rock keeper in my place. Oh, it is a grand game."

"Come on, Auntie. You used to be a great runner, I know."

"Oh no, I am much too old."

"I resent that, Miss Murray. If you are too old, then I am too old. But I am not too old and therefore you are not too old. Come away. We will show these children something. I will be rock keeper."

Fast and hard they played the ancient game till it was agreed that the minister could beat them all, and they were glad to sit down and rest.

"Well, padre, you are a regular top-notcher in that game," said Jack. "You put a tent over me all right."

"Yes indeed, Mr. Matheson, you are a marvel," said Aunt Elizabeth.

"Oh, there are certain tricks in the game. I am getting slow."

"Another of the exploded myths, Mr. Matheson," said Professor Hale. "Every science and every art has them. But I fancy here comes our man."

"A quarter to nine," said Sylvia looking at her watch.

A cavalcade of rather dejected looking horses made their way down the winding path toward them, led by a heavily built man with a heavy cheery face, a loud voice and a hearty manner.

"Hello folks," he cried, waving his hand in salutation. "Arrived all right, eh? Lovely day for your picnic."

"Good morning, Mr. Hample," said Sylvia pleasantly. "I am Miss Rivers, the secretary."

"Oh, by jinks, say! I thought you'd be about forty. Awful glad to meet you. Going to start right away?"

"Just as soon as we can get going, Mr. Hample. Perhaps you will be good enough to get our stuff packed and loaded as soon as possible. Have you any tump lines?"

"Tump lines? What for?"

"They are easier to pack with. Well, I brought them in case--and a rope. The stuff is in the cabin. It is five miles to your first camp, I understand, and ten to your second. We will make the second before noon, if the road is not too bad. Good-bye, Jack, awfully sorry we had to keep you."

"But I'll see you loaded up and away."

"No, no, Jack, we are all right now," said Sylvia, adding in a low tone, "Get right off, I can handle this man better if you are not here. Please do get off."

"All right then," said Jack, "I shall be here on Thursday evening at say, eight. That will get you home in good time, won't it?"

"Quite all right. Your third camp is about fifteen miles from here, isn't it Mr. Hample?"

"Well, let's say about fourteen or fifteen, I guess. But it's only a pack trail, you understand."

"I understood it was a wagon road," said Sylvia, her blue eyes holding Mr. Hample's steady.

"Well, of course, you can call it a wagon road," said Hample with a cheery laugh, "depends on what you mean of course."

"You can make five or six miles an hour on it, I suppose," said Sylvia.

"Oh well, see here, I haven't ever exactly timed myself on it. But don't expect too much and you won't be bitterly disappointed," said Hample cheerfully.

"Jack, you will be here at half-past eight, and we will meet you then. Good-bye."

"Good-bye, and good luck to you all. Wish I were staying with you."

"Hold on a minute," said Hample, hurriedly. "Could you run me down to the Highway. I've got to get some things."

"And bring you back here, Mr. Hample?" asked Sylvia. "I'm afraid you can't do that, Jack. You are two hours and a half behind your schedule now. Good-bye, Jack," she said giving him a little nod.

"But hold on! I got to get--" Hample began.

"Good-bye," said Jack, throwing in his clutch and slipping away. "Thursday, eight-thirty."

"Eight-thirty, Thursday, Jack," said Sylvia. "Now we'll get away as soon as possible. You understand packing, Mr. Hample. Perhaps you will be good enough to help me to get this stuff loaded up. Mr. Matheson, will you and Aunt Elizabeth, as soon as your packs are loaded, please move on. I suppose the trail is quite easy to follow, Mr. Hample."

"Oh, it's easy enough to follow," said Hample rather crossly. "But say, I got to get something at the village."

"What things, Mr. Hample?" asked Sylvia sweetly.

"Oh mail and stuff--private--"

"Well, the mail can wait for a day, I suppose, and perhaps the other things too," said Sylvia smiling at him. "You see we are now nearly three hours behind our schedule. I can't possibly spend more time here. There are such a lot of things to see. Now Mr. Matheson, you have your loads, you go. We will catch up to you. And," she added in a low voice, "make the best time you can. Auntie is a good rider."

Mr. Matheson, followed by Aunt Elizabeth, with an understanding nod set off at a good pace up the trail.

Reggie, who knew something about packing, had meantime got his pack lashed to his saddle, leaving a biggish bundle for Hample and two smaller packs for Sylvia.

In a few minutes Hample, who had not spoken a word since Jack's hurried departure, got his bundle in place and mounted his pony, his face reflecting bewilderment and wrath.

"Well, we are away at last, Mr. Hample. It is a perfect day for our trip. I do hope the rain keeps off. You haven't had much rain for the last month, I understand."

"Not a drop," said Hample.

"Rain is such a bore in camp, I always think. Gets your clothes and things soaked. I hate it." Pressing her pony to a canter she kept up a stream of pleasant chatter, flinging swift glances and brilliant smiles at her glum escort, 'till the poor man between rage and bewilderment was driven into a state of silence quite unusual with him.

The leading horses, ridden by Mr. Matheson and Aunt Elizabeth, made such excellent time that they were not overtaken till the first camp was reached. At this point Hample proposed a rest for the midday meal.

"What is there to see here, Mr. Hample?" asked Miss Sylvia.

"Oh not much, we have only about fifteen men here, mainly clearing up roads and that sort of thing. Finishing up as it were."

"How many teams have you here?"

"About eight. Ain't it, Paddy?" turning to the stable man.

"Four," said Paddy.

"I suppose they are all out on the roads, Paddy?" Sylvia's smile woke a responsive radiation in Paddy, a red-headed, thick- shouldered squat son of Erin, with a rich brogue and a humorous twinkle in his blue eyes.

"Not to-day, Miss. They're kind of restin' up, so they are, the crathers."

"Resting up, Paddy?"

"Ye see they were workin' yisterday."

"And why not to-day, Paddy?"

"Aw, they're kind o' ketchin up to their feed."

"We are a little short of feed at the present. I didn't know till to-day. They didn't report the shortage," said Hample hurriedly. "They'll be all right to-morrow. We have a load coming in."

"When? To-day?"

"No, to-morrow," said Hample.

"Let's take a look at them."

"There is really nothing to see, Miss Rivers."

"But I love horses. Don't you, Reggie. Come along, Paddy."

"Sure, I do. I used to have a lot to do with them out west," replied Reggie.

The stable was banked up to the doors with manure, the stench was almost unsupportable. Inside, the place was almost dark. The horses were standing in filth over their hoofs.

"I would like to look at them. Take them out, Paddy," said Sylvia. "I just love horses you know, Mr. Hample."

"Oh, they are really not much to look at," protested Hample. "These are really our culls. You will see better horses at Camp number three."

"Oh, never mind. Take them out, Paddy."

"Indeed then they're better out than in," said Paddy untying his horses and turning them loose.

Slowly the wretched creatures stumbled out into the light and stood dazed, lifeless, blinking in the sunlight.

A heavy silence fell upon the group. Shaggy haired, unkempt, ribs, hip bones showing through their skins, one with galled back, another with a horrid gash in the flanks, both wounds black with flies, they stood in eloquent, silent condemnation of the callous inhumanity of man.

For a few minutes Sylvia stood looking at the poor creatures with white stricken face and horror filled eyes, then covering her face with her hands she groaned miserably.

"Oh Paddy, take them all out! take them out please. Take them out," she cried vehemently. "Wouldn't they be better outside, out of the dirt?"

"They would that!" said Paddy.

In a white fury Hample turned on Paddy and cursed him for his carelessness. "What the devil do you mean, letting your horses get like this? You're fired!"

"An' phat about the man that sint me to hell when I besought him for time to clean them, the poor bastes?" said Paddy in a low desperate voice moving slowly upon the manager. "What about him, I'm askin' you?"

"Paddy!" Sylvia's voice rang out sharply. "I want you, please."

Paddy paused in his advance. "Come here!" He slowly came to her. Pointing to the horses she cried. "Can't you get something for these poor wounds?"

"Shure I can, but I'm fired."

"Perhaps Mr. Hample will reconsider. I do want these sores looked after."

"But--but--" began Hample.

"Ye may, but--but if it wasn't for the young lady and the blue eyes av her, I'd see ye slitherin' in hell before I'd sthay an hour in this mess of a mudhole, an' I'm tellin' ye."

"I am very sorry and very shocked at the conditions of these horses, Miss Rivers. The truth is I haven't been down here for three weeks."

"Except when ye be passin' through on yer way to the town," growled Paddy, tying up the horses to a tree. "I'll fix them up an' the rest av them inside that's as bad or worse then thimselves. But I'm givin' ye warnin' as I did before," he added turning savagely on Mr. Hample, "that I'll tind yer cookhouse and the crathers here, but no more. None of yer bunkhouse, nor yer grubshack for me, an' I'm tellin' ye."

"Carry on, Paddy," said Hample.

The party visited the cook house, a Chinese cook in charge. At the back of the house a heap of rotting refuse furnished a convenient and luxurious ground for millions of flies of all kinds, from the infinitesimal gnat to the vicious deer fly and the voracious bull dog.

"Let us go on!" said Sylvia. "We must hurry."

Another hour and they were at the second camp.

"Sylvia, I can't go another foot, no matter what happens," wailed Aunt Elizabeth. "I am fainting with hunger, and I am sure these poor men are too."

"Ravenous, Miss Elizabeth," said Mr. Matheson, "ready to slay any living thing--except a horse perhaps--and devour it raw."

"We will camp here," said Sylvia alighting from her saddle. "Though I can't bear the thought of food. Think of those flies at the last camp."

"I saw some lovely looking bread in there," said Aunt Elizabeth. "And biscuits, and the coffee smells good."

"And there are no flies!" exclaimed Sylvia.

"I'm afraid we haven't much accommodation for ladies here, Miss Rivers," apologized Mr. Hample.

"Oh, never mind, Mr. Hample. My aunt and I will go down to this lovely little stream, and have a rest. And then perhaps we can get a cup of coffee."

"You will have dinner in fifteen minutes, Miss Rivers," said Mr. Hample. "I may say that our Arsene here rather fancies himself as a chef."

"Let me see him, Sylvia," said Aunt Elizabeth briskly. "Please introduce me,

Mr. Hample. Then Sylvia, we shall choose a nice little spot by the brook. You are fagged out."

"Not a bit," said Sylvia, throwing herself down upon a bank of moss under a spruce tree.

Had she been the late Empress Eugénie, Arsene could not have received Miss Murray with greater empressement, as he swept her a profound bow.

"What lovely bread, Arsene! And pie! What? Surely not blueberries!"

"But certainement Madame! of the best! as you see."

"We thought we would picnic by the stream down there under the trees, Arsene!"

"Ah! Fête châmpètre!" exclaimed Arsene. "Beautiful!"

"Your coffee smells divine, Arsene."

"Ah, non! For de men? Yes. For ze lady non non--I shall make you coffee. Ten minutes only. Also some egg--non! Some omelet n'est ce pas!"

"Arsene, I shall leave it with you! Oh, I am starving."

"You like pancake, Madame?"

"Pancakes, Arsene? You don't mean it."

"Fifteen minutes, Madame--one small fifteen minutes--you will see."

"I leave everything with you, Arsene," Aunt Elizabeth slipped away with Sylvia into the woods.

"My dear, I feel it in my bones that we are to have a wonderful feast! But I do wish I had said ten minutes instead of fifteen."

A shady spot close to a purling stream free from infesting flies, carpeted with pine needles, they selected for their table.

"Mr. Matheson! Professor Hale! come here!" called Aunt Elizabeth. "Do come here! Did you ever see anything lovelier?"

"Never! never--saw anything lovelier," said Mr. Matheson gazing rapturously now at one lady and then at the other. "You both--"

"Nonsense, this picnic ground here, I mean."

"Oh, picnic ground. Of course perfect! Eh, Hale?"

"What about some cedar or balsam branches for a table cloth? I'll cut some. I know about them, see?" said Professor Hale, but Arsene appearing at this moment spread down upon the pine needles a snow white table cloth.

"Dis is more better," he said. "She keep de leetle bug from your grubs, n'est ce pas? De sapin! C'est bon for your seats."

"Splendid, Arsene!" said Aunt Elizabeth. "Permit me to introduce my niece, Miss Sylvia Rivers. Professor Hale, Reverend Mr. Matheson." Arsene's bows would have graced the court of Louis Quatorze.

"Ah! Madame, it is one occasion! Now one leetle cocktail, pour l'apéritif, non?"

"Oh, no thank you, Arsene. The gentlemen do not wish it. Besides we are famished!"

"At once! Madame! You will see!"

"Let me help you, Arsene," said Sylvia.

Arsene held up his hands with a volley of excited French expletives significant of horror.

"Non non! It is impossible! Fifteen minutes! your bouillon!"

It must be confessed that it took slightly more than fifteen minutes. But they were profitably spent by the party in bathing hands and face in the cool running water of the brook.

"I'm going to wade," said Sylvia. "Come on, Auntie. Mr. Hale will get some towels."

"Hurray!" cried Mr. Matheson. "Me too. Come on, Miss Murray. Let us paddle!"

A moment's hesitation and Aunt Elizabeth with a rosy face exclaimed, "Of course, the very thing. My riding boots are so very hot and uncomfortable. But do let us hurry! Arsene will be here with the bouillon."

They were still paddling when Arsene appeared.

"As you are, Madame!" he exclaimed. "In de bat' is it not, as in Ancien' Rome. Ha ha!" To each one he handed a bowl of delicious soup with toasted buttered biscuits.

Shouts of delight welcomed his service, while he rushed away to return with plates, knives and forks, following almost immediately with a large covered pan.

From the pan he swept the cover with a bow.

"Voilà!"

"What? Arsene!" shrieked Aunt Elizabeth, "not partridge?"

"Pardon! It is not time only to fry!"

The rapturous exclamations from the whole party banished Arsene's regrets.

"Oh, where is Mr. Hample? Arsene present our compliments to Mr. Hample and ask him to join us."

"Mr. Hample is desolate. It is not possible he come to you."

"Ah, we are sorry, tell him please!" said Sylvia devastating Arsene with a radiant smile.

Biscuits, pancakes, omelet, cake followed in succession accompanied by Arsene's most profound apologies for the meagreness of the feast. If he only had received warning.

"My dear Arsene, the Ritz has nothing so perfectly cooked and served as this," exclaimed Sylvia, who had regained her spirits and who obviously, as Professor Hale declared, set herself to drive poor Arsene into a state of helpless imbecility.

"One hour's complete repose would seem to be indicated," suggested Mr. Matheson, after the dishes had been cleared away.

Lighting their pipes the men stretched themselves in luxurious ease upon the balsam.

"You might now converse, dear ladies, for our delectation," suggested Professor Hale.

"Why not you, Professor Hale?" replied Sylvia.

"No, no, Not Hale! Who would dare to desecrate this heavenly peace with rude jargon as to economics."

"What are your plans, Sylvia?" enquired Aunt Elizabeth.

"We shall ride to the Fifteen Mile camp. I think I have seen enough in these camps for my purpose. But at the next camp we shall see men at work. It is all pretty bad."

"You didn't see Arsene's cook house. It was a joy to behold. Clean, tidy and no refuse about."

"I think I shall ride on, Miss Rivers," said Hample, making his appearance. "You can come at your leisure. You cannot mistake the road."

"Thank you, Mr. Hample. We shall follow more slowly."

As they approached the Fifteen Mile camp they could hear sounds of noisy shouts, hoots, groans. Pushing on they came upon a scene of wild confusion and excitement. Some thirty men were milling about in front of a small building, which proved to be Mr. Hample's office. Standing in a doorway, Mr. Hample stood looking out upon them with an easy smile upon his face.

As he caught sight of the party riding up he shouted to the mob.

"Here, you fellows, get out of this. I'll see you tomorrow. Come on, clear out. Come, move! Can't you see I've got visitors?"

"Sorry Mr. Hample," said a young giant of a lad with a good-natured face. "We want a definite answer now, and we are going to have it."

"May I ask what is the trouble, Mr. Hample?"

"Oh, nothing at all that you have to do with, Miss Rivers," said Hample politely.

"Who pays the wages?" said a rough voice.

"Why, I do," said Sylvia.

"Why don't you do it then?"

"Here! you shut up Terry! Aw, cut it out!"

"But your wages are always paid on the fifteenth of the month. Is not that so, Mr. Hample?" asked Sylvia.

"Quite right, Miss Rivers. The fact is I haven't got round to it this month yet."

"This month is it?" laughed Terry scornfully. "What about last month? And the month before that?"

"The fact is I have been a little crowded with extra work and--"

"Ha ha! extra work! Aw come off!"

Sylvia's eyes fell upon the young giant's face.

"Mr. Hample please introduce me to this gentleman?"

"Roderick Macdougall," said Mr. Hample gruffly.

"Would you ask this young man and another to step in to the office with us?" she said.

"Excuse me, Miss Rivers, I am not going to be bullied by any gang of hoodlums. I do my business in my own way, and if you will excuse me I must ask you to keep out of this. I am manager of this camp."

"Oh, of course, Mr. Hample. I have no idea of interfering, but as to wages, you know the wages are paid on the fifteenth of every month."

"I have explained that, I think--"

"But these men complain that their wages have not been paid for two months. That is my business. I am responsible for wages, as Secretary-Treasurer. Mr. Hample will you please ask Mr. Macdougall to come into the office?"

"No. I am not going to be dictated to by this bunch. And I am not going to have any one interfering with the discipline of this camp," said Hample in a loud voice.

"Very well, Mr. Hample," said Sylvia. "Mr. Macdougall, please tell the men that the wages will be paid tomorrow at noon. Will that do, just now?"

"Certainly, Miss," said Roderick, blushing scarlet under her blue eyes, and her ingratiating smile.

"Come on boys!" said Roderick.

"Hold on Roddy, what have you got?" asked Terry. "Don't let her diddle you, Roddy." While another began whistling, "Two lovely blue eyes."

"You Terry! Get out of this," said Roddy, in a low voice, "or I'll knock your block off."

"Mr. Hample," said Sylvia, following him into the office, "I am sorry even to appear to intrude. But you must know that as Secretary-Treasurer I must know what has become of the payroll for the last two or three months. If you cannot explain I shall be forced to put an accountant into this office to-morrow morning." Her indignation forced her to become more personal. "You knew my father--he was a Glengarry lumberman. No lumberjack ever suffered injustice at his hands, nor ever shall at the hands of his daughter."

"It is just carelessness, Miss Rivers," said Hample in a very humble voice.

"Do you pay in cash or by cheque?"

"Cash. The men like it better."

"Can you have the cash here to-morrow noon?"

"I'm afraid not."

"When can you?"

"A week or ten days. I am a little low just now."

"Very well, I shall have the money here to-morrow and you will give me your cheque dated two weeks ahead. Are you agreed?"

"Certainly. It is quite simple," said Hample.

"Now, what other grievances are there, Mr. Hample?"

"Miss Rivers, I must decline to let you come into the camp and interfere with the management."

"Very well, I have no right to interfere with the running of your camp. But learning that there is a threatened strike I must ask for a full statement of the particulars. We cannot get the best results if there is discontent. Can you let me have that statement to-morrow morning?"

"No, I decline. I shall report to the Company, the President of the Company."

"In that case, Mr. Hample, I must ask for your resignation."

"You? Absurd, you didn't appoint me. I had my appointment from Mr. Huntington."

"You were recommended to me by Mr. Huntington, Mr. Hample. It was I who appointed you."

"Well, I guess I'll have to see about that. I rather think I stand in pretty well with the directors," Hample smiled pleasantly.

The afternoon was spent by Professor Hale and Sylvia exploring the roads, the work accomplished and the general condition of the camp.

In the evening Professor Hale rode back to the nearest telephone office and was able to make such arrangements that all back wages were duly paid by noon the following day.

CHAPTER XII

The matter of the back pay being satisfactorily attended to, the party took their leave about one o'clock.

Hample was quite cheerful.

"I am sorry for the little misunderstanding," he said as he bade his visitors good-bye.

"So am I, Mr. Hample. You are forcing me to do what I never thought I should have to do."

"And that is?"

"Dismiss any one from my employment."

Hample laughed cheerfully. "Oh, I do hope you will not be forced to that, Miss Rivers. Indeed I may tell you that Mr. Huntington and I are very old and very good friends. So please don't be sore with me. I can promise you that everything will be quite satisfactorily adjusted."

"It will be, Mr. Hample, and for your sake I am very sorry indeed."

"Oh, please, don't worry about me. Good-bye. A pleasant trip home. Sorry I can't go with you. But just tie the horses up in the old cabin and one of the boys will go over for them this evening."

"Good-bye, Mr. Hample," said Sylvia very gravely.

At Ten Mile camp the party were halted by Arsene with the offer of a cup of tea.

"Oh splendid," cried Aunt Elizabeth. "But, Arsene, we don't want to put you to any trouble."

"But it is a mos' great plaisir," protested Arsene, who had a room prepared for the ladies where they could refresh themselves.

There followed another petit fête châmpètre for which Arsene had made more elaborate preparations.

"What Arsene? Not doughnuts? And cake? And pie? But this is extravagant! Your chief will be calling you to account."

"Pouf! Dat fella!" The snap of the fingers, the tone of voice made words unnecessary.

"Arsene, I like your cookhouse. What do you do with your refuse?"

"I show you, mamselle. Come up with me." He took her to the rear of the camp among the trees and showed her an incinerator improvised out of an old oil tank.

"Voilà! No smell, no flies, no notting."

"Splendid Arsene! I wish we had you in all the camps."

Arsene looked at her shrewdly. "Maybe, it is possible. It is quite easy. Dat cook! Bah! Sacr-r-e!"

Sylvia had an inspiration.

"Do you think? I mean could you supervise all three camps?"

"Sure ting! Ah, dose fly! Dose mess! Dose smell! Mon Dieu!" Arsene's hands were eloquent.

It was grey dusk when the party riding quietly came to the last clump of trees, a thick underbrush of spruce, before issuing into the clearing. Professor Hale and Aunt Elizabeth were riding at a slow walk in front with Mr. Matheson and Sylvia a hundred yards in the rear discussing the situation at the camps.

Suddenly in the thick spruce underbrush there was a crash of breaking limbs, and a loud snort. Instantly Sylvia's broncho, a hard mouthed brute leaped high in the air throwing her rider half out of her saddle, and plunged down the declivity at a terrific gallop.

At Sylvia's shriek, and the rattle of the galloping hoofs, Professor Hale turning in his saddle saw the horse coming, running low with Sylvia half out of the saddle and clinging desperately to the pommel.

"Get to one side," he shouted to Aunt Elizabeth and stood braced to check the runaway.

"Let him go! Let him go! I'm all right," shrieked Sylvia.

But Professor Hale facing his horse down hill set him off at a gallop and as the racing broncho drew level he leaned far down, snatched the dangling reins and held on.

Thrown out of his stride the broncho stumbled and pitched headlong flinging his rider clear into a thick spruce tree where she lay dazed, and at the same time dragging Hale out of his saddle among the kicking scrambling hoofs.

Hurriedly coming up Mr. Matheson pulled Hale free and then turned to Sylvia.

With a gay laugh she greeted him.

"What do you think of that?" she cried. "You couldn't do that, eh?"

"Are you hurt?" the minister gasped.

"Not a bit. It must have been a cow, I think. How are you, Reggie?"

"All right--I think. A bit--shaken up--but--oh--" he groaned hoarsely and lay back insensible.

"Water!" cried Sylvia and springing on her horse she dashed down to the cabin, only a few hundred yards away and returned with a small pail of water.

In a few moments he revived and smiled wanly upon them.

"You are--all right--Sylvia?"

"Oh, yes, but you? Where is your pain, Reggie?"

"Just here," he said laying his hand upon his chest. "I can't-- breathe--very well--Thank the good God--you are--not hurt--Sylvia--"

"Legs and arms all right, I think, except for some superficial cuts," said the minister, who had been examining him for broken limbs. "Some marks on his chest may mean kicks."

"Oh! There is Jack, just on time," said Aunt Elizabeth.

Sylvia dashed off to meet him.

In a few swift sentences she told of the accident.

"Get in," said Jack. "I can drive up there, I think. Wait! Can he sit up? No?"

He dashed into the cabin and returned with a ragged old mattress. "Nothing too clean, I fear, but it will do, I guess."

In a few minutes he was kneeling beside the injured man. "Legs and arms all right? Yes? Chest, eh? Pile your blankets and wraps in the back seat. Fix up this mattress, Aunt Elizabeth, and you get in behind."

"I'll go, Jack," said Sylvia.

"Get in there, Aunt Elizabeth," ordered Jack. "No stimulant with you? Whiskey?"

"Of course not! Whiskey indeed!"

"Ought to always carry a little whiskey, Aunt Elizabeth. Very careless! Now then, Aunt Elizabeth, sit up in this corner and support his shoulders."

Meantime Sylvia and the minister had run off to tie the horses in the cabin. With great care Reggie was lifted in.

"Fairly comfortable, old chap?" asked Jack. "All right, now? The first part will be a little rough, but once on the highway it will be better. Now then, let's see-- about forty miles, eh? Half an hour ought to do it."

"Now Jack, that is eighty miles an hour. It is very dangerous and poor Mr. Hale, this way."

"Oh, forty or eighty won't make any difference to Reggie if we hit anything, but we will moderate the pace," said Jack, whose indicator after he had reached the highway rested steadily about seventy.

"How is he looking?" he asked Sylvia, after a few minutes had passed.

"Oh, awfully pale, Jack," she said with a catch in her voice.

"All right, we will turn in here." He drew up at a road-house and dashed to the bar.

"Hello Julian! Awful hurry," he snatched a bottle of whiskey, with a glass and dashed out again.

"Aunt Elizabeth, give him a teaspoonful as a medicine, you understand. We don't want him playing any tricks on us you know. By the way, where are we going? Royal Vic. I suppose? That is another forty-five minutes."

"Nonsense, drive straight to Hilltop House," said Aunt Elizabeth with indignation.

"Of course, Jack," echoed Sylvia.

"All right. It is certainly where I should choose if I broke any bones."

In exactly thirty-five minutes after reaching the highway, they turned into the drive to Hilltop House. Immediately Jack took command again.

"Sylvia, will you please phone the doctor before we move him. Aunt Elizabeth perhaps you will see about the room, bed, etc. Mr. Matheson you stand by till the doctor comes."

Sylvia came running out. "Dr. Lang will be right over."

"Meantime, if I remember my first-aid stuff," said Jack, "there being neither bleeding nor concussion, another spot might be good. I am rather doubtful of Aunt Elizabeth's measurements. In a little water, not too much. Well, here's the doctor. I resign the patient into more capable hands."

"Principal pain, where?"

"Here!" said Reggie, laying his hand upon his chest.

"Ah, no other pain?"

"Oh yes--all over--but--sharp pain--just here--"

"Well, well my lad, don't worry."

"I'm not worrying--mighty lucky."

"Ah well, don't. We will soon set you to rights."

"How soon?" gasped Reggie.

"Tut tut! Now my dear lad--be reasonable. I think we shall use the mattress as a stretcher. Fortunately he is not unduly developed--a hundred and fifty pounds."

"A hundred--and--forty-seven," said Reggie.

"Ah, very good. Now young man, have you ever carried men who were hors de combat, so to speak."

"Often," said Jack. "Off the football field."

"You will take the shoulders then; Mr. Matheson, you will support the legs; I the body--move easily, but swiftly without jar or hesitation."

"Ought to have another man," said Reggie fretfully.

"Here am I," said Sylvia. "I'm as good as most men."

"No!" exclaimed Reggie. "You'll hurt--"

"Thank you, Miss Sylvia, you will do excellently."

Swiftly, without too much jar or hesitation, the task was completed, the Professor fretfully protesting all the way, against Sylvia's taking part.

"Apart from various contusions and abrasions, a fractured collar bone and three ribs, the patient has escaped serious injury," the doctor announced gravely to the little company assembled in the drawing-room.

"Hurrah!" cried Jack. "Lucky devil. He might have had a couple of teeth knocked out or something."

"The broken ribs might easily have been driven inward and perforated the lung. A broken rib has an extraordinarily piercing quality," replied the doctor gazing at Jack with grave disapproval.

"Yes, indeed," cried Aunt Elizabeth, reproach in her tone, also.

"Of course, or the heart," said Jack earnestly.

"The location of the cardiac organ and the structural conformation of the chest would render that difficult though not impossible," said the doctor.

"How long will he be laid up, doctor?" asked Jack.

"That is, of course, quite impossible to say. Probably two or three weeks," replied the doctor.

"Rather a nuisance," said Jack.

"Jack!" Sylvia's blue eyes were turned reproachfully upon him.

"I mean, his job you know. His classes at Cornell begin in about two weeks, I guess--of course, if he can't--I mean--we can fix that up. You can't promise--"

"What do you mean, Jack?" asked Sylvia in bewildered amazement.

"Well, I'm off. I'll just run up and say good night to Reggie."

"The patient has settled down and will probably be better left alone. The nurse is in charge and quite competent and trustworthy. Quiet and rest are important for at least forty-eight hours. After that a little pleasant excitement."

"He'll get it too. I mean--I'll run out now often. Well I'll push off. Good night."

Sylvia followed him to the door.

"Oh Jack, what a mercy you came along. I mean you were so efficient. Poor Reggie, you helped him so. Poor boy!"

"Lucky beggar, if you ask me," said Jack grimly.

"Lucky? Why Jack!"

"Forty-eight hours quiet, and then, the Lord only knows how many hours of pleasant excitement to follow. Feel like a spin round the block? No? You look awfully tired dear. You are a plucky sort, you know. Now go right to bed."

"Not for an hour or so yet, I'm afraid. I must do some thinking."

"Thinking?"

"Yes. About that perfectly terrible and messy camp."

"Oh! The camp? Well good night, dear." Jack somehow found it difficult to take his final departure.

After he had gone, Sylvia went to her room and set herself to do some hard thinking. But instead, she found herself preoccupied with Jack. "How funny he was! He never acted like that before. What could be the matter?" Suddenly a light shone in her eyes and overflowed her face. A tender pitying smile touched her lips. "I wonder if it could be that. Poor dear! What a silly boy!"

With a much lighter heart she took up the work before her. If a touch of jealousy were all the trouble with Jack she could easily remedy that at their next meeting. But this messy camp, and this impossible camp manager--these were quite different.

Before she had laid her weary body to rest Sylvia had the carefully prepared outline of a letter to the President, Mr. Huntington, announcing the dismissal of Mr. Hample as superintendent of the Lumber Camps in the region of the upper Ottawa for the reasons set forth in the report which she begged to enclose.

CHAPTER XIII

The head office of the Central Canada Lumber and Furniture Corporation was one of the most commodious and imposing in James St., and the president, Mr. J. B. Huntington, one of the most impressive of the "Big Business" men doing business in that famous street.

The president was a keen, hard-featured, hard-headed man. As a stock manipulator he was dreaded by every stock selling house as utterly ruthless, and preternaturally uncanny in his premonitions and prognostications as to stock movements.

In his relation to the Central Canada Lumber and Furniture Corporation, however, he was no mere stock operator. He was determined that the Corporation should become one of Canada's great industrial concerns, developing with the national development, and helping to exercise a steadying influence upon the whole industrial life of Canada.

The merger was making fair steady progress. The various concerns, large and small of which it was composed were each and all working out their various problems and destinies, some toward permanency, others toward elimination.

Into the head office there came a daily report from each unit in the merger, which received the swift and searching study, first, of the chief of staff, Mr. Piper, and then of the president himself. At the close of each day the president and his chief of staff could tell you just how each unit stood individually and relatively to the great Corporation as a whole.

On the morning of the second day succeeding the visit to the camps the chief of staff, Mr. Piper laid some papers upon the president's desk, with the attached memo "special attention and immediate." The combination of "special" and "immediate" was quite unusual and therefore arresting. The documents consisted of: (1) A memorandum setting forth the terms upon which the Riverside Mills had entered the merger; (2) A summary of the monthly reports from the Riverside Mills since reorganization; (3) A report of a visit paid to the camps upon the Blackwater River; (4) A letter from the secretary of the Riverside Mills dismissing from the service the superintendent and manager of the Camps, Mr. E. J. Hample.

A hasty glance through the documents and the president rang Mr. Piper's bell.

"Now Piper, who the devil is this S. Rivers, secretary of the Riverside Mills? And what the devil does he mean by this sort of high handed stuff, dismissing Hample, our manager at the Lumber Camps? What do you know about him?

And who the devil does he think he is anyway?"

With perfectly unmoved face Mr. Piper proceeded to answer his chief's demands categorically and in order.

1. He knew Rivers only by his reports, which are always punctually rendered and in perfect order.

2. He was acting strictly within the terms of their contract with him.

3. He knew nothing personally about him. Never had met him.

4. He evidently was a man of prompt and decisive action.

"Who knows about him? Who put through this deal? Who made this fool contract anyway?"

"Tim Brady was the agent in the case. The greatest difficulty has been experienced in getting the Riverside Mills into the Corporation. The Riverside Mills was considered to hold a place of great strategic importance because of its location, and its efficient management.

"Get Brady," ordered the chief.

Mr. Piper hesitated a single moment--a most unusual proceeding.

"Well, what?"

"I would venture to suggest, sir, that you read this report, a very clever and very complete document."

"Get Brady," ordered the president.

It took an hour or so to get Brady, but during that hour the president had a rather disturbing visit from Hample, the superintendent in the Blackwater River district.

The relation between the president and the superintendent were of old standing, and evidently of a very intimate nature.

Without ceremony Mr. Hample pushed into the president's private office.

"Good morning, Hample. So you're in trouble again?" was the president's greeting.

"Trouble? Well hardly," replied Hample with a smile of easy assurance.

"Well I have a letter this morning that makes rather bad reading."

"Let's look at it."

"Private letters of the Company are not for public inspection."

"Well, I'm telling you, Huntington, that I'm through with that job. Unless I can run my own camp, according to my own ideas, I'll see the thing to hell. It's only a one horse job anyway. You gave it to me only as a temporary thing. My work is office work. Do you think I'm going to stay up in the woods there all winter, buried in snow to the neck and run a couple of hundred men? Not me. And the sooner you get that the better. You can't shunt me into any back yard like that, Huntington."

Hample's bearing was that of a man who has the whip-hand and who knows it.

Mr. Huntington showed amazing self-control, indeed almost obsequiousness in the presence of this truculent bully.

"Well well, Hample. I'll look into the matter. But this is really serious, you know, rather ugly, in fact. That holding back of the payroll funds has an ugly name you know."

"Ugly name? Not so ugly," Hample's language became highly sulphurous, "as some other matters we know about."

The president's face changed subtly. A look of hate gleamed in his eye, but his manner of suave geniality remained unchanged.

"Well, I'll see what can be done, Jim. I must get through my morning correspondence. Drop in--eh--in a day or so--"

"Day or so? Not much. This has got to be settled and quick. I don't want to be unreasonable," he hastily added as the president rose to his feet, with a look of desperate resolve on his face. "I want a new job, and in the meantime a perfectly free hand where I am."

"All right, Jim. I'll fix it up somehow. But I must get on with my work. Good day, Jim."

"Good-bye, Huntington," said Hample moving out. "Those are my only terms. Fix it up."

"Terms, eh?" He swore a deep slow oath. "'Fix it up' eh? You polecat--you cur--. Yes, as God in Heaven lives, I'll fix it up, and I'll fix you up, too, my boy. You think you can bulldoze Jim Huntington, do you?"

His great fist closed slowly into a hammer. "I'll smash you, my boy. Give me a little time. You fool, you ass."

A knock came to the door and Tim Brady appeared, smiling and debonair. "You sent for me, Mr. President."

"Come in, Brady, sit down. You were the agent of the corporation that negotiated the contract with Riverside Mills?"

"I was, and a divil of a time I had with that same," said Brady, who was an old friend of the president.

"Well, you have let us in for serious trouble with the secretary. Just read that letter and that report, while I look at some letters here."

Brady read with his eyes all atwinkle, then sat back waiting for his chief with a look of benign complaisance on his fat, red face.

The president rang his bell for his chief of staff.

Mr. Piper appeared with a terrifying pile of letters in his hand, which he laid in the basket at the president's right hand.

"Now then, Brady. You are the man that let us in for this contract with this--this--fool secretary--what's his name? Rivers."

"It's meself is the man, and never was I prouder than I am at this blessed moment."

"Look at your fool contract! You allow this man the right to hire and fire. And what does he do? Butts into Hample's Camp upon the Blackwater--that's where you have those valuable hardwood stands, isn't it?--and finding things not exactly to his taste he fires our superintendent without a single reference to me. What do you say to that?"

"Not a word. Not a blessed word. But first I will read that report to you. You just gave it a glance. I'll bet you a hundred dollars you can't tell me but one thing and that is that Hample is fired."

"Done!" exclaimed the president. "He says he found the horses with galled backs, all eaten up with flies."

"Bedad, you've got me!" exclaimed Brady much chagrined. "I ought to have remembered you were a horse man. Well, here's your money." And from his roll Brady peeled off ten $10 bills, and handed them over to the president.

"I'll teach you to monkey with a buzz-saw," said the president gleefully pocketing the money.

"All right! Now if ye have any sport in ye I'll lay ye another bet, two hundred dollars that if ye drive out with me to Riverside Mills and let that secretary talk one half-hour with you over that same report, ye'll take it, and ye'll thank God for the kind of secretary you have. Come on now if ye have any guts in ye!"

"Come on, Piper, we'll have dinner at the Royal at Riverside, the loser pays the dinner."

"Done it is!" said Brady.

In high glee the president, accompanied by Brady and his chief of staff, drove out to Riverside and turned in to the office of the Riverside Mills.

"Rather neat, eh?" said the president as his glance took in the smooth gravelled front with trimmed borders of green grass edging the flower beds.

Ushered by Tim Brady they entered the outer office. Spotlessly clean it was with flowers in the windows, and two clerks, neat, busy and prompt in their response to a request to see the secretary.

Entering the inner office with something of a flourish, Mr. Timothy Brady presented the president to the secretary.

"Miss Sylvia Rivers allow me to have the honour of presenting to you the president of the Central Canada Lumber and Furniture Corporation, Mr. J. B. Huntington. Mr. Huntington, Miss Sylvia Rivers, secretary of the Riverside

Mills. Mr. Piper, Miss Rivers."

Shy, blushing, her blue eyes wide open with surprise and dismay, Miss Sylvia shook hands with the two men and offered them seats.

"Miss Rivers," said the president, "before I sit down I want to tell you that this man Brady is a low down creature who has played on me and on you a mean and dastardly trick."

"Mr. Huntington, Mr. Brady has always treated me fairly, but--I can quite believe--oh, Mr. Brady, you didn't tell him who S. Rivers was!"

"Never a hint!" exclaimed Mr. Brady rocking with delight. "But I'm not through with him yet." He took out his watch and laid it on the desk.

"Miss Sylvia, Mr. Huntington is a very busy man. We have exactly one half hour. It is about the Blackwater Camps. I have read your report. Mr. Huntington has only glanced at it. Will you please now tell us just what you found out there. And please we are in a hurry. Begin by telling us why you went out at all--"

"Do you wish this, sir?" asked Sylvia.

"No! Unless you would like to do so," said Mr. Huntington with a bow.

"Please sit down, Mr. Huntington." She opened her desk and took out copies of her letter and the report sent that morning to the head office.

"I am sorry Mr. Hample is not here. Would it not be better that we should wait."

"Never mind Mr. Hample," said Mr. Huntington. "We really don't need him to-day."

"To begin with I found it difficult, indeed impossible, to get detailed reports of the work in the camps, the kind of information which you apparently desire. I could not just see the work going on. I have been in lumber camps before, but somehow Mr. Hample didn't seem to understand just what I wanted. There were other things too. So I thought it would help all round if I went out."

In simple, clear concise narrative she presented a picture of the camp, with apparently every effort to be quite fair to the facts, and to make such apology as was possible for the conditions existing.

At the end of half-an-hour, Mr. Brady interrupted.

"The time is up, Mr. Huntington. Are you ready?"

"Shut up, Brady. Please go on Miss Rivers."

"There was practically a strike on at Fifteen Mile Camp on the ground of non-payment of wages."

"And you sent the money?"

Sylvia rang a bell.

"Frances, this is Mr. Huntington, our president, and Mr. Piper." The gentlemen rose and made their bows. "Please bring the cash book and the cheque register."

"These entries show you our method of checking the cash payments, Mr. Huntington."

"Quite all right. Please go on."

"Mr. Huntington, remember, I am not suggesting misappropriation of funds, only carelessness and unfairness to the men who have weekly obligations to meet."

"Exactly so, I quite understand," said Mr. Huntington, his lips drawn in a hard line.

"These were the reasons why I felt I could not allow Mr. Hample to continue to represent our interests in the camps. I love my work and I want to be happy in my work. I could not be happy when I was not sure that the work was going on as the company and you would like it to go on. I couldn't bear to think that the men were not sure of their monthly pay. They have their homes and families I know. And it made me really ill to think of the poor horses, and there were other things too."

"It is enough, by Gad. It's more than enough. Miss Rivers I wish to Heaven we had a secretary as conscientious and as capable as you in every unit of our Corporation. And Brady, blast your ugly Irish mug, here's your $200. I was a fool to bet with you, but how was I to know that the secretary of Riverside Mills was--was a--Miss Rivers. I can't just trust myself to say just what--"

"Put yer money in yer pants, Mr. President," said Timothy Brady. "Bedad it was worth a hundred to see your face when ye walked into this office, and another hundred to have you see just the kind of secretary it was I got for ye in this plant."

"Get to blazes! Here's your money."

"It's himself that took a hundred off a me this morning. As to the other hundred, well, we'll see. Now Miss Sylvia, can you take us through this factory, as you took me once. Just half-an-hour, and then dinner. He owes us a dinner. Oh, it's a great day entirely, so it is--"

"Can you spare the time, Mr. Huntington? We have only a small plant and nothing great to see."

"Can you spare the time, Miss--Miss Sylvia--if I may call you so?"

"Oh, I should be glad to show you our place and our people. We are rather proud of our people, you know." Her radiant smile quite took Mr. Huntington's breath away.

"My dear young lady, I'm sure they are a very lucky lot," he said earnestly.

It was Mr. Brady who undertook to show the party the various points of interest in the plant. As they reached the large room where the machine girls were busy at their sewing and decorating, the bell for the noon hour blew.

"My dear Miss Sylvia, could you now, could you just let the president hear them do one of them songs I heard. Do you remember?"

"Oh, Mr. Brady, it is nothing worth while. We do encourage them to sing at their work."

"Sing? You don't mean it?" exclaimed the president.

Miss Sylvia clapped her hands.

"Girls, you remember Mr. Brady?" Mr. Brady swept them a bow. "It is a great honour to introduce you to our president, Mr. Huntington and to his secretary, Mr. Piper. They would like to hear you sing."

At once a girl began singing softly a French-Canadian chanson. Immediately the whole group took up the song in beautifully arranged harmony.

"Now what was it we sang once for Mr. Brady?" asked Sylvia.

After a moment's hesitation, a girl began, "The Old Londonderry Air."

"That's it!" cried Mr. Brady in ecstasy.

"Thank you girls," said Mr. Huntington, who was deeply moved, when they had finished their song. "I only wish that in all our factories we could have such conditions as make it easy for the workers to sing as you sing."

"Ye've got it, Mr. Huntington," said Mr. Brady in a loud tone. "It's easy to sing when people are happy and contented. They don't sing much out in them camps, I bet ye."

What Mr. Huntington said was too low to be caught by any but Mr. Brady.

"Thim's the words," he said with emphasis.

"And now then, Miss Sylvia," said Mr. Huntington, "there is that dinner, if you would be so good as to honour us."

"Oh, thank you, I should love to dine with you," said Sylvia, her beautiful face aglow with delight. "But I have only an hour for it, more's the pity."

The dinner, though hurried, was a great success. Mr. Huntington and Mr. Brady were both on their mettle and kept Sylvia rocking with laughter.

"I am behaving shamefully, I know," she said. "And in my home town too. They will all be shocked."

"Won't they, then?" said Mr. Brady. "I've heard them. She has the men all eatin' out of her hand."

"I don't doubt it," said Mr. Huntington.

"You see, a lot of these men here have some of their people somewhere in the mills. They are not like ordinary working people. You see their fathers all worked with, or for my father. They are all dear folk. And their children now work with me. That is why, Mr. Huntington, that clause about hiring and firing is in the contract."

"You know she has a dozen clubs and things, boys, girls, men and women, music, dancing, reading, dramatics," said Mr. Brady, in warm admiration.

"How are they supported?" enquired Mr. Huntington.

"They are self-supporting, or were till very recently."

"Falling off, eh?" said Mr. Huntington.

"The girls unfortunately are all in the stock market. It is so bad for them. Oh, I forgot--Mr. Brady--" A quick hot flush covered her face.

"Oh, never mind me. I guess I don't help them much. But if I didn't get their money some other fellow would get it. And anyway I make money for them. And for some of them a lot of money."

"I don't like it, Mr. Brady. It is very disturbing. They are forgetting their Club work. They are all going mad. And they are spending too much money." Sylvia's face showed its distress.

"Never mind. They will have to learn their lesson," said Mr. Huntington. "People like them have no right in the stock market."

"How can you keep them out?" said Sylvia. "I wish I knew how. They are withdrawing their money from the Savings bank and putting it in stocks. The crash is coming, Mr. Huntington, isn't it?"

"Just as surely as that sun is going down this evening. They must learn their lesson. People like that have no business in stocks."

"What can one do?"

"What indeed?" said Mr. Huntington. "The whole world has gone crazy, but more than any others the Americans and our people."

"Now I must run. Thank you, Mr. Huntington for the lovely dinner, and for the good time. I am sorry about Mr. Hample."

"No chance for reconsideration?" said Mr. Huntington observing her intently.

"No, I would be unhappy all the time about the work, and the men and their families."

"And the horses," said Mr. Brady, with a smile.

"The poor horses! Oh, they were terrible."

"And what about his successor?"

"There is a man in Fifteen Mile camp whose grandfather worked once for my father. I have asked him to carry on for a few weeks, till we could see. Was that right, Mr. Huntington? You see, I didn't know you then." Again her smile disturbed Mr. Huntington's equilibrium.

"Quite right, my dear. You go right along. I wish I was as sure of the other units in our corporation as I am of Riverside Mills. Now for your clubs, I am quite sure Mr. Brady will put up fifty of the hundred he made out of me to-day, and I'll meet him with another fifty."

"Oh, thank you, but I would rather not. If you will let me ask you when I need it any time, I would like that better, Mr. Huntington. Now I'm off."

The men lingered over their cigars after the girl had left, smoking in silence.

"How is this Riverside plant coming on, Mr. Piper?" asked Mr. Huntington thoughtfully.

"Best in the lot. I have been following it closely. I am expecting great things from the enlargement of the sawmill. The hardwood stands up there are very promising, bird's eye maple, beech, butternut and birch. The maple and birch will make fine veneer work. I know woods, and you have some very fine stands, if carefully handled."

"And this young lady, she seems to have an extraordinary gift for business. She apparently can handle anything," said Huntington. "She has that plant working like a clock."

"Do you know why?" asked Brady. "She has two great qualities. She thinks of her workers as folks and she has a conscience. She has taught me something."

"Eh? A little sentimental, Brady? That's the Irish in you."

"Let me tell you something," replied Brady. "I've been poking round that plant a good deal. She knows those people of hers like as if they were her own family. There's an old Scotty engineer in that plant. He sits up nights with his engine. Why? Because she looks after his sick baby. Those girls now. She keeps them busy in the evening, clubs, singing, reading, dancing. But she works them like slaves when they are on the job, and pays them for it too."

"She's evidently got you eating out of her hand, Brady, eh?"

"It's myself that isn't ashamed to say it. I went in there ready for any devilment with those clerks of hers, but by the Holy saints and Heavenly Powers she has me playing the guardian angel to them."

"She surely is some kid, if she did that to you, Brady," said Mr. Huntington, with a laugh. "But let's go. It is a hard world, a devil of a hard world, and what is coming to us the next six months, the Lord only knows. If the market only holds. Well let's get into the game. You are operating an office here, Brady. Go easy! Those kids and their fool racketing."

"Will you, or will any man tell me how?" asked Brady bitterly. "God knows I hate shearing lambs. The old bucks now. I'd take the hides off them and rejoice in it--but--"

The following day Roderick Macdougall was standing in the Riverside office, now on one foot and then on the other, listening to the young lady setting forth the duties of the superintendent of the camps.

"I can't do it, miss," he said. "Not with the staff there. You are asking for clean camps and cook houses, well kept horses. You are asking for a logging gang that is up to its job, and keen on the bit, you are asking for road building and you are putting in a new store and new payroll system. I can't do it to your liking and I won't do it any other way."

"Think it over, Roderick, till this evening. Then come and tell me what staff you want. Your grandfather was camp boss for my father."

"Lumbering was different then," said Roderick.

"And our appliances and equipment are different, Roderick. Take half a day to think it over."

As Roderick was passing through the outer office he was halted by Frances.

"Here are some papers you might look at," she said. "You will find them useful."

"Useful?"

"Yes, in your job. Record sheets and that sort of thing. Also price lists for your store things."

"Price lists?"

"You must keep a price list unless you have a wonderful memory."

"Say, Miss--"

"Frances is my name," she said demurely.

"Well mine is Roderick Macdougall and--"

"I know."

"You seem to take for granted, Frances, I'm going to take on this job?"

"Well aren't you? She wants you. And she thinks you can do it."

"What does she know about me?"

"She heard you speak for the men to Hample in camp. And besides she knows. She says you can do it. And she wants you, and--well-- she needs you, Roderick."

"Say, you're sold on her, eh?"

"Yes."

"I don't wonder. She's a peach and that's why I'd hate to disappoint her." Roderick's eyes were glowing.

"You won't disappoint her. But young man, let me tell you something. Don't lose your heart to her. She is already taken up."

Roderick's face flushed a deep wrathful red.

"Say! What do you think I am. A darned fool?"

"Just as well you should be warned, or you would be falling for her. Hard too. They all do. I'd hate to see you break your heart. But of course, you may have a girl of your own?" Frances' smile was very alluring.

"Not me. Haven't the time nor the cash."

"Time? Cash?" Frances laughed scornfully. "What have time and cash to do with it?"

"A mighty lot as far as I'm concerned," replied Roderick shaking his handsome black curly head.

"Well, you'd better read that stuff over. Perhaps you would like me to go over them with you. It would save you time."

"Say! Would you? When? Now?"

"No, come at half past twelve. I could rush through lunch."

"Look here! Let's eat together." Roderick could not check the flush on his cheek.

"What about the cash? What about a Dutch treat?" suggested Frances.

"Not with me," he said quietly.

"All right," said Frances quickly. "I know a nice cheap place."

"You will come with me to the Royal Hotel," Roderick's tone brooked no dallying.

"My what a boss!" exclaimed Frances.

"That's me. I'll call for you here at twelve exactly."

"With your car, I suppose," said Frances meekly.

"You will walk on your two feet," replied Roderick firmly.

"I think you will make a fine camp boss, Roderick," said Frances smiling up at him.

"At any rate no woman pays for her eats with me," said Roderick in a haughty tone.

"Highland chief, eh? Well, forgive me, please."

"I will--but--"

"No, no, I'll never do it again Roderick Dhu."

"Aha! Where did you get that?"

"Well, I will tell you. My minister knows your minister."

"God pity me. Has he been telling you? And will you still come with me?" asked Roderick aghast.

"I will, Roderick," said Frances, a very kind look in her eye.

The second day after, Roderick was in camp and explaining to the men gathered in the grub-house how he came to take on his position as superintendent. "I can't rightly tell you how I came to do it. But my grandfather was camp boss for her father in the old days. And--well she asked me to do the best I could. And I'm going to-- and if any fellow doesn't like it, his money is waiting for him, right here and now. I am going to promise you a clean camp, good grub, lots of hard work and regular pay, according to what you earn. I'll give you a week's try at it, and then you will sign up till the end of the season. I promise you my best--and I ask from you your best. Anyone that doesn't want to stay at the end of a week, his pay is waiting him. That's all."

"All right boss! Go to it! Suits me!" cried a voice.

"Me too! Same here! Let's get going!" came responses from the gang.

Ten days later the president of the Central Canada Lumber and Furniture Corporation sat reading a report handed him by his chief of staff.

In reply to his bell Mr. Piper appeared.

"Piper, you have read this report?" asked the President.

"Yes, sir."

"Piper, that is the first real report I've had from those camps on the Blackwater. It's all there, every detail. Say, we can't really close up that Riverside plant. That Secretary is too good to be lost. And besides there may be something in those hardwood stands. Veneers in bird's eye maple and birch are coming up well."

"Whatever is in it she'll get out. But the whole thing is in a very uncertain condition," replied Mr. Piper doubtfully.

"Well, we will try everything else first, but the stock is slipping badly," said the President. "There's a monkey somewhere in the woodpile."

"Monkey?" said Mr. Piper as he sat down to his desk. "Not much monkey or any other land bird. It is them," at this point the chief of staff allowed a careful selection of adjectives to flow from his lips, "water rats that have swamped the blasted ship."

CHAPTER XIV

Professor Hale and Sylvia were sitting upstairs in what had come to be known as the Professor's den, a small room adjoining his bedroom. It had become their custom to spend the time between Sylvia's return from her office and the dinner hour, in intensive study of certain books, dealing with the subject of economics, which the Professor had selected for his pupil.

"Now then, Sylvia," said the Professor, lying back in his armchair. "Just give me the points in that last chapter."

Without an instant's hesitation the girl was able to give him in a perfectly coordinated sequence the contents of the chapter.

"You are an amazing girl," said the professor. "I have been teaching economics now for more than three years. I have had hundreds of students pass through my hands. Never have I had a pupil of such keen insight into the essentials of a subject or such marvellous capacity for getting at the heart of a discussion."

"But--Professor Hale," said Sylvia.

"Professor Hale? To me, Sylvia?"

"Well then, Reggie--I am sure it is perfectly delightful to hear you say that, and I am extraordinarily uplifted."

"It is the simple truth," said Professor Hale.

"But you see, Reggie, to me this is not the study of a book; it is a study of the things that make up my life. It has to do with my business, my responsibilities. Look at this awful merger. It has the terrific power of swallowing, of obliterating all personalities. Look at me, for instance. There is my little business, expanding enormously, a practically new sawmill for preparing veneers and other materials for furniture. Then there are those hardwood camps with a hundred men and more employed. Also there is that fantastic equipment for fanning mills, apparently for the sole purpose of advertising and pushing my poor little patent.

"I understand," said the Professor, "at least someone has told me, Jack perhaps, that it is a most excellent device."

"Oh, it may be," said Sylvia. "I don't know, but think of all this expansion, with the responsibility attached. No wonder I am keen on the study of industry and economics. Then too," she continued, eagerly, "there is my future. This whole business may blow up some day. I have a dreadful sense of insecurity. That word 'security' has taken on a new meaning for me, I assure you. Besides, I have had almost two years' experience in the practical affairs of business, so that these books do not represent to me mere ideas and theories, they are practically my very life. James MacDonald says, I have a business head. I don't know how true that is, but sometimes I wish I could escape from all this responsibility."

"I wish to God you would, Sylvia my dear."

"One thing I have quite decided to do, and that is, I shall get rid at once of all my stock in this terrible corporation. Mr. Brady offers me one hundred and fifty for my stock, but he advises me to hold on, for he is quite sure it will go over two hundred. That is why I want to sell now, for I know quite well that it will never be really worth two hundred. How could it become worth two hundred? We have sold very little of what we are manufacturing, and where the market is to come from for all the stuff, furniture and fanning mills and the rest of it, nobody seems to know. That is what makes me anxious. How can a little business like mine compete with the great concerns and their mass production? That is why I am selling all my stock in the merger. I should like to be done with it all. Indeed I should like to quit and give it all up. But how can I quit? I have double the responsibility now that I had a year ago. How can I quit?"

"No! That's the devil of it," agreed the Professor. "You can't quit."

Suddenly the Professor sat up very straight, his eyes blazing, his pale cheeks tinged with color. "I wish to heavens I could take you out of it, Sylvia," he exclaimed. "Why doesn't Jack take you out of it?"

"Jack? Oh, I do wish--" exclaimed the girl, a tone of despair in her voice. "Oh, poor Jack, he is very tired and very worried. He is working dreadfully hard, and then he is anxious about his father, who is not at all well, and is also worried and anxious, Jack says. And that is another reason why Jack cannot possibly take me out. He wants to but I can't see my way out."

"The Lord pity him," said the Professor. "I hear about Jack from everybody. They tell me he is one of the rising young men among the stock brokers, and becoming quite a power in the market, that he has developed a marvellous instinct for what they call 'the market pulse' and that he is getting tied up, more and more deeply, with that pack of wolves."

"What do you mean exactly?" enquired Sylvia, a note of anxiety in her voice.

"Why that bunch dominated by that wolf pack leader Scaiffe, Sir James Scaiffe. I consider him the most dangerous man in Canada to-day. And before long there will be a big killing, Scaiffe will get away with the carcase, the rest of the wolves will be left fighting for the bones."

"Sir James Scaiffe," said Sylvia. "Why I have met him. I met him last week at dinner with Jack. I found him most fascinating."

"Fascinating?" echoed the Professor. "So is Satan, I believe."

"And they say he is very kind," said Sylvia. "He often helps people."

"Helps people! My God!" ejaculated the Professor.

"Jack says that he often helps men who are on the point of a crash, and sets them on their feet again."

"Helps men? On the verge of a crash?" Suddenly the Professor seemed to lose control of himself. "Sylvia, Sylvia, my dear girl. Jack ought to be out of all that. You! You are far too good, too fine a girl to be involved in all that mess. Why should you be forced to touch it with the point of one of your fingers? A girl like you! You! who are fitted for high things, for noble things." The Professor became more and more excited, "I wish somebody--oh--I wish with all my soul I had the chance to lift you out of it all, to lift you to the high place for which you are fitted. I could do it too. I know I have a future and a great future. I am no egoistic ass. I know myself. Oh Sylvia--" suddenly he reached forward and caught her hand in both of his. "I am mad, Sylvia, I love you. I would give my life if I had the right this moment to take you in my arms."

Startled, shocked, Sylvia sat rigid a moment staring into the Professor's burning eyes. Then quickly recovering herself she pulled her hand free of his grasp, and with a loud laugh, verging on the hysterical she cried:

"But Professor Hale, think of your cracked ribs! Besides," she added running to his desk, "there is Pearl." She lifted up a photograph of a young girl, and held it up before the Professor's eyes.

"Pearl," groaned the Professor. "Poor little soul, she is tired of me. Indeed we bore each other to death. Oh! That was one silly blunder. A bit of summer madness two years ago. Oh Sylvia--"

"Hush! hush! Professor Hale," her face had become very sad, her eyes kind and pitiful. "You bore each other? Surely you don't know what you are saying. Oh, I am so sorry for you. Besides you see how impossible it is. First, there is Jack,

Jack loves me. And then there is me, I love Jack."

"God pity me!" he said with a groan. "Don't I know it? It was the maddest folly! Try to forget it Sylvia! Try to forget."

"Hush hush, Reggie," she said in a low voice. "I hear Aunt Elizabeth coming."

"Of course I will forget and you will forget," the Professor's laugh rang out loud, and a little wildly as the door opened.

"Oh, Aunt Elizabeth," exclaimed Sylvia. "You've come at a most exciting moment. The Professor had been telling me about his love affairs."

"Yes," said the Professor again with a loud laugh. "I have been boring Sylvia with my love affairs. All love affairs are boring except to the lovers, and indeed sometimes even to them."

Aunt Elizabeth glanced sharply from one face to the other. "Love affairs?" she said. "Well, they are as a rule very interesting, but we didn't talk about them so much in my young days."

"Oh Auntie," exclaimed Sylvia. "You had your own love affairs."

"Love affairs," again said Aunt Elizabeth, a little color tingeing her cheeks. "Yes, we had our love affairs. And sometimes they went deep, deep as life," and after a bit she added, "deep as death. But hurry child, dinner is just ready and Jack will be with us in a very few minutes, and poor boy, we must not keep him waiting."

"Lucky Jack!" said the Professor in a low tone.

Sylvia hurried to her room, her mind dazed, her heart in a turmoil. During her young life she had had the usual experiences in love affairs that fall to the lot of the modern girl. Possessed of such attractions as were here, men young and old, had made love to her, lightly or desperately, according to the nature of their malady. But these experiences had ruffled the serenity of her soul no more than does the summer breeze the calm placidity of a land-locked lake in the bosom of the hills.

This experience with Professor Hale, however, was something quite different. Here was a man ten years her senior, a man of brilliant intellectual power, a man of extraordinary force of character, a man who commanded the respect and confidence of the members of his own profession, and of any community with which he became associated. That such a man should have become so desperately infatuated with her as to confess his love openly, to a girl whom he knew to be engaged to his friend, completely overwhelmed her.

As she attempted to perform the mysteries of her toilet, she found her hands all atremble, so that she was forced to abandon the attempt. She flung herself down upon a couch and took herself severely to task.

"Now, don't be a little fool," she said to herself. "The man is nervously overwrought, poor dear, and he has been seeing far too much of me these last three weeks. Naturally he imagines himself in love."

She recalled his burning eyes, his drawn, pale face, the fierce nervous grip of his hands upon hers.

"He must feel dreadfully," she said. "And really it must be a terrible thing for a man to love somebody who does not care for him."

As for Pearl, she found herself strangely indifferent. If the girl frankly acknowledged that the man to whom she was engaged bored her, there was little use wasting pity upon her, and with Reggie it was quite otherwise.

"Poor Reggie, he is a dear after all. I should not have laughed at him with his cracked ribs." In spite of herself, however, a smile touched her lips. "Now, there must be no more nonsense." Once more she sprang to her dressing. "It will be perfectly awful at dinner," she said, continuing her soliloquy. "I must get Jack and Reggie talking economics. I am afraid Aunt Elizabeth suspects something. She is so very sharp, and I didn't like the look in her eye. I really must do my very best at dinner."

And it must be confessed that her very best at dinner was rather bewildering to them all. Never had Jack seen her so brilliantly fascinating. Never had she kept the professor so completely at his very best on all his pet themes. Before the dinner was over Jack had been driven out of the conversation, and had relapsed into gloomy silence. Thereupon Sylvia took on the Professor herself in argument, and in such brilliant fashion as to completely engross his attention and make him quite forget for the time the painful experience through which he had just passed.

In the full tide of an unusually severe attack upon the modern economic system, Sylvia interrupted him.

"Excuse me, Reggie, but you must remember that it is a comparatively easy thing to play the role of critic. No system can stand up under the handicap of a perverse and selfish human nature, which has been the ruin of every civilization in past history."

The Professor turned sharply upon her. "You acknowledge then that the present system has broken down?"

"Well partially, but hardly beyond repair. The foundations may here and there require shoring up, but surely it is rather a drastic method of improving a building by setting fire to it."

"But my contention is that the very success of the present system is its chief condemnation. This tremendous development in modern industry--the vast increase of wealth in the hands of a few, the obvious and unprecedented prosperity which every bank manager in Canada has acclaimed in his annual address this year, these are the features which condemn the present system. For, coincident with all this magnificent prosperity, losses totalling almost a billion dollars mark last year's transactions."

"But Professor Hale," began Sylvia.

"Excuse me," cried the Professor riding high upon the crest of his oratorical wave. "Allow me to give you a few illustrations, not in regard to stock values, but in regard to actual money losses. The losses of the Canadian Pacific Railway for instance, a most magnificent and solidly based Canadian industry, amount to $55,000,000; Shawinigan $54,000,000; Brazilian the pet investment of the market $64,000,000, and if you consider the most important and most secure stocks you find Abitibi dropping 36 points, Consolidated Mining and Smelting 57, Steel of Canada 75. These are statistical facts that have shaken the confidence of our great bankers."

"But Hale," interposed Jack, "you are giving us rather old stuff. You don't know that within the last few days there has been a very definite recovery in the industries mentioned and in the stocks as well. But for Heaven's sake can't we talk of something else. Pardon me, Aunt Elizabeth," Jack continued, "but really I am somewhat wearied of this everlasting economic argumentation. I get it everywhere and all day long."

"But Jack," said Sylvia brightly, "I am trying to prove that Professor Hale is wrong."

"My dear," said Aunt Elizabeth in her most dignified tone, "I think we have had enough of economics. Jack is tired and I confess that my poor brain is somewhat in a whirl."

"Jack tired?" said Sylvia with a quizzical smile.

"Tired?" said Jack. "No, not in the least. Only, if I may very humbly suggest, I am rather bored with disputations that appear to be both interminable and inconclusive. Frankly, you behold me as a part of a vast machine, which however imperfect is organized under our present government and operated in accordance with our laws. Confessedly it has defects, but under it I must carry on whether I like it or not, or whether I am attacked or not."

"But Jack, I am not attacking you," exclaimed Sylvia.

"Nor am I, my dear boy," said the Professor. "Except in so far as you defend a system whose evils are so apparent without--"

"Reggie, for Heaven's sake! I am only suggesting the futility of this endless economic discussion."

"But Jack," broke in Sylvia, "it is so very interesting, and to me it is so very important, so very vital, for you see I am involved--"

"Exactly," interrupted Professor Hale. "We are all involved, Miss Sylvia as an industrialist and as a financier, I as a professional expert, more or less competent in the science of economics."

"Pardon me," said Jack in a tone of excessive and deliberate courtesy. "Am I right in saying that you and this young lady spend the hours in which she is free from her business routine in these same economic discussions and studies?"

"I am afraid that that is true," said the Professor.

"Yes indeed," said Sylvia, "to poor Professor Hale's sorrow."

"Delight," cried the Professor. "Unbounded delight."

"Our mutual delight," exclaimed Sylvia.

"Very well," continued Jack with an excess of calm courtesy, "as a mere matter of variety of occupation, might I suggest that since there are so many interesting and delightful subjects of conversation--"

"Such as?" enquired Sylvia simply.

"Love affairs, eh Reggie?" exclaimed Aunt Elizabeth, with a wicked little smile.

"Love affairs?" gasped Professor Hale, flushing a deep red.

"Love affairs?" exclaimed Sylvia, her cheeks also hot.

"Love affairs?" said Jack casting a swift glance from one pair of flushed cheeks to the other. "Splendid! But whose--not yours, Aunt Elizabeth?"

"Certainly not," cried Aunt Elizabeth with a gay little laugh. "Let's have something much fresher--the Professor's for instance, I understand the Professor was--"

"Auntie!" cried Sylvia, in a shocked and indignant voice, her cheeks flushing a still deeper red.

"Well, my dear," said Aunt Elizabeth cheerfully, "this evening you both seemed to be engaged in a most hilarious discussion, as I understood you to say, of the Professor's love affairs."

"Really?" exclaimed Jack, "I am most intrigued; truly we have lighted upon a subject of fresh, absorbing, indeed passionate interest. I am all for it. The Professor's love affairs! Will it be a serial? Let's begin with number one." Jack was enjoying himself hugely. Not so the others.

"Oh, I do think, Auntie, you are really--" began Sylvia, in a voice of indignant surprise.

"Tut, tut child," said Aunt Elizabeth. "A little bit of pleasantry. Surely there is no place either for indignation or surprise. What were you and the Professor laughing at so hilariously this evening as I entered the room, may I inquire?"

"Something quite private," said Sylvia.

"Quite personal and private," echoed Professor Hale.

"Ah!" said Jack. "Quite private? The interest deepens. Personal? Well most love affairs are marked by both qualities. Did you get any particulars, Aunt Elizabeth?"

"None whatever," said Aunt Elizabeth, who for some reason appeared to be enjoying herself vastly. "None were offered and of course I couldn't ask."

"Certainly not," said Jack. "I am quite sure you are not guilty of the slightest indiscretion, not to say indelicacy."

"What nonsense, Jack," cried Sylvia, with great indignation. "The Professor was merely--"

"In short, if you are at all interested," said the Professor. "I was merely--"

"Professor Hale--Reggie--" interrupted Sylvia, her cheeks now a deep crimson, her voice trembling. "I forbid you to refer any further to the subject."

"I shall certainly not," said the Professor, bowing gravely toward her.

"Dear Aunt Elizabeth, I really can't understand how you--"

"Pooh, pooh! pray don't 'Aunt Elizabeth' me in that tone of voice. You remember I came in upon your stories and found both the Professor and you in gales of laughter, which you said was caused by the recital of the Professor's love affairs. You remember, I simply made the remark that we did not make a practice in my young days of discussing our love affairs, after the manner of our modern young people. Why should it be that what seemed to you both a subject of hilarity this afternoon should now suddenly become a shocking or improper thing?"

"My dear Miss Murray," implored the Professor.

"But darling Auntie," exclaimed Sylvia.

"May I suggest that the matter appears to be quite unimportant and has even ceased to be interesting. Shall we go into the drawing- room and have some music?" Miss Elizabeth's tone and manner were on her grandest scale, the scale reserved, in short, only for great occasions. So much so that no one thought for a moment of continuing the discussion.

"Aunt Elizabeth," said Jack following her into the drawing-room. "I regret greatly that I must hurry away. The truth is my father is not at all well. Nothing serious, but he is overdone, tired and somewhat worried. These are rather trying days for him."

"I am so sorry, Jack. I do hope you will find him better. Let us know in the morning."

"Good-night, Reggie," said Jack, with a cheerful grin on his face.

Sylvia accompanied him to the door.

"Good-night, Sylvia," said Jack, "or will you come for a turn round the block. Perhaps it is too cold."

"I am going," said Sylvia, in a quite determined voice. And putting on her fur coat, for the night was sharply cold, and a fascinating little blue toque, she ran out and climbed into the car.

"Well this is very nice of you, my dear. If you are not too tired," said Jack. "Though I must say you developed a new brilliance in conversation to-night, you quite astonished me. Sorry I was so dull, but I was played out. These are hard days." He snuggled down a little closer to her, "It is really lovely to have you all to myself, even for a few minutes. We do not seem to have much time together, do we? You are so terribly occupied with your economics, and your professor and all that." Jack's voice faded off into silence.

"My professor," said Sylvia rather sharply. "Poor Reggie!"

"Poor Reggie," echoed Jack. "Lucky beggar, if you ask me. Comfortable home, capable, fascinating, sympathetic attendants, nothing to do but worry about his love affairs," said Jack with a little snicker. "Of course I am not in his confidence in that regard. By the way, wasn't Aunt Elizabeth killingly funny to-night! A perfect scream, I thought."

"Yes, you evidently did, but I want to say I was surprised and indeed shocked at Aunt Elizabeth, and at you too, Jack. If you only knew the facts," Sylvia paused abruptly.

"Tell me," said Jack in a tone of deep sympathy.

"Now Jack, you are being horrid again."

"But you see I am not informed, nor apparently is your Aunt Elizabeth."

"How could I tell you what was given to me in confidence?" exclaimed Sylvia.

"But you both apparently regarded the whole thing as a huge joke. Aunt Elizabeth speaks of hilarious laughter. Why then the pity for poor Reggie?"

"If you only knew," said Sylvia in a low voice.

"Well, I won't you see," replied Jack, "and I am not particularly anxious to know, and I have no particular desire to pry into his love affairs; but apparently he has confided in you something that struck you both as being enormously funny."

"Funny, Jack?" Sylvia repeated. "Why it is a perfect tragedy."

"What is?" asked Jack.

"How can I tell you," said Sylvia.

"Well," said Jack. "He has shown me a photograph of a very lovely girl, his inamorata I gather, which he keeps upon his table."

"Yes," bursts forth Sylvia, "and he bores her to death. There," she said crossly. "I shouldn't have told you that."

"Ah, he bores her to death," said Jack. "Probably because he talks economics to her. I must say I am not entirely surprised. Economics and love-making really don't mix too well. Personally, my sympathy goes out toward the poor girl. Possibly she bores him as well. That should be the natural reaction."

"Jack, you are not nice. Indeed you are most unkind."

"But my dear, if they bore one another to death where is the tragedy?"

"Isn't that tragedy enough that after ten years' engagement these two should bore one another to death?" retorted Sylvia. "There! You've got that out of me."

"My dear Sylvia, it was rather obvious, I must say. But I fail to see the tragedy."

"And isn't it a tragedy?"

"Tragedy?" said Jack, "no, stupidity. If they bore one another to death why the deuce don't they end it."

For answer there was silence.

"But apparently," continued Jack, "your Aunt Elizabeth suggests that the thing was something at which he laughed hilariously."

"Laughed?" exclaimed Sylvia. "It was a horrible laugh. It was very like hysteria."

"But you laughed also, I understand," continued Jack relentlessly.

"Well, Aunt Elizabeth had just opened the door and of course I had to laugh too."

"And quite right, I should say," said Jack. "If two people bore one another after ten years' experience, why shouldn't they laugh about it, and treat it as a huge joke, and be done with it?"

"Ah, but this is not the tragedy. If you only knew! And I am not going to discuss the matter any further."

"Very sensible indeed, my dear." Jack's voice was full of consolation. "By the way," he went on, "when is the Professor going away? He seems to be fairly recovered by this time."

"He is not," said Sylvia emphatically. "He is miserable, nervous and lonely."

"Lonely? With two charming ladies to spend their spare hours in happy converse with him?"

"He is very unhappy, Jack, and you are certainly not very sympathetic with my friend."

"Your friend?"

"Yes Jack, and yours as well."

"I am not so sure there," said Jack.

"Not your friend, Jack?"

"Well," said Jack recklessly. "You've asked for it, and I might as well be frank with you. I have had a very high regard for Hale. He is a brilliantly clever man, but as to friendship, after what you've told me, I am not quite so sure. A man who announces that the girl to whom he has been engaged for ten years bores him to death, I have another name for him than that of friend. But for Heaven's sake, let us forget him for the present."

"But I cannot, Jack. You don't know the sad part of it, and you can't understand."

"Oh well, Sylvia, it is rather obvious, and I may as well be frank about it. If I am wrong you can correct me. I fancy your friend, Reggie, has allowed himself to fall in love with you, and he knows it is no use. That is indeed a tragedy, I grant you the most terrible tragedy that can befall a man. But if you ask me to register woe in this connection I am afraid I shall have to disappoint you. The tragedy is there, but the tragedy is, not that his own girl bores him, but that he had the nerve to allow himself to fall in love with a girl whom he knew was engaged to a man whom he called his friend. I confess I have little sympathy for a man that behaves like a cad."

"Jack, will you please take me home?"

"Certainly, my dear," said Jack, "if you wish me to." And soon the car was on the way to Hilltop House.

As they approached the end of their drive Jack said gently, "I am sorry for this Sylvia. It is extremely unpleasant for you, and it is hard lines upon Reggie."

"Please don't talk about it, Jack," she said in a low voice.

"I shall not! Not to-night, nor ever again," said Jack as they drove up to the door.

"Good-night, Jack," said Sylvia kissing him lightly.

"Oh good-night. Well! is that all? Well, good-night, Sylvia. I am sorry I have hurt you."

"Oh good-night! Oh go! Jack, I can't bear it--oh go!" She ran to the door and opening it passed hurriedly into the hall and stood there with her heart beating hard as if it would choke her.

Suddenly it came upon her that Jack was going away. Anything might happen before she saw him again. Immediately she tore the door open, ran out into the drive and cried, "Jack! Wait! wait!" But the car moving swiftly was disappearing through the gate. "He is gone," she said in a grief-stricken voice.

She came slowly back to the house, removed her wraps in the hall and was passing upstairs when Aunt Elizabeth called to her, "Are you coming in for some music, Sylvia?"

"I think I shall go to bed, Aunt Elizabeth, I have a headache." She ran downstairs, kissed her Aunt and said: "Say good-night to Professor Hale for me," and disappeared upstairs to bed.

To bed, but not to sleep. "What has happened?" she asked herself. "What have I done to Jack, and why?" Over and over, as she tossed sleepless, she rehearsed the conversation at the dinner table and later with Jack in the car. Most of it seemed now to her to be entirely silly. Why had she been so indignant with Jack? She was dismayed to discover that she could not recall any just reason for her treatment of him. For Reggie she could arouse little sympathy, or pity. He had certainly not behaved well, either to the young lady to whom he was engaged or indeed to herself. She made up her mind that she would phone Jack the first thing in the morning. The present situation was perfectly intolerable. With this resolution in mind, and thanking God for another day, she at length fell into a troubled slumber.

CHAPTER XV

Mr. Timothy Brady was early at the office of the Riverside Mills. With his usual aplomb he entered the outer office and beamed upon the clerks.

"Hello, Miss Frances, my dear, is my lady in and can she spare me a few minutes? I am rather rushed this morning and regret to say have no time for even such charming young things as you are. These are strenuous days. Great doings are afoot, Canada is going to see big things."

"Oh, dear Mr. Brady," cried Sally, the blonde typist under her breath. "Tell me what shall I do with International Nickel? They want me to sell, but yet everybody says it is going very much higher."

"My dear," said Mr. Brady solemnly, "my advice is to do the exact opposite to what everybody says. In regard to International Nickel, let me say, the deluge is surely coming, still not just to- day. International Nickel is the one stock which I should say it was a quite safe bet to hold for at least three months. On general principles my advice is don't be a hog, let the other fellow have something. Now, my dear Miss Frances, can I see my lady?"

"Sit down, Mr. Brady," said Frances moving toward the door of the inner office.

"Thank you, Miss Frances, I have no strength to sit down. You see it requires so much more energy to rise than to stand, and I need all my strength to keep moving. My dear Miss Sally," he continued, "how many stocks are you holding at the present time?"

"Only five," said Miss Sally sadly. "You see it is so hard to hold when they offer you a good price."

"Five stocks, you blessed little idiot. Get rid of four. Do you hear me? Or you will be biting the blankets some of these fine nights. As I have said, don't be a hog, let the other fellow make a dollar."

"You may go in," said Miss Frances, returning from the inner office.

"Oh, thank you my dear," said Mr. Brady. "If I can help you any time, let me know."

As he entered the inner office he exclaimed. "Hello! Miss Sylvia what is the matter? Market hit you?"

"Good morning, Mr. Brady. No the market gives me little trouble. I am perfectly all right. Though I didn't sleep as well as usual."

"Thank God, then that you have no market troubles. Lots of them have these days. And now I want to relieve you of possible trouble. I want your Central Canada Lumber and Furniture stock. I offered you last week one hundred and fifty, I told you it would go to two hundred. It is on the way. To-day I offer you one hundred and seventy-five. But I am telling you it is going to two hundred sure as you're a foot high."

"All right, Mr. Brady. Last week you offered me one hundred and fifty. I will take one hundred and fifty."

"Not now!" expostulated Mr. Brady. "I don't steal candy from a baby. You will sell me your stock at the market price or not at all, and the price to-day is one hundred and seventy-five and going up."

"Very well, I shall sell at one hundred and seventy-five."

"Remember, I am telling you that the market will close to-day at one hundred and eighty-five. Do you want to hold on?"

"No, certainly not," said Sylvia firmly. "It isn't worth one hundred and eighty-five. It isn't worth one hundred and seventy- five, but since you insist, one hundred and seventy-five it is."

She rang a bell and gave orders to her secretary for the transfer to be made.

"This means a lot of money, Mr. Brady," she said, as he proceeded to make out the cheque for $52,500.00.

"Not so much as $60,000.00," said Mr. Brady, "where it will be by the end of this week. You are just handing me $7,500.00."

"Mr. Brady, I am sure all this stock inflation is wrong."

"Now, my dear, don't worry your pretty head. You can't make the world right, you must take it as it is and do the best you can to play the game."

"I wish I was done with it all," said Sylvia.

"Say young lady, don't talk like that. What you want is a rest. What is wrong with you?"

"Mr. Brady," said Sylvia earnestly. "Will you do something for me?"

"Will I do something for you? Tell me something real hard."

"Telephone Mr. Jack Tempest for me the moment you reach town. Ask him to call me at once."

"Ah!" said Mr. Brady, "So that's what it is? Pardon me, Miss Sylvia. That telephone will be the first thing, before I sell a dollar of stock. Remember the sun is high in the sky and all the clouds will roll by. I didn't mean to make poetry. Cheer up, my dear, good-bye."

In response to Miss Sylvia's bell Frances brought in the daily reports. First there was the report from the camps.

"Anything important there," enquired Sylvia.

"The camp seems to be in good order," replied Frances, "everything running smoothly--horses got fit again--roads being cleaned up--the cutting is progressing satisfactorily, and the men are quite content though there is a hint of trouble between the French and English--nothing to speak of. Roddy--I mean Mr. Macdougall--says he would like you to go up in about two weeks' time to look it over."

"I'm afraid not. That seems to be a fine boy."

"Yes, Miss Sylvia," said Frances demurely. "He says they have found quite a stand of white oak, which is very valuable. The bark itself is worth a lot for tanning, so Roddy--Mr. Macdougall says."

"We must keep that in mind, Frances. Of course we are doing no tanning just now. What next?"

"There are several enquiries, Miss Sylvia. The first is about fanning mills. Here's a letter asking if we will sell your patent outright."

"Well, let that rest just now, Frances. Report to Headquarters. They will decide that point."

"Then," continued Frances, "we have two or three enquiries as to our nursery furniture. The decorations seem to be making that rather attractive."

"Frances, we shall push that a little harder. You might put two or three of the girls on that department. What next?"

"A letter from Headquarters," said Frances. "The usual thing, hard times, must cut overhead expenses."

"Make the usual answer, Frances."

"They ask us to hurry with the hardwood."

"Just tell them we cannot move much hardwood till the snow flies; though we might possibly run a raft down before freeze up. Has Mr. Macdougall any men fit to run a raft? You might ask him. Anything else?"

"Nothing but mere routine."

"Very well then, Frances. Here are some letters: I have indicated the answers as usual, and I think that is all this morning. Oh, by the way, are many of our girls buying stocks?"

"Yes, Miss Sylvia, quite a number of them."

"Can't you persuade them to give up this nonsense?"

"Mr. Brady says International Nickel is good for three months, at least."

Sylvia remained silent a few moments.

"Frances, Mr. Brady is an enthusiastic Irishman. He has got the booming blood bouncing in his veins at the present time. A friend of mine, an excellent judge and very well informed, assures me that bad times are coming. Tell the girls that I would be much pleased if they would get rid of their stocks at the earliest possible moment."

"It is no use, Miss Sylvia. They won't listen to me and some of them are making quite a lot of money."

"Do your best, Frances. I am sure this stock booming is all wrong. I sold all my stock to-day."

Frances paused a moment as if she could make reply, but changed her mind and went slowly from the room.

A few moments later the telephone rang.

It was Mr. Timothy Brady.

"Sorry, Miss Sylvia, but I can't get in touch with Jack Tempest. He is not at the office, and the house will not answer. The report is that his father is rather seriously ill."

"Thank you, Mr. Brady," said Sylvia and rang her bell.

"Frances, please order my car around at once. I shall run into town. How long I shall remain I cannot say. Telephone my Aunt that I shall not be home for lunch. Please do not say anything of my whereabouts."

An hour and a half later Sylvia was standing at the outer desk in the office of Tempest, Boyle, Brice and Company.

In reply to her inquiry concerning Jack, the clerk could give her no satisfaction. Mr. Jack Tempest had sent word that he would not be at the office to-day, the reason given being that his father was seriously ill.

"Can I see Mr. Boyle?" inquired Sylvia.

"Mr. Boyle is engaged at present, but I will make inquiry."

As he spoke the door of the private office opened and out came Mr. Boyle, accompanied by Mr. Cameron Ogilvie. They both came forward to meet Sylvia.

In answer to her anxious inquiry, Mr. Boyle replied:

"I am sorry to say that we have very bad news in the office to-day. And Miss Sylvia, I am rather pressed for time. Matters of great importance are awaiting my decisions. Perhaps Mr. Cameron Ogilvie will explain."

"My dear friend," said Mr. Cameron Ogilvie. "Can I take you some place?"

"Thank you, Mr. Ogilvie. My car is at the door. Tell me, what is it? Is Mr. Tempest dangerously ill?"

"He is gravely ill," said Mr. Cameron Ogilvie. "In fact, he has had a stroke, the issue of which is quite doubtful. But besides that I may as well tell you, for the whole world will know it to- morrow, a terrible disaster has befallen this office. One of the partners, Mr. Brice, has been found guilty of very serious irregularities, indeed deliberate dishonesty. He has used the firm's name and authority to make heavy purchases in the stock market, Pulp and Paper, in fact, buying on margin, a practice utterly contrary to the practice and tradition of this office. The market slipped a few points yesterday, and the demand for cover came into the hands of Mr. Tempest. Inquiry revealed an appalling situation. I am telling you this to save you the pain of learning it on the street. I have been using my utmost endeavors to prevent a complete collapse of the market, but I have not been successful. I am on my way to see Sir James Scaiffe. He is the only man who can do anything. I have been unable to get him so far. I fear, however, that I can do little with him. He is a hard man, a ruthless man indeed. If Mr. Jack Tempest were free he is about the only man who can handle Sir James, but of course Jack cannot leave his father's bedside."

"Oh," cried Sylvia, with quickening breath. "I think I must see Jack at once. Do you think I could?"

"Miss Sylvia," said Mr. Cameron Ogilvie, "I do think it would be a kind and wise thing to go to him at once."

"But, Mr. Ogilvie, I do hope you can see Sir James."

"I shall do my best with him, but have little hope of influencing him. You have my sympathy, my dear. Goodbye."

As in a horrible nightmare Sylvia made her way slowly through the crowded traffic toward Mr. Tempest's residence. At a cross street the traffic held her up. Close to the curb, as her eyes were wandering dully over the faces of the passersby, suddenly she became aware that Sir James Scaiffe was standing on the pavement and looking at her. Instinctively she raised her hand, beckoning him to her.

"My dear Miss Sylvia," said Sir James, greeting her with a fascinating smile. "And what are you doing in this mess at this hour of the day?"

"Oh, Sir James," said Sylvia breathing hurriedly, "I am on my way to see Jack Tempest. I must see him, his father is very ill, and there is trouble at the office. I wish--" she paused abruptly.

Sir James's face fell.

"Oh--yes--of course, I have just heard the very sad news."

"Can I drive you anywhere, Sir James? Will you get in?"

"Why, thank you, my dear, yes, I am rather in a hurry at this very moment. Indeed I am on my way to catch a train."

He glanced at the girl's stricken face. "My dear, I am grieved for you," he said. "I remember now, you are engaged to Mr. Jack Tempest."

Sylvia made no reply, unable to command her voice.

"I really am very sorry," Sir James continued. "Mr. Tempest and I were once very close friends. In later years we have not seen eye to eye in matters of business, in fact we are in opposite camps. Still he is an old friend, and it grieves me to hear of his serious illness. I am sorry, very sorry for his son Jack. I regard him as a fine boy, a young man of great promise."

With a tremendous effort Sylvia took herself in hand. She suddenly remembered Mr. Cameron Ogilvie's word that Sir James Scaiffe was the only man who could save the situation for Jack's father. She resolved to take her chance and make an appeal to him.

"Sir James," she said in a quiet voice, "Jack Tempest is very dear to me. He is in terrible trouble. I have no right to talk to you, but Mr. Cameron Ogilvie has just told me that you are the only man that can help. Please let me speak?" she said, as Sir James made an impatient movement. "You see, Jack has only his father. There is besides a little lame boy, Nickie, a wonderful, a very dear little chap, very nervous and needing care."

"Yes! yes! I remember," said Sir James hurriedly. "But what can I--"

"Sir James, Mr. Cameron Ogilvie says you are the only man that can deal with the market. He says you know all about what is being done, and you are the only man who can prevent disaster."

"Ah!" said Sir James. "Did Mr. Cameron Ogilvie say nothing else?"

Sylvia hesitated remembering what Mr. Cameron Ogilvie had said about Sir James. "Yes," she said in a very low voice, "but if you please I would rather not--"

"Never mind," said Sir James. "They will blame me of course. But if men will play the fool and the rogue they must suffer for it. Of course," he added hurriedly, "I am not blaming Roger Tempest, he is neither one nor the other. He is their victim to-day."

"Yes," said Sylvia in a sudden rush of tears. "And he is dying and Jack is alone."

"Miss Sylvia," said Sir James suddenly. "Will you drive to the Montreal Club, the side door please."

Arrived at the Club, Sir James alighted briskly.

"Come in," he said, and ushered her into the Ladies' waiting room. "Let me order you a glass of sherry."

"No, thank you, Sir James, I never take any."

"Then, let me see. I shall be busy for a few minutes. A pot of tea, waiter and a biscuit. Now will you excuse me, wait here."

"Certainly, Sir James," she said, catching his hand in hers. "And oh--Sir James--Thank you for trying."

"Trying?" replied Sir James, his lips coming together in a straight line. "Make your mind easy. I will do something!"

It was quite half an hour before Sir James reappeared. "Cheer up!" he said. "I have succeeded in checking a run on the Pulp and Paper stock. Things will be steady for a couple of days at least. Tell Jack that I say to him that he has no need to worry about Pulp and Paper for a few days at least."

The sudden accession of hope completely broke down Sylvia's self- control. "Oh, Sir James," she said, holding his hand as he bade her good-bye, her lips trembling, the tears running quietly down her face. "They tell me you are a hard man, but I know you have a kind heart."

"I hope you will always be able to say that, Miss Sylvia," he replied, gravely. "Now run away to Jack."

By noon it was known that Sir James Scaiffe was buying Pulp and Paper, with the result that there was a swift upward swing of the market.

CHAPTER XVI

Sylvia found Mrs. Foster and Julia in the morning room.

"Dear child," exclaimed Mrs. Foster. "What a shock to you, to all of us. Poor Jack, he is in a dazed state, and all that terrible affair at the office. Tom says it is quite serious too."

"Mother," said Julia quietly, "Jack would like to see Sylvia."

"Shall I call Jack?" asked Mrs. Foster.

"No Mother," said Julia. "Take Sylvia in."

With a grateful glance at Julia, Sylvia followed Mrs. Foster into the bedroom. Jack looked up and came forward quickly to meet her. Sylvia put her arms round him and murmured, "Jack--Jack--Jack dear," clinging to him. The nurse placed a chair for her near Jack's, at the bedside.

"He is resting more quietly," she said and left the room.

"Sylvia, this is more than good of you, to leave your business in this way."

Sylvia took his hand and held it very tight, but for some moments was unable to say a single word.

When she had regained her self-control she gave him Sir James Scaiffe's message.

Jack listened astonished. "He said that, the old devil? Well, it is decent of him. But," he added, "he cannot bring Dad back again."

At this point the doctor entered the room and Sylvia moved away toward the bay window, where she stood vaguely taking in the room and its furnishings. It was a large, square bedroom with heavy old fashioned furniture, a beautifully carved, ornate mantel over the fireplace where a fire was burning. On the walls were hung some old fashioned prints, a large photograph of Jack's mother and on the wall opposite an illuminated Scripture text with the words: "My Peace I give unto you."

The doctor finished his examination and said, "He is better this morning, distinctly easier. Of course, it would be wrong to give you any false hope. We must wait for his recuperative powers to come into play. He must have perfect quiet, no attempt at conversation. But if he seems anxious, try to understand and relieve his anxiety."

"Dr. Strang," said Jack, "may I introduce my fiancée, Miss Sylvia Rivers."

"Ah, I remember her quite well--sings--lovely girl--good sense, too."

"Shall I go now, Jack?" whispered Sylvia.

"No, no," said the doctor. "Stay with Jack. Mr. Tempest likes you. It would be a great help. Watch his eyes. Try to understand him. Keep his mind at rest."

Immediately after the doctor's departure the nurse came in.

"Mr. Jack, I think you should try to get an hour's rest."

"I am all right," said Jack. "Besides there is Nickie."

"Jack, you need your strength, therefore you must rest. I shall take Nickie home with me, if you promise to go and lie down an hour or so. The nurse is here, Mrs. Foster is in the next room, everything will be all right."

To this Jack finally agreed.

In the next room they found Nickie. Jack who had not seen him for some hours was shocked at his wan, pale appearance.

"Nickie," he said in a cheery voice. "Dad is better, he is sleeping quietly now and Sylvia is going to take you out to her home for the night. You will come in to-morrow morning."

"Dad is better?" said the boy, a wave of colour flooding his cheeks.

"Yes, the doctor says so," answered Jack.

The boy turned to Sylvia. "Yes, I should like to go with you."

"Come along then, Nickie, and we shall bring your violin with us."

On her return to Hilltop House, Sylvia found Aunt Elizabeth in a state of great anxiety. She gave the little boy a warm motherly welcome, and soon had him quietly seated before a comfortable fire in the morning room with a cup of cocoa in his hands.

"Professor Hale went away this morning, Sylvia," said Aunt Elizabeth. "He left this letter. I tried to persuade him to remain, but he said no, feeling that your preoccupation with Jack and his trouble made it better that he should depart."

"It was very thoughtful of him," said Sylvia, taking the letter and going upstairs.

After she had dressed for dinner she opened the letter and read:

Dear Miss Sylvia:

Nothing I can say can fully express my grateful appreciation of the care, the loving care, I have had from the dear friends in this house, nor am I able to tell you how greatly your companionship has stimulated and cheered me. There is one thing more for which I am grateful. You have shown me the wrong which I have been doing Pearl. That at least I can and will make right at once. Any pretence at engagement where love has ceased to exist is both foolish and wrong. As for my love for you, that will remain a sacred experience, but as to my speaking, I pray you, forgive and forget that sudden madness, and regard me as your true and loyal friend.

REGGIE

Sylvia was surprised to find how slightly the letter moved her. "Poor Reggie," she said, and put it away.

Next morning the papers announced a slight improvement in Mr. Roger Tempest's condition. He had had a quiet night, but he was by no means out of danger. On another page of the paper it was announced that Pulp and Paper stock showed a distinct recovery, and was already on the upward swing.

A phone call from Jack informed her that the newspaper report was unduly optimistic.

"Shall I come in at once?" asked Sylvia.

"No, it is not necessary. You will have your morning work to do. If any change occurs I shall let you know immediately. How is Nickie?"

"He looks very much better this morning. He had a good night and has apparently enjoyed his breakfast. I am going to take him down to the office with me. One of the girls will show him about. I think he will be quite happy."

The morning Sylvia spent busy with the routine duties of the office. This being attended to, she took Nickie herself through the more interesting parts of the factory. At two o'clock, however, a phone call from Mr. Tempest's house announced that he had taken a turn for the worse, and indeed was rapidly sinking.

In a little more than an hour's time Sylvia, with Nickie, reached the house. Leaving Nickie with Mrs. Foster and Julia, Sylvia passed into the sick room where she found Jack with the nurse in attendance.

The sick man was obviously much weaker and apparently very restless. As Sylvia took her place at his bedside he made a slight movement with his hand. Sylvia took it in hers and kissed it. The sick man's eyes remained steadily fixed on hers. There was no mistaking the enquiry in the eyes.

"Is it Nickie?" asked Sylvia. "If so, close your eyes."

Immediately the eyes were closed.

"Oh, Nickie had a very happy evening with us," she said, "and a good night. He is very much better. Jack will bring him in."

Nickie greeted his brother eagerly. "Is father better?" he asked.

"No Nickie," said Jack slowly. "He is not quite so well."

"Jack," cried the boy, "is Daddy going to die?"

Jack picked him up and took him in his arms and carrying him to the bay window sat there with him.

"Nickie," he said quietly. "Nickie boy, can you be brave for Daddy's sake? The doctor says Daddy must not be disturbed. Can you be brave and quiet?"

The little boy was silent for a moment, then with a deep breath he said, "Oh, is Daddy going to die?"

"Nickie," said Jack very gently, "you remember mother went away. Daddy was very lonely. He is going now to meet mother. Isn't that wonderful?"

The boy's lips began to quiver, his eyes slowly filling with tears.

"Jack, I am afraid I cannot help crying. If Daddy is going I think I would like to go too."

Jack drew him tight to his breast. "I know, Nickie, I know just how you feel, but I don't want you to go yet. You see I need you with me, I need you."

It was the right word. Nickie put up his thin hand and stroked Jack's face. "All right, Jack," he said with a deep sigh. "I will try--I will try my best, Jack."

"Brave little man," said Jack. "You are just like Daddy. He was a very brave man. Do you think now you could go in and say good night quite quietly?"

"I think so," said the boy. "Just wait a minute or two."

In a few minutes Jack said, "Are you ready, Nickie?"

"Yes, Jack," said the boy.

Then Jack carried him in and laid him beside his father on the bed.

"Say good night to Daddy, Nickie," he said.

"Good night, Daddy," said the little boy, his clear boy's voice ringing out steady and true. He put his arm round his father's neck and kissing him, held him fast.

The father's eyes were on Sylvia's face gravely enquiring.

"You want something," said Sylvia.

The eyes closed. Then opening again fastened upon Sylvia's face.

"Is it something about Nickie?" enquired Sylvia.

The eyes closed again.

"I am going to take Nickie home with me. Is that what you want?"

Again the eyes closed.

"Now, Nickie boy, say good night," said Jack in a firm quiet voice.

"Good night, daddy dear," said the boy and kissed his father.

Jack lifted him in his arms and carried him out into the next room.

"Good stuff, laddie," he said. "Brave boy!"

"Jack," said the boy suddenly, his arms convulsively clutching his brother about the neck. "Jack," he cried, "I want him."

"God help us, laddie," said his big brother in a broken voice. "So do I," and sitting down before the fire, held him tight in his arms till Julia came and took him away.

"Come with me, Nickie," she said. "Jack must go to Daddy now."

"Yes, yes," whispered the lad.

Again Jack went into the bedroom and sat with Sylvia at his father's bedside, waiting for the slow deep breaths as they came one by one.

For some minutes his father lay with eyes closed. Then suddenly the eyes opened wide, bright with intelligence, and turning first to Sylvia and then to the wall opposite and once more back to Sylvia's face. The lips moved. Quickly Jack bent over trying to catch a word, but in vain. Once more the eyes travelled from Sylvia's face to the wall opposite. Following the glance Sylvia found her eyes resting upon the illuminated text: "Peace I leave with you."

"Is it 'peace' you mean?" enquired Sylvia.

The eyes closed.

Quietly Sylvia said the words over very clearly, "My Peace I leave with you," and finished the quotation from memory, "Let not your heart be troubled, neither let it be afraid."

"Is that what you want?"

Once more the eyes opened, held her face steadily for a moment, turned to the face of his son and slowly closed.

A deep breath--a long pause--another long deep breath--and again a long pause. Once more and again a longer pause--once more a long deep--deep breath. They waited. There was a little sigh--again they waited--and waited--and waited--but there was only silence, eternal silence.

"He is gone," said the nurse.

"Gone?" echoed Jack in a hollow moan. He leaned over his father, put his arms round him and held him close to his heart. "Oh, Dad-- Dad--I want you--you were a great man--a good man--I want you."

For the first time in his life there was no response to his cry. He sank on his knees, his head on the bed. Sylvia knelt beside him, put her arms around him, drew him close, but no word she uttered, only the warm strong clasp of her arms.

Mrs. Foster came softly in.

"He is gone," she said in a broken voice. "For forty years he has been my friend--a great man--a great gentleman--a great Christian. Thank God for him and for all such men. Come Jack," she said, "you must tell Nickie."

"God help me," he groaned.

Mrs. Foster passed out and left the two together. Jack rose, stood looking into Sylvia's eyes. "Sylvia," he said in a quiet steady voice, "whatever may come to us two, never, never shall I forget what you have been to us--to my father--to Nickie--to me--these days." Sylvia went quickly to the bedside and kneeling took the still hand in hers, kissed it once, twice, thrice. Once more she came and stood with her arms round Jack.

"Oh, Jack, he was a good man and I loved him. I shall take Nickie home with me until everything is over."

"Oh Sylvia," said Jack. "How understanding you are. I am a foolish and weak man. Be patient with me, Sylvia. The other night I was foolish and wrong and unkind."

"The other night," said Sylvia. "What was it? What was wrong? Oh, that silly old Professor. Forget all that nonsense. Oh Jack, come and get Nickie for me."

CHAPTER XVII

Returning from his father's funeral, Jack found awaiting him Mrs. Foster with Sylvia and Nickie.

"Come, Jack," said Mrs. Foster. "You have eaten nothing to-day. We have a cup of tea waiting for you."

They had no sooner seated themselves about the table when the phone rang.

"Let me answer it," said Mrs. Foster.

"Yes, he is here. I beg your pardon. Hold your telephone, please. Jack there is a very excited man on the telephone. I can't make out what he is saying."

"Yes. Who is it?" said Jack, placing the receiver to his ear. "Oh, Brice," he said.

"Can you give me three or four minutes," said Brice. "I am not going to explain, nor am I going to ask forgiveness."

"Don't you think that anything you might say now is quite unnecessary?"

"No," replied Brice. "I believe I can make it a little easier for you if I give you these facts. Do give me a chance, I shall never trouble you again."

"Go on, but please make it short."

"God knows I wish to make it short. I had inside information in regard to Pulp and Paper. The stock had declined sharply. I was assured on the best authority there would be quick recovery. I bought heavily on margin. The market caught me in half a dozen places next day. Never did I have such damnable luck. I couldn't cover. I borrowed the firm's name for a day, only for a day. The market went to pieces, and I couldn't meet it. The crash came. Jack, I never knew a father. For fifteen years Roger Tempest was a father to me. If he had asked for my life I would gladly have given it, that is what hurts me now. You loved your father. You loved him no better than I did. I wanted you to know this. Good-bye, Jack."

"Where are you going?" asked Jack. "Are you leaving town?"

"No, I am not leaving town," answered Brice.

"What are you going to do?"

A mumbled reply came over the telephone.

"I can't hear you. Where are you now?" asked Jack.

"At home, Jack. Good-bye. Jack, remember I loved your father and that is what kills me now."

"Wait a minute, Brice. Hello!" cried Jack. "Hello! Hello! He is gone," said Jack turning with a ghastly face from the phone. "Julia, listen to me. I must speak quickly. Telephone Dr. Strang-- a matter of life and death--send him to Brice's house. Tell him possibly a case of suicide--carbon monoxide--or some such stunt, and for God's sake tell him to hurry up."

Without hat or coat he dashed from the house, leaped into his car and within six minutes was at the Brice's home. Driving to the garage door he heard a car running within, with the garage doors closed, locked from the inside. He rushed to the side door. That also was locked. Looking around wildly his eye fell on a spade. With a single blow he smashed the lock and was within the garage.

In the driver's seat he saw the figure of a man slumped over the wheel. He leaped at the car door, tore it open, seized the man by the shoulders, dragged him from the car and on to the gravel walk outside. There was no sign of life in him.

Jack was skilled in the technique to be applied in drowning accidents, but he knew well that these would be of but slight use in the case of poisoning by monoxide.

Within five minutes of his arrival, Dr. Strang drove up in his car, and came running with his case of instruments in his hand.

"I'll shoot this into him," said the doctor, thrusting a hypo into the flesh.

Together they worked frantically over the inanimate form of the asphyxiated man. After some minutes of desperate work the doctor exclaimed, "There, I believe the breath of life is in him." In a short time the eyes of the unhappy victim slowly opened. With a groan he closed them again, gasping, struggling for breath.

"Jack, there is a pulmotor in my car. Pump a little oxygen into him." As a result, the eyes opened once more, and the breath began to come steadily.

"Confound you, Brice!" exclaimed the doctor in an angry voice. "What the hell do you mean by this fool stunt? Haven't you done enough mischief already without this?"

"Why--didn't--you--let--me--go?" moaned Brice in bitter agony.

"And leave your wife and kiddies to struggle on alone? Not much, you poor coward. We won't let you go out yet!"

"Get hold of him, Jack, lift him into your car. We'll take him to the Royal Vic."

After leaving Brice at the hospital, comfortably resting, Jack drove Dr. Strang to the home of the rescued man.

"Must keep this quiet," said Jack.

"Keep it quiet?" said the doctor. "The thing will certainly leak out."

"Well, he will never be nearer the pearly gates than he was to- day," said Jack.

"Pearly, eh?" grinned the doctor. "Darned idiot! Suicide is the coward's back door of escape from himself. Drive round the block, Jack, you are all shot to pieces. Have you a flask?"

"Never carry one," answered Jack.

"Well, it is lucky for you that I do," said the doctor, rummaging in his bag. "Here, take a good mouthful of this mixture. You need it. So do I."

"Yes," continued the doctor, "a man like Brice has no business to be in the stock game. It is a devil's game anyway. There are three classes of money madmen in the world. (1) The miser, who loves money for itself--psychic. (2) The man who loves money for the things it can buy. He wishes to make a pyramid of things and climbs to the top and sits there where all may behold him. Vulgar beast! (3) The man who seeks money for power. Brice belonged to the second class. He had no resources within himself, therefore must accumulate a pile of things for his glorification, thereby confessing his poverty of mind and soul. Old Scaiffe represents the third class. Money to him means power. He loves to make men jump at the crack of his whip, and the more men the better. Hundreds of thousands of men in Canada to-day jump at the wave of his hand. Humiliating, eh? He can't make me jump. He has nothing to offer me."

"Unless his appendix gets funny," said Jack.

"Ah!" said the doctor. "Old man La Roque down in Trois Rivières, the millionaire, poisoned by his money, had a tumor two weeks ago that bothered him. I extracted the tumor and incidentally with it $6,000."

"Quite a fee," said Jack with a grin, "for a man who despises money."

"Sure!" the doctor said. "It did me a lot of good and him a lot more. Besides it pays for the cure of two hundred and fifty little children otherwise condemned to lifelong bondage to crooked backs and legs. I love to make millionaires pay up some return to the people who make their money for them. But Jack, you have the gift of making big money. Old Scaiffe told me so no earlier than last week."

Jack cursed below his breath.

"That is why I am talking to you to-day," the doctor continued. "Your father was my friend. Twenty years ago he helped me to finish my college course. He backed me again and again, but more than that he showed me what was the big thing in the world. Not money, nor the things money can buy, but something beside which money is mere dirt--life--high quality of life--that is why I am what I am to-day--a surgeon. My assets are in myself, my brain, my hand, my nerve. That is my fortune. Besides that there is the possibility--not to speak cant--of rendering a great service to humanity. Your father did that for me, Jack. I am speaking now to his son on the darkest day of his life. I know what you are planning, Jack. You are planning revenge, not on Brice, poor fool, but on the man whose manipulation drove Brice to dishonour and suicide.

"Let me say two things to you, Jack. Revenge is not good enough. Complete revenge for the blow dealt your father would involve that whole wretched gambling crew, who support this present damnable system. The man you think of is only a figure head. The second thing I want to say is, revenge is not satisfaction to a man of such heart qualities as you have. That was the cause of your father's death, not the loss of money. Not in the least. But the blow over the heart killed him. These are the lethal blows. The man he had loved and trusted and treated as a son for twenty years betrayed him. The heart shock killed your father. Jack, I wish you would get out of the game. But, anyway, for God's sake and for your father's sake, forget old pirate Scaiffe."

"Never," said Jack in a low, level tone. "Listen to me--as God lives--"

"Jack, I won't listen to you. Come to me in six months and I will listen. Don't be a fool. Think of that poor creature in the hospital. A desperate deed now might ruin your whole future."

"No, no," Jack replied with a little laugh. "Don't imagine anything crude, no shooting, no beating up, but I want to see that man where he can't hurt people like my father any more."

"Jack, don't deceive yourself. There is nothing high minded in revenge. I have spoken, my boy, for your father's sake. I have spoken for your sake. I have said what I know he would say. That is all."

"Thank you, doctor," replied Jack. "You have done all you could. Never shall I forget what you have done for me these days. Never! Never!"

"All right," said Dr. Strang. "Here we are at the house. I suppose we must run in and see the wife. Well, let's say Brice has had a seizure. Fortunately, you and I happened along. That will do as well as any other story."

As Dr. Strang drove away he held Jack's hand for just a moment. "Old man, think carefully of what I have said."

"I've thought the whole thing over, doctor, very carefully indeed."

"Looks ten years older," said the doctor to himself as he drove away. "God help him, and God pity the man whose trail he is following."

CHAPTER XVIII

It was Sally Long, Miss Sylvia's blonde typist, who was responsible for the Riverside sermons, which made such a sensation, not only in that hamlet, but in the neighbouring city as well; Miss Sally Long and her special boy friend, "the enterprising news hound" as he called himself, who honoured the Montreal Evening Courier with his services.

It fell upon an afternoon that Miss Sylvia found Sally emerging from a bout of tears, with Frances striving to lend aid and comfort in the case. Now Miss Sally was not of the tearful kind. She had a cool brain and a steady little heart. But the loss of six hundred dollars was more than her cool brain and steady little heart could bear with equanimity. The six hundred dollars were dedicated to the paying off of the last installment of the mortgage on their home, and this was to have been a Christmas present for her mother. The tears were tears of disappointment at her loss, tears of humiliation at her own stupidity, tears of fury at Bertie Bingle on whose advice and assurance that Consolidated Aeroplanes were bound to go "away up," she had invested her six hundred dollars. And so they did, but alas! their subsequent career only demonstrated the truth of the old adage that "whatever goes up must come down." Her red eyelids and tragic gloom could not escape the observation of her chief.

"What is wrong, Sally? Come into my office?"

Sally followed her in trepidation for her chief, she knew, possessed not only a kind heart, but in case of need the power of searching penetration and of cold and biting comment.

Having listened to Sally's tale however, Miss Sylvia, who might have said: "Well, Sally, I told you," but she did not, or "I hope it will be a lesson to you, Sally," which also she avoided, listened patiently to her story. She thereupon sought to comfort her typist with soothing words; "Never mind, Sally, perhaps we can find a way to help out." This she did later on, by double pay for extra work which Sally took on in overtime. This overtime engagement, however, excited the disappointment and wrath of her boy friend the "news hound," who had arranged for Sally's overtime in quite another fashion.

The following evening Sally, in discussing her woes with her boy friend, a red headed North of Ireland youth, only a year out from the ould sod, carrying the cognomen of Andy McGarrick, announced with obvious satisfaction: "But they are all going to catch it next Sunday."

"Not them," said Andy, "the devil himself can't catch those burds."

"No, but the minister can," said Sally. "And he is going to hold them up to public reprobation."

"What?" asked the news hound, his nose to the trail.

"He is going to preach a sermon on them," said Sally.

"A sermon? Is he then? What minister? When? Where? Is he any good at all?" questioned the hound.

"Our minister. In St. Paul's and a fine man he is. He is going to give the first of three sermons next Sunday evening."

"He may be a fine man for St. Paul's, but will he give those fellas hell like the Rev. Tommy Bailey, for instance, would in the People's Church?"

"Andy, our minister is not a sensational preacher. He would despise such stuff as Tommy Bailey gives. He is a scholar I would have you know, and a gentleman, and he knows what he is talking about."

"Oh rats! my dear," ejaculated Andy. "It isn't a scholar those fellas want, it is the broth of a bhoy who can put the fear of hell into them. But Sally--you know--a scholar, well, and a gentleman? I will go and see him, Sally. Is he the kind of a man now that a chap like meself could call on without the fear of being kicked out of the back door?"

"I am telling you, Andy, he is a gentleman. He is a perfect dear, and awfully kind."

"Och now, hold your horses! Is that the kind of a man to set after these lads of the Stock Exchange for instance? Howsomeever, I will have a look in on him. He can't do more than kick me out, and that's in my day's work."

"Don't mention my name or say I sent you," cautioned Sally. "I wouldn't for anything like him to think--"

"Listen to me, my dear. Andy McGarrick wasn't born yesterday."

Andy's interview apparently strengthened his resolve to persuade his chief to allow him to get a story out of the Rev. Malcolm Matheson's three sermons.

A modest note in the regular St. Paul's weekly announcement had advertised the first of three sermons to be preached in St. Paul's by the Rev. Malcolm Matheson, on the general theme: "The Kingdom of Heaven and Modern Finance." But the news had gone through the little town like wildfire, and in consequence St. Paul's was filled, as the reporter put it "to the cross beams," with a congregation representative of all classes and all creeds in the community, which goes to show, the reporter commented, "that when preachers preach to-day on themes of interest to the people of to- day, the people will be there to hear."

It took Andy McGarrick's full powers of persuasion to secure from his chief the assignment of St. Paul's for the Sunday evening sermon.

At the close of the service Andy had no time, even for Sally.

"Sally, my dear, I have got the blessed stuff burnin' in my heart, and if I can only get it out, and if I can only persuade the chief to run it, there will be something doin' on the streets of Montreal, or my name isn't Andy McGarrick."

At ten o'clock a weary and worn reporter with pale face and burning eyes, laid his copy upon his chief's desk, and waited developments. The chief fell upon it, blue pencil in hand. But soon the blue pencil was laid aside. The copy ran as follows:

In style of delivery the Rev. Malcolm Matheson is frankly a disappointment. A poor, thin voice, and a bad delivery. We venture to suggest that a few simple lessons in the art of elocution would undoubtedly make Mr. Matheson's services to his congregation more acceptable. The minister apparently is a humble- minded, gentle soul, with an ingratiating manner and a disarming smile, but he has the little grey matter packed above his kindly blue eyes, and he knows his European history, from Versailles to the last date and the last dollar. If only the late M. Poincaré and Mr. Lloyd George had been present, their tempers might not have been improved, but their souls might have benefited, and no one would have had to keep them awake either.

The minister knows his economics as well, and no mere book stuff, but the economics which the present day world desperately requires.

He is strong too on theology. His theme, we must remember, was the Kingdom of Heaven and Modern Finance, and his definition of the Kingdom of Heaven was a little poem which we would like to insert verbatim et literatim, but for fear of the chief who wields a blue pencil with a penetrating point. What struck one about the minister's understanding of the Kingdom of Heaven was that it appeared quite remote from the religion which churches are trying to give people to-day. Here is his definition: "The Kingdom of Heaven is an organized state of existence in which the principles of the spirit of Heaven prevail. It is something not for the life after death only, but for life here and now in this present evil world."

And then in his gentle voice he read a bit from the Book descriptive of the City within the Gates of Pearl, where gold is used to pave the streets and where the River of Life flows down between avenues of the Tree of Life, whose fruits come every month, and whose leaves are for the healing of the nations.

"There are strange absences from this city," he cried with his gentle smile. "No pain--no sorrow--no tears--no sin--no curse--no death. Everybody healthy, everybody kind to everybody and everybody happy. What a City to live in!"

"Here, here!" says I to myself. "But get down to real life."

Which the minister proceeded promptly to do by leaning over the pulpit and saying confidentially, in his ingratiating voice, to the congregation: "This church of St. Paul's exists to promote that sort of experience in the daily life of thousands of the people in your town, in Montreal, in Canada. If the church is not doing this, then whatever else it may do cannot save it from the just condemnation of Almighty God."

There was no sleeping in the church that night; even the lads in the back seats were leaning forward eyes and mouth wide open.

The preacher then proceeded to draw a contrast between the organized form of existence in Riverside and the Kingdom of Heaven, in regard to one single test, that was the happiness of its people. And he sure had his facts about Riverside. As he pictured the town, the homes of the poor, their daily burden of toil, their inadequate wages, the sickness and suffering, the dreary monotony, the haunting fear of poverty--says I to myself, says I; "No Riverside for me." But when he proceeded to describe the great city nearby I found myself even more determined that Montreal was no place for a decent man to live in. Before the picture was completed I was dismayed to discover that there was no place in all of Canada where I could safely and happily live. Pain, sickness, sorrow, poverty flourished, the result of cruelty, meanness, lust and greed. Again the minister leaned over the pulpit, with his disarming smile, but he did not catch me this time, I knew he was reaching for the solar plexus. "The church that is content," he cried, in his thin little voice, "in a world so unlike Heaven is a church that is false to its charter, forgetful of its mission, and traitor to its Lord. It has ceased to have any right to exist."

For the first time in my life I was conscious of a feeling of satisfaction and relief that no church could claim me as a member.

The preacher then turned to the subject of finance. Here, says I to myself, he will make a slip or two. But again I was disappointed. Just as he knows his European history, his economics and the social conditions of his people, so he knows finance. If I knew his college where they give this stuff to their students I would gladly devote a small percentage of my princely income to its support. Here are a few of the tender titbits dropped into the open mouths of his people. But the disarming smile was gone, and in place of the smile tears which did not fall, and agony which twisted your vitals and wrath which made your conscience turn summersaults within you. "Finance," said the preacher, "is the science of money, and money is the marker of value in exchange. Business is human activity organized for the equitable exchange of the fruits of man's toil, for his happiness and well being."

If I knew the book where he got those definitions I should do my utmost to borrow it.

After elaborating upon the magnificence of the opportunity in the hands of the men of finance in this country, and after lauding to high heaven the splendor and glory of the service that business men might render, and have rendered, to humanity, the minister once more leaned over the pulpit and dropped a few burning coals upon the consciences of those who have to do with certain methods of finance and business. "The man that uses his superior power of hand or brain to secure for himself more than he honestly earns is a predatory pirate, and should be removed from human society. The man that takes advantage of his superior knowledge to deceive, cajole or allure simple people into the purchase of mere wind or water in the form of stocks, is a thief and a robber and should be denied a place among honest men.

"The man that uses his power, whether of brain or money, to oppress, enslave or injure his fellow men is the enemy at once of humanity and of God. He deserves and will receive his just judgment.

"The man, who in the happy enjoyment of great material blessings and privileges, is forgetful of and indifferent to the miseries, sufferings and wrongs of his fellow men has nothing in common with Him who came to share the burdens of the unhappy and suffering and lost children of men. These men should not sit at any communion table in a church bearing the name of Jesus Christ. These men are of the tribe of Judas, they are traitors to their Lord."

A swift glance I cast about me. It seemed to me I could detect all the church members by the ghastly expression on their countenances.

I was waiting for him to walk in upon the Montreal Stock Exchange. I was disappointed. He cheered me, however, by announcing his intention to deal with these gentlemen on the following Sunday evening.

This minister has the supreme gift of the great orator. He knows when he has said enough. His concluding words were spoken, again leaning confidentially over his pulpit, his ingratiating manner and his charming smile had returned to him, but there were tears behind both.

"The question, my beloved brethren, for us here tonight, is not what the financiers, what the business men, what the Stock Exchange is going to do about it. This is not the first question for us here. But the question for this church, for its members, for its office bearers and for its minister, is, what is the church going to do about it? The Lord have mercy upon us all."

To which this reporter said: "Amen! and go to it!"

The chief laid down the copy and turned his eyes upon his young reporter: "Look here young fellow! What do you suppose you're writing? a novelette? This is a newspaper office. You've got some good stuff here. But say, cut out all that goo, and give us the facts in clean journalistic English!"

The boy's face fell.

"Say chief, I can't do it into journalistic English, and I don't want to do it. That man got me and I am wid him, I am all for hell and blazes for that bunch of robbers getting fat with the earnings of the poor and ignorant and having a good time while these poor devils sweat blood."

"Aw, get out!" roared the chief. "You're a darned bolshie, a blasted communist, as red in your politics as you are in your hair."

"A bolshie, is it?" said the boy standing up. "I never knew what kind of a baste he was, but if he is like that soft-voiced gentle faced hell fire of a volcano out at Riverside I am one, and I don't care who knows it, and you can fire me if you want to, and go to hell with the rest of them. Me! I'm for the poor divils outside of the church, forgotten by the church, but not by the Man that died for them."

McGarrick turned to leave the room.

"Come back here you red-headed Fenian."

"A red-headed Fenian is it you're callin' me?" answered the boy indignantly. "It's an Ulster Presbyterian I am, so it is."

"Here," said the editor. "Take your stuff to the composing room and we'll run it as it is and be darned to you."

And thus it came that the first of Mr. Matheson's three sermons appeared in the Courier on the following Monday in the form as reported by the Ulster Presbyterian, bolshevist and communist, Andy McGarrick, and with portentous results to McGarrick himself and to others as well.

The first of these results came to no less a person than the editor of the Courier. The editor happened to be an Ulster Irish Presbyterian, by blood and training, whatever his daily practice might be.

The chief was not in his office on Monday evening after the issue of his paper.

His first phone call on Tuesday morning was from the President of the Stock Exchange: "Is that you McIvor? Cuthbert speaking."

"Yes sir," said the editor. "Good morning Mr. Cuthbert."

"What sort of blank, blank reporters have you on your staff anyway?"

"The livest reporters in the City. They give the news and they serve it up hot. What do you like best in yesterday's edition?"

"Look here, McIvor! That darned stuff about that blankety blank preacher in Riverside is sheer bolshevism."

Mr. McIvor listened patiently to what Mr. Cuthbert had to say, then he replied in a polite businesslike tone.

"Excuse me, Mr. Cuthbert, I am very busy just now. If you don't mind, would you please call me in an hour and I shall be happy to talk to you."

For two hours Mr. McIvor was occupied in answering phone calls. They came from all sorts and classes of men. Men of the Stock Exchange, Bank managers, presidents of Loan and Insurance companies, in fact Montreal big business men seemed to be taking the morning off in their eager desire to enter into conversation with the editor of the Evening Courier. Mr. McIvor's reply to one and all was in the same terms as he had used with Mr. Cuthbert.

During the second two hours of the morning the editor made a point of calling up each gentleman who had phoned him earlier to discuss the sermon of the Riverside minister, and to each he made the following proposition. He had carefully noted what his interviewer had said and he proposed to publish in this evening's edition these remarks and similar remarks of other gentlemen who had called him up on the phone, duly signed with the appropriate names. The profanity, of course, would be indicated merely by dashes. He was very particular about the kind of language that appeared in his paper. He wished each gentleman a brief good morning, and shut off the telephone.

The following two hours his chief clerk spent in receiving apologies, appeals, threats, from these gentlemen, who all gave the clerk a definite indication that they had no desire whatever to make any public statement in regard to the report of Rev. Malcolm Matheson's sermon, which had appeared in the Monday evening's edition.

At noon the chief called in reporter McGarrick.

"Look here you dod blasted Ulster Irish Presbyterian! You've got me into a hell of a mess, but I am Irish myself and I want you to stay with that gentle-voiced volcano of yours for the next two Sunday evenings. We will give you double space and let the blank gold bugs go the way this minister evidently has them ticketed for. And McGarrick your salary is up ten percent, but don't you weaken or you're fired. Now get out of my sight, you red-headed communist."

CHAPTER XIX

The second Riverside sermon was duly reported by Andy McGarrick and, if the report lacked something in originality of style and naïveté of expression, it gained in exactness of record and logical articulation of the argument. However, the report attained the distinction of an editorial in the paper and in addition, a front page insert of "Titbits Dropped Over the Pulpit." These titbits consisted of pungent and juicy dicta taken verbatim from the sermon, which challenged some of the fundamental principles underlying the practice of the Stock Exchange artists in Canada and the United States, but which set forth certain principles enunciated by Jesus Christ in his conception of the Kingdom of Heaven. The Monday edition of the Evening Courier ran to over double the size of its usual issue. The Riverside sermons indeed, proved to be extremely good copy, outclassing the most spectacular bank robbery, or millionaire kidnapping incident.

So great was the interest aroused by this arraignment of the principles and practices of the Stock Exchange that a group of leading members of the Exchange and others held an informal meeting to consider what action, if any, should be taken. Opinions varied with the character and experience of the speaker. After some desultory and diffused discussion, Mr. Cameron Ogilvie, President of the Empire Bank rose and addressed the gathering.

"Gentlemen, I have been waiting for some one to make a definite charge against the minister of Riverside, of inaccuracy of statement in his criticism of some of the practices of members of the Stock Exchange. Apart from all considerations of the wisdom and propriety of bringing these matters into the pulpit of a Christian Church, it strikes me that the primary question to be considered by us here, is, whether the statements made in the sermon are true or false. Is there any gentleman present who can indicate a single utterance which represents a departure from truth. Can any gentleman here present challenge any statement as reported in this paper?" Here Mr. Cameron Ogilvie held up a copy of the Evening Courier of Monday's issue.

There was no reply.

"Then, Gentlemen, it seems to me that the first business of the members of the Stock Exchange, to which I have the honour to belong, though I do not indulge in the stock selling game, is to investigate certain practices of some of its members, and to condemn those who are guilty of the practices condemned."

This daring challenge by a gentleman of the standing of Mr. Cameron Ogilvie so disturbed the company that the meeting broke up without action.

In the office of Sir James Scaiffe the matter of the Riverside sermons was discussed by Sir James and his principal partner, who generally represented him in his stock operations.

"Mr. Macnamara, have we no representative in Riverside? Have we none in this minister's congregation?"

"I do not know of any one, but I can find out," said Mr. Macnamara.

"But surely," Sir James went on, "something can be done to make this man see the unwisdom of such utterances. The first thing we know the whole pack of preachers, who are desperately hunting up sensational subjects to fill their empty churches, will be buttonholing every fool who has been caught in the market for hot stuff for his evening sermon. Look into this Mr. Macnamara."

"I shall do so, Sir James. I think I can promise you that something effective can be done. I remember now that we have in Riverside, Mr. John Henderson of the Canada Imperial Loan Company, who I think is a member of St. Paul's congregation."

"Another thing," said Sir James, "that fellow Brice, you know, the partner of the late Mr. Roger Tempest, stopped me on the street and asked for an interview. As a matter of fact he wants a job. Think of the audacity of the man! I asked him to call at the office on Friday."

"A job!" exclaimed Macnamara. "For a man who sold up his chief!"

"Well!" said Sir James. "I turned him over to you. Who can conscientiously offer such a man a job? Think of the effect on the public mind. We cannot be too careful in these days in keeping high the moral standards of our business men."

"I will see the man, Sir James," said Macnamara. "You can leave him to me."

"Well, of course," said Sir James, "I am sorry for the fellow and should be glad to offer him a cheque, if he is in need of money. You understand?"

"A cheque?" said Macnamara gruffly. "I'll check him all right."

In the Riverside congregation the reaction following the minister's sermons was very definite and very varied.

For instance the manager of a leading bank in the town frankly and definitely supported the minister in his attitude towards stock gambling. At the same time, however, he gravely questioned the wisdom of introducing these matters into the pulpit.

"I am old-fashioned, in my reverence for the pulpit," he said. "The pulpit should be reserved only for sacred and spiritual themes. The people want something for their souls' good when they come to church."

There were others, however, and more particularly those who had been fortunate in their stock transactions, who were indignant at their minister.

Mr. Bertie Bingle, a young man who had been notoriously fortunate not only in his own dealings in the stock market, but also in his advice to his clients, was one of this class.

"Why don't he attend to his own business?" enquired Mr. Bingle of the young man at the filling station. "I used to think a lot of Mr. Matheson, but when he butts in to--to--well to things that ain't got nothing to do with religion and--and--that sort of thing I have no use for him."

"No religion in your business, eh Bertie?" replied Joe Piggot, the filling agent. "I guess perhaps you're right."

"Well, you know what I mean, Joe," said Bertie. "Every man should stick to his own job. How would this country get its railroads built, its power projects, its big industrial firms organized unless they sold stock?"

"That's what he said, Bertie," said Joe. "You must have been asleep."

"When I sleep, I sleep at home," answered Bertie.

"Well, I read the papers," said Joe, "but I never sleep in church, Bertie."

"No, nor keep awake either," replied Bertie.

"One for you, Joe," said a bystander.

"Well," said Joe, "I've got to fill her up for you and your crowd I guess on Sunday night same as Saturday."

A more formidable opposition, however, arose after Mr. Macnamara had found it necessary to run out to Riverside to interview some of his clients on some very promising new issues, about to be placed on the market.

One of these visited, Mr. John Henderson, Chairman of St. Paul's Kirk Session, became deeply concerned for the good name of his church, and for the success of its financial activities.

"This is no time to be stirring up strife and creating division among our people, when we are planning a campaign for the renovation of our church, and especially when we are organizing to meet our allocation for the Missionary and Maintenance Fund. It is a very bad policy. The session should take action and that immediately."

Mr. Henderson had no difficulty in securing the support in his attitude toward the minister, of the members of session, who had been called together to discuss matters of importance to the congregation, especially the questions of church renovation and the Missionary and Maintenance Fund. It was decided that a carefully chosen delegation should wait upon the minister and point out to him the very grave consequences that might ensue if the third sermon advertised should take the same line as that of the first two.

The deputation reported that the minister had received them most cordially, and had assured them that he deeply appreciated their concern for the welfare of the congregation, and promised that in his closing sermon of the series on the Kingdom of Heaven and Modern Finance, nothing should be said to endanger the spiritual well-being of the church.

"I made it quite clear to him," reported Mr. Henderson, "that I could not see how we could successfully hope to carry through our renovation campaign, or meet our allocation for the Missionary and Maintenance Fund, if a large number of the most important and most liberal members of our congregation were alienated, as they were being alienated at the present time, so I think there will be a change next Sunday."

Towards the end of the week, however, two events happened which stirred deeply the community of Riverside and of the neighbouring city as well. The first of these was the arrest of two prominent members, the President and the Secretary-Treasurer of one of Montreal's oldest and most honourable financial corporations. The firm had recently been reorganized and new blood introduced in the person of the Secretary-Treasurer. With the reorganization new methods were employed, the effects of which were seen in a very large increase in the extent of their business. Branches were opened up in every important city in the Dominion, and the firm took a leading place among the financial concerns of Canada in the promotion of industrial and utility enterprises. The firm appeared to have almost unlimited credit and its various ventures were invariably attended with enormous success. Without the slightest warning, came the announcement that the President and the Secretary- Treasurer of the company had been arrested, charged with conspiracy to defraud and theft.

At the preliminary hearing they were both committed to stand trial and were immediately committed to bail under heavy bonds.

The shock of this event was felt throughout the length and breadth of Canada. The offices of the company were immediately closed, accountants placed in charge of their affairs and the whole clientele, whose investments were in the company's hands, were thrown into a panic of dismay. A preliminary inspection of the books and a careful estimate of the values of the securities held revealed a situation more serious than was at first suspected. A sense of uneasiness and anxiety thrilled through all Canadian financial circles, and ominous premonitions of disaster threw the Stock Exchange of Montreal into temporary confusion and uncertainty, while everywhere on the street, men began to ask one another if the collapse so frequently predicted by a certain school of economists, might not indeed be at hand.

The second event was of a much more terrible and tragic nature.

As Mr. Edward Macnamara, Sir James Scaiffe's partner and representative was sitting in his office on Friday afternoon, a clerk handed him a card.

"Send him in," was the reply, and into the room, pale, nervous, trembling, and with the appearance of a beaten dog, came Mr. Brice, former partner and friend of the late Roger Tempest.

"I have an appointment to see Sir James Scaiffe," he said in a weak and trembling voice.

"Your business," enquired Mr. Macnamara gruffly.

"Sir James Scaiffe asked me to call and see him."

"Sir James is busy," said Mr. Macnamara. "He has asked me to see you."

Mr. Brice, without being invited, sat down in a chair across the desk from Sir James Scaiffe's representative.

"I need not explain to you, Mr. Macnamara," he said in a low and trembling tone, "the reason for my presence here to-day. I have made application to Sir James for a position in some department of his business. I understand it would be a very minor position of course. You know my record. I want to get another chance to redeem myself, and Sir James Scaiffe is the only man in this city who can give me this chance."

Mr. Macnamara's cold blue eyes had rested with a relentless gaze upon the man's pale face while he was making his plea.

"Brice, I have to say you have a colossal nerve to come into this office, and make such a request, after you have been practically charging Sir James with the responsibility for your crime."

"That I did not, Mr. Macnamara," said Mr. Brice. "I accept full responsibility for my own act. It is true, of course, that owing to Sir James' action in connection with the Pulp and Paper stock I was misled. I am laying the blame upon no one. I made my mistake-- the only mistake in my career. All men make mistakes."

"All men are not traitors, Mr. Brice."

A rush of hot blood came to the pale face before him, and receding rapidly left it more ghastly than before.

"Have you never made a mistake, Mr. Macnamara? Have you never done wrong?"

"I never sold up a man who had trusted me for twenty years, as you did, Mr. Brice."

"Give me a chance, Mr. Macnamara," pleaded Brice. "Just one chance."

"A chance in this office?" was the reply. "You amaze me. Do you know where you should be this morning? You should be in the penitentiary."

Brice suddenly rose to his feet, his hands trembling, his breath coming quick, his eyes blazing.

"And you, Macnamara, you should be in hell, and your boss, too. I did betray my chief, the best man God ever made, but where I betrayed one, you and your chief have betrayed thousands, yes, hundreds of thousands in this country. Your chief went into Pulp and Paper. He obtained control with fifty million dollars, he watered it to one hundred and fifty millions. He slid out and left his victims with the empty bag. I alas, was one of them. You were his agent, his chief agent in the business. You knew what you were doing. I am a traitor, you say. As God judges, I am a saint compared with men like you and your chief. You say I should be in jail," here his voice rose to a scream, "and you are right, I should be in jail, but if you had your rights you should be in hell, and by God that is where you are going now." Suddenly he pulled out a gun. Macnamara sprang to his feet.

"For God's sake don't shoot. I will give you--" He stepped back toward the door of the inner office, his hand clutched at the door knob. Brice fired once. Macnamara staggered against the door. Again Brice fired and Macnamara fell to the floor.

"And now you will go where you belong, and maybe I will go too, but not to the same hell." He put the gun to his mouth, fired and fell dead across the desk, the red blood streaming over the white paper.

The stock gambling madness had once more claimed its victims.

CHAPTER XX

"How is it that our friend the padre is not here with us, Aunt Elizabeth?" asked Jack. "In fact I have not seen him for many days. I hope I have not offended him by my capitalistic opinions."

"No fear of that Jack, he is really very fond of you," said Aunt Elizabeth.

"Though of course he cannot help thinking of you as a dangerous and reactionary character," said Sylvia.

"I have the greatest admiration for him. He is a fine old boy, and his arguments are hard to resist, however much one is opposed," replied Jack.

"But Jack," said Aunt Elizabeth, "you are not really opposed to his opinions. In your heart you agree with him."

"Well Aunt Elizabeth, I believe he is right to a very great extent, but if I may make such a remark in this house, I am sincerely sorry that he has dragged matters of business into the pulpit; I believe it is a bad thing, not only for business, but for the church as well."

"Why," exclaimed Aunt Elizabeth, "you haven't even heard him preach."

"I read the newspaper reports however," said Jack.

"But Jack," said Sylvia. "That is quite a different thing. I am quite sure that if you had only heard him preach these two sermons you would have been tremendously impressed, and I believe you would have entirely agreed with him."

"Of course I can only speak of the effect upon the public mind as I get it from the press. The congregation consists of a few hundred people, the press reaches many many thousands."

"Is Mr. Matheson responsible for that?" enquired Sylvia.

"Yes, he cannot escape responsibility for he knows quite well that-- they are being reported. Are the reports not accurate?" enquired Jack.

"The reports are really very well done, and very cleverly and clearly give the line of thought, but as Aunt Elizabeth says, you cannot begin to get the full effect of the sermon, nor can you catch the spirit and purpose of the preacher by reading the press reports. Why not come to-morrow evening and hear him for yourself? You ought to come, Jack," she added earnestly, "for he is to speak upon the subject of the Kingdom of Heaven and the Stock Exchange."

"Terrible!" said Jack, "Just think of it! No thank you. I go to church for something quite different. I get enough of the Stock Exchange throughout the week."

Suddenly little Nickie broke in.

"Jack, I like the minister and you should not speak that way about him."

"Why do you like him, Nickie," asked Jack.

"Because he is kind and he tells splendid stories and he loves Mozart."

"These are all fine reasons, Nickie boy," said Jack kindly, "and I am sure he is all that you say. But I am speaking of something quite different."

"But Jack," replied Nickie, "the way you were speaking made me think you didn't like him."

"Well Nickie, to be quite candid," Jack answered, "I do not like what he is doing now. No," he added turning to Aunt Elizabeth, "I must say I deeply regret the course Mr. Matheson is taking. I think a minister should preach religion. I go to church to worship, to get something good for my soul, to get a change of atmosphere. It annoys me terribly to go to church and hear a man tell me how to run my business. I will have to ask you to excuse me from going to-morrow night."

"Why certainly, Jack," interposed Sylvia, "we wouldn't for the world urge you to do anything that you don't think right."

"Now Sylvia, I know I have hurt you, but you must allow me to have my own opinions about this, and I cannot help my feelings. Perhaps I am old-fashioned about this but I can't stand these sensation- mongers in the pulpit."

"My dear Jack," exclaimed Aunt Elizabeth, "sensation-mongers!"

"Jack," said Sylvia gravely, "I do think this is quite unfair to call Mr. Matheson a sensation-monger. Nothing is further from his style, and nothing further from his nature than to be a mere sensation-monger."

"Well, you can't deny," said Jack--"and I don't want to discuss the matter--you can't deny he has succeeded in springing the greatest sensation that this part of the country has experienced for many a long day. But will you excuse me, Aunt Elizabeth? I am sorry, I must run away. I have an important meeting to attend, one I am afraid, neither you nor Sylvia would greatly approve of."

"But why not?" asked Aunt Elizabeth.

"Well, it is a meeting of the junior members of the Stock Exchange. We are getting a little fed up with the old game and the old bunch, we think they are a bit out of date."

"And in what particulars?" asked Sylvia in a deliberate, almost cold tone.

"Well, for one thing we wish a little closer checking upon the brokers. We are opposed to bucketing, and oh--well--there are other matters. But I need not go into all this business for I am sure you are not interested, Sylvia."

"Oh, but I am Jack. I am awfully interested in anything that will get rid of the shameful and terrible practices that are carried on by members of the Stock Exchange, and surely with what has been recently seen in Montreal, there is no doubt that certain changes should be made. The whole country is going mad with this stock gambling. I get it among my girls and boys." Her face had grown very pale, her voice began to tremble. "I do wish with all my soul that you had nothing whatever to do with it."

"My dear Sylvia," replied Jack a little impatiently, "I am afraid I cannot discuss this with you. I know that you have studied a good deal about this matter, and I am not going to condemn your opinion, but all the same I am certainly not going to accept wholesale condemnation of the business carried on by the Montreal Stock Exchange of which my father was one of the founders, and all his life an honourable member." Jack's voice ended upon a low and husky note. He was obviously deeply moved.

"Why Jack," cried Sylvia, "you should not speak to me that way. You know that not for the world would I suggest any criticism of such practices and methods in the business of the Stock Exchange as your father used."

"I must go," said Jack hurriedly. "I really must."

Sylvia followed him to the door. "Jack," she said putting her arms round his neck, "please don't imagine--" her voice broke.

"No, no, Sylvia, I don't imagine that you cherish any opinions that would reflect upon my father's memory," said Jack. "But I am afraid we do not see eye to eye upon this stock business."

"But Jack," said Sylvia, still clinging to him, "surely we are not going to allow this to come between us in the very slightest degree."

"God forbid," said Jack. "Good-night, darling." He kissed her tenderly and hurried away.

Sylvia came from the door, kissed her aunt good-night and went upstairs to her bedroom. A little later her aunt tapped upon the door.

"You are not feeling well, Sylvia," she said.

"Yes, I am feeling quite well--I mean I am not ill."

"Sylvia," said her aunt, "I am afraid there is something between you and Jack. Somehow you don't appear to be getting on well together."

"Oh Auntie!" cried Sylvia, her reserve breaking down completely, "I don't believe Jack cares for me. He is all bound up in that business of his and I hate it!" she said vehemently. "It is a wicked, wicked business. Just think what it is doing with us here in Riverside and in Montreal, and just look at the New York papers for the terrible accounts of defalcations and suicides. I hate the business! Oh Auntie! I am afraid it is dragging him away from me every day."

"Now Sylvia, you must not speak in that way. You are speaking like a foolish child. Jack loves you truly, sincerely, anyone can see that, and though he may differ from you in his opinions on many things, that does not affect his love. As to this business of his, you must remember that it was his father's business before him."

"But it is different now," exclaimed Sylvia. "Mr. Tempest never did carry on business in such a way as to drive men to ruin. Jack is quite different from his father in that; he says every man must look after himself."

"Sylvia, no son is like his father. Besides you can't undertake to be conscience for any man. If Jack thinks he is doing right, what right have you to step in and demand that he should do as you think?"

Suddenly her aunt came to her, put her arms round her and cried: "Oh my dear, be patient. Only one thing matters--love--love--only love. Listen to me--I know what I am speaking about--I know from bitter experience--be patient--put nothing before love."

"But Auntie," began Sylvia--

"Oh, go to bed, Sylvia. You are far too opinionated," said her aunt impatiently. "You are not the only one who has loved a man who insists upon taking his own way. And why shouldn't he, that is his responsibility?" Without further word Aunt Elizabeth turned and left her.

CHAPTER XXI

The tragic news of the past week had produced a state of mind in the whole country almost akin to panic. The congregation that met in St. Paul's Church on Sunday night when the third of the series of sermons was being preached by the Rev. Malcolm Matheson were obviously in a mood of solemn expectancy. The minister also was evidently under a strain of deep emotion.

He prefaced his sermon with a brief account of the two events that had taken place during the last week in the city. By the mercy of God, the attending physicians gave promise of life to the wounded man. For all those more immediately connected with both families concerned, the minister expressed the deepest pity and sympathy.

The minister announced that he had been approached by some members of his congregation with a request that he should postpone, or altogether abandon the sermon, as announced, upon the theme "The Kingdom of God and Modern Industry." After earnest consideration he felt it more than ever to be his duty to deal with this subject. The subject was as announced, but he acknowledged that the sermon he had prepared was not the sermon which he would preach to-night.

The report of the sermon sent in to the Evening Courier by Andy McGarrick, reflected the atmosphere and spirit of the whole service. There was a complete absence of McGarrick's rather flippant asides, but the reporter not only clearly reproduced the line of argument, but he caught the spirit and atmosphere of the whole service.

Industry, the minister defined as "The co-operative activity on the part of the people in the production of things for the use and service of all the people." He thereupon proceeded to picture the Canadian people thus actively engaged in the service of the Canadian people and showing forth the spirit of the Kingdom of Heaven. The Kingdom of Heaven, conceived as industry, would bring about a state of existence in which all workers would be protected in their essential rights of security, freedom and growth.

Jesus definitely forbade the mad pursuit of wealth as the chief aim of industrial activity. The true objective of industry was service of the whole body of the people. The badge of rank was not the power to command men, but the power to serve them. The greatest man in the community was he who could serve most men in the community. Industry should never be carried on under such conditions as would enslave and degrade men, but rather ennoble them and develop their highest powers.

Jesus thought of humanity as a great brotherhood, whose members were bound together by ties of love and mutual responsibility. Egoistic individualism is a denial of brotherhood of man and of the fatherhood of God. The unhappy, the unfortunate, the poor, the sick, the outcast, Jesus conceived to be his very brethren. Service to these unhappy creatures He considered as service to Himself.

There was little argumentation in the sermon and almost an entire absence of oratorical declamation. Quietly, impressively, simply the minister stated the principles of the Kingdom of Heaven in relation to industry. He concluded his sermon, however, with an entrancing and moving picture of a community in which all the members lived to express in their life and work the sacrificial love represented in the life of Jesus.

At the close of the sermon, during the singing of the last hymn a young man, tall and with a fine, strongly marked intellectual face came and stood beside the minister and said a few words to him. Mr. Matheson nodded his head. After the hymn was finished the minister said, "Mr. Graham Douglas, president of the Young Men's Club will make an announcement." Thereupon Mr. Graham Douglas made the announcement:

"The Young Men's Club has been asked to hold its regular open meeting to-night here in this auditorium. The subject to be discussed is: 'What are we going to do about it?' All young men will be made welcome. I might add that all men who feel young are young men in the opinion of this club."

Immediately the President of the Ladies' Association, one of the modernistic and strong-minded type, rose in her place and said:

"May I respectfully inquire if there is any reason why a similar invitation should not be extended to the women in this meeting?"

Promptly Mr. Graham Douglas made reply:

"There is no reason why women should not be present at this meeting. I believe I represent the opinion of the young men of the club when I say that all who care to remain will be entirely welcome. I may add however, that the discussion will be confined to the members of the club."

In consequence of this announcement the report of the third sermon was greatly curtailed, a very considerable amount of the space assigned to it being taken up with the report of the Young Men's meeting.

After the benediction, as some of the people began to pass out of the church,

Sylvia became conscious of a hand gripping her arm and an excited voice speaking in her ear.

"Jack's here! We're going to stay. Is that all right?"

"Why Peggy, you here? Of course it is all right. Stay if you like."

"You bet we'll stay," cried Peggy excitedly. "Jack was with us for lunch. I wanted to hear this wonderful minister of yours. Mother said Jack ought to come too. He has been awfully dull and quiet lately, and mother thought--Oh here he is."

"Good evening, Sylvia," said Jack. "I thought I might as well be hung for a sheep as a lamb, so here I am, staying for an after meeting no less." As he spoke he crowded into the seat beside Peggy.

"Aunt Elizabeth, may I go in beside you?" asked Peggy.

"Come along, Peggy," said Aunt Elizabeth, and Peggy moved to the other side of Aunt Elizabeth.

In the meantime the people seemed to be of two minds as to whether they should go or stay. But when the president of the Young Men's Club called the meeting to order, and when at his request those remaining in the gallery had taken their places in the body of the church, it was seen that the church was comfortably filled with the congregation that remained.

"Glory!" exclaimed Peggy excitedly, "will you look at the crowd at the meeting. Will there be a discussion? I hope there will be a first-rate row."

"Shut up! you little idiot," said Jack. "Don't you know you are in church?"

"But this is the Young Men's meeting," said Peggy.

"Hush, Peggy," said Jack, "they are going to begin."

The president opened the meeting and in a few compact sentences explained how it was the Club had come to hold this open meeting in the Church. There were three main reasons:

(1) The Club had been deeply stirred by the sermons on the Kingdom of Heaven and Modern Finance, preached by their minister.

(2) The Club was of the opinion that the questions raised were of such importance to demand earnest study and discussion.

(3) The public interest awakened by the sermons seemed to indicate a widespread desire that the discussion of these questions should be open to a larger number than the members of the club. Hence this meeting.

"We do not consider it wise," he continued, "that discussion of the questions raised should be carried on this evening. The program will therefore be confined simply to one question: 'What are we going to do about it?'

"The sermons preached in this church the last three Sundays have created a new world of thought for many of the members of the club. An attempt to enter to-night into a discussion of the problems raised without due time for preparation and study, would not be treating the great moral, religious and national issues raised, with the consideration they deserved, nor would it be respectful to their minister whose treatment of these questions gave evidence of much study in their preparation. The committee, therefore, have prepared three resolutions which they hope the members of the club will accept. (1) The Young Men's Club of St. Paul's Church, Riverside, hereby express their grateful appreciation of the great and valued service rendered this congregation, and the whole community, by the able discussion of the important themes presented in these sermons by our minister the Rev. Malcolm Matheson. (2) The members of the Young Men's Club beg respectfully to assure their minister of their confidence in his integrity of purpose, their admiration for his courage, their appreciation of his fair minded, able treatment of the questions presented, and their undiminished affection and esteem for him as their minister and spiritual guide. (3) The members of this club pledge themselves to begin immediately the earnest study of the questions raised in their relation to their present lives and to the well being of the whole community."

The President thereupon presented the first resolution. Two young men, in glowing terms, as mover and seconder of the resolution, proceeded to eulogize their minister, and to express their gratitude for the service he had rendered the church and the members of the club in the sermons delivered. They believed that in saying this they represented the opinion of the whole body of the young people of the congregation.

After a very brief discussion the resolution was unanimously adopted by a standing vote of the members.

Suddenly a man from the congregation rose and cried excitedly.

"Mr. President, I move that we--this whole congregation--support the resolution."

Immediately the suggestion was seconded and before the president could speak the whole congregation, with very few exceptions rose in support. The president, however, apparently did not approve of this action.

"It is not in order," he said, "that in our open meetings resolutions should be voted upon by any who are not members of the club."

The second resolution and the third were proposed in like manner and carried. Thereupon the chairman who had conducted the meeting with prompt despatch, announced that he would now accept a motion to adjourn.

"No," came a voice, loud, sharp and stern, as a man in the back of the church rose and came slowly forward. When he reached the front of the church he began to speak in a clear penetrating voice that reached to the farthest corner of the building.

"My name was once on the roll of this congregation. I have not attended this or any other church for thirteen years, because I felt that all the churches were false to the principles of the Founder of our faith. But when I saw the advertisement of these sermons in the paper, I decided that I would hear what the minister had to say. I have not been disappointed. But I am disappointed in the action taken by the young men of this club. The last resolution pledged its members to study these questions discussed by the minister. Study? Why study? These principles stick up into the light of truth as the spire of this church into the light of the sun. I had hoped for a different answer to the question: 'What are we going to do about it?' Do? That is the point! Will this young men's club demand that these principles become conditions of membership in the church? Study?" The man's voice was now ringing out like a trumpet over the congregation that sat spellbound, with eyes riveted upon his white face and gleaming eyes. "What are you going to do about it? If nothing, then why not in God's name dissolve this church and come out in your true colors before the world, not as Christians, but as anti-Christians. Is this only another instance of humbug and sham?

"Will you stop chasing money?

"Will you work together and share together with all the people?

"Will you count those poor wretches, outcast from your society as your brethren for Jesus' sake?

"If not, then you are a lot of damned--I am not swearing--the minister said 'condemned'--I am using the simpler English word--you are damned hypocrites."

The people sat gaping at one another while the man went slowly back to his place, picked up his hat and coat and made for the door. There he paused and turning back thundered at them this last word:

"Jesus Christ is waiting your action. What are you going to do about it?"

For some minutes not a soul moved. The president sat as in a trance. Finally the minister rose and for a few moments stood facing his people. "Who he is that has spoken," he said, "I know not; that matters not. But it does matter that he has spoken the truth for Jesus Christ this night. The question for me and for you my friends, is: 'What are we going to do about it?'"

For some tense, breathless moments he stood regarding his congregation, then he raised his hands for the benediction. "God be merciful to us sinners." The words came in low, clear, penetrating tones to the congregation's ears, then after a pause, "Amen."

Slowly the people moved out of the building in deep silence as if under a spell.

"Come home with me," whispered Sylvia to Peggy. "The others will follow."

Catching her arm Peggy whispered in reply: "Wasn't it great to see that man? He sure had them all buncoed; not one of them could wink an eye. Even the minister was paralyzed."

"Yes," said Sylvia, "because he is an honest man; I too felt paralyzed I assure you."

Before they had reached the door Aunt Elizabeth and Jack had caught up to them.

"You are coming in for supper," said Aunt Elizabeth.

"You bet I am, I am starved and so excited. Aren't you?" said Peggy turning to Jack.

"I'm afraid," began Jack.

"Now Jack," said Sylvia, "you have no meeting tonight. Come along. I will just dash on before and see about things, you follow on with Aunt Elizabeth," and she ran away, leaving Jack to bring the others home.

As they opened the front door they were surprised to hear shrieks of laughter coming from upstairs.

"Who is that?" exclaimed Peggy. "Not Nickie, surely. I never heard him laugh like that in all my life."

"Oh, he and Sylvia are carrying on some prank or other," said Aunt Elizabeth. "They do all sorts of wild and funny things up there in the attic."

"May I run up?" enquired Peggy eagerly.

"And me, too?" said Jack.

"Certainly," answered Aunt Elizabeth. "Run along!"

They both ran upstairs to the top floor and reached a closed door.

"Hush!" said Peggy, "let's see what they are about." She opened the door and peeped through the crack, then immediately drew back, wonder, almost awe on her face.

Jack then looked in, and he too drew back with a like look on his face.

Slowly they both opened the door. There was Nickie swinging on his arms on a horizontal bar, his poor little legs dangling about in pathetic helplessness. Immediately as they entered the room, with a whoop the boy took a flying leap at Sylvia, who caught him in her arms and lowered him to the floor. Never had Jack been so surprised in his life, and seldom more deeply moved. That his little brother, who since his accident, three years ago, had been a poor miserable, helpless, petted and spoiled child should make this display of physical activity and of exuberant joy, was almost a miracle.

"For Heaven's sake, Nickie," he said. "How did you learn this trick? Are you not afraid that you will fall or knock Sylvia over?"

"Huh! not a bit. I can't fall and she is as strong as you are yourself, Jack. Why I have been swinging on this bar here for two weeks every day, and Sylvia says I am going to learn to swing on my legs too."

Jack gazed in silence at Sylvia, too moved to speak.

"What were you laughing about a little while ago?" enquired Peggy. "We could hear you out on the street."

"Oh, that was at my pictures," said Nickie.

"Pictures?" echoed Peggy.

"Yes," said Sylvia, taking up a portfolio. "Here they are. The girls in the designing room have been teaching Nickie all sorts of things, and he has gone far before them all in design. We use these things in our nursery furniture department, you know. We try to make them as funny as possible."

Suddenly Peggy, who was turning over the portfolio of comic sketches of children and animals, went off into a series of giggles.

"Look, Jack, at that pig. 'This little Pig went to Market.' Isn't he a perfect darling? So cocky, you know."

"Yes," said Sylvia, "that is one of our prize table covers. Nickie is beating them all. The girls, of course, are crazy about him. He demoralizes the whole room, and then, too, you know, he is transforming their singing. I couldn't have believed that two or three weeks would have made so great a change."

Meantime Jack, as he listened, was studying the boy's face.

"By Jove, Nickie, you look a different creature. Whatever they are doing to you, I hope they keep on doing it."

"Why he is the busiest boy in town," said Sylvia, "from early morning till--"

"What? Early morning? Do you mean EARLY morning? Whose job is it to get him up EARLY in the morning?" Jack's voice had a quizzical note of unbelief in it.

"The 7.30 bell wakens him and he is ready for breakfast at 8 o'clock," replied Sylvia. "We are at the office at exactly 8.45."

"Seven thirty?" exclaimed Jack.

"Of course. Why not?" asked Sylvia. "He goes to bed at nine."

"What? Bed at nine?" said Jack, amazement in his voice, "and who gets him to bed at nine?"

"I go myself," said Nickie proudly.

"Of course he does," said Sylvia, "Why not? A big boy like him. A boy who is beginning to earn his own living."

"Earn his living? You are joking."

"Not I," said Sylvia, "Why shouldn't he draw a regular salary for the instruction he gives these girls? But now he must go right away to bed. Come Nickie, good-night. I will see you later."

Nickie looked wistfully at Jack and at Peggy, then in a grave and manly voice he said quietly, "Good-night Jack. Good-night Peggy."

Peggy rushed at him, flung her arms round his neck and kissed him: "Oh Nickie, Nickie," she said, tears in her voice and eyes. "It is too--too wonderful." She paused abruptly and rushed from the room.

"Good-night, Jack," said Nickie, as Jack put his arms round him and kissed him. "Jack, I am going to do a lot of things, Sylvia says, oh, a whole lot of things."

The full pathos of the words only Jack understood, for he could not help thinking of the dull and colorless life of the boy, who was never allowed to do things for himself or for any one else, but who had things always done for him.

"Do things!" cried Sylvia, "You just wait, he hasn't begun yet. Take him down Jack, not in your arms like a baby. Let him climb on your back. He is going to have a pony next spring."

The eager light in the little lad's eyes smote Jack into silence.

Throughout supper both Jack and Sylvia took very little part in the conversation. Peggy and Aunt Elizabeth carried on a vivacious discussion in regard to the extraordinary evening service, through which they had passed.

"I just love your minister," Peggy exclaimed. "He made me cry over and over again. I couldn't exactly tell you why. And I understood every word, or almost every word he said. And do you know Aunt Elizabeth, when he was talking about all those poor people in our towns and cities I seemed to see them with their sad, hungry faces. I feel horribly mean when I think of all the money I spend in silly things, like shows and sundaes. Don't you Jack?"

"Sure thing!" said Jack, "at least I mean--I ought to."

"Just think, Aunt Elizabeth," cried Peggy, "this dress of mine--of course it is my best dress--would cost enough to keep a family for a whole month. It seems terrible, doesn't it?"

"It really doesn't seem quite fair, does it?" said Aunt Elizabeth.

"Fair? It is a dirty deal, and think of all the girls! Ethel Wiley's coming out dress cost a hundred and fifty dollars, without the jewelry and frills. Why it would keep two families for two months in food. I have been working it out. It is a beastly shame."

"A good deal longer than two months," said Sylvia.

"Why don't they do something about it?" indignantly enquired Peggy. "Just as that man said. Wasn't he splendid? He had the whole bunch absolutely paralyzed."

Sylvia gazed in wonder at the girl. In her fine new dress she looked quite a grown-up young lady. She had indeed developed amazingly during the last few months. Her features had grown finer, her figure had developed new curves of loveliness, she had somehow shed some of the hoyden awkwardness of girlhood. The promise of rare beauty was strongly apparent in every line of her lovely figure and every feature of her vivid face. Sylvia was conscious of new and strange emotions as she watched the girl's countenance, and listened to her shrewd, almost brilliant remarks on the various happenings in the church.

"Well," said Jack, "I think we must go. I am due at the office at 8.30 A. M. and this young lady is in my charge, and must be ready for her classes at 9."

"He is really thinking of himself, you know," said Peggy. "And indeed he ought to be in his little bed. You know, Jack, you don't get sleep enough."

"Well, you at any rate should be there now," replied Jack. "For if you don't make your matriculation there is no European trip for you."

Peggy made a face at him. "That beastly matric. I know I shall be plucked," she said.

"You are not to be plucked," he said. "You know," he continued, "I am teaching Peggy to run my car on the condition that she makes the grade in her reports every month."

"Yes," cried Peggy with enthusiasm. "He is teaching me everything. He shows me where he keeps his gun for hold-up men, and all the rest of it. And when we get out of the traffic, I can drive his car as well as he can. You see I will need a car for myself when I am at the University."

Sylvia listened with queer little qualms in her heart. This child would be a University undergraduate in a few months. A very advanced, self-confident, capable young lady, she was becoming rapidly experienced in the ways of the world of men and things. Her devotion to Jack was apparent in every tone of her voice, and in every flash of her brilliant brown eyes. And Jack in his "big brother way" was obviously very fond of her.

"I am coming out again to see Nickie at his work, Aunt Elizabeth," she said as they made ready to go. "I can't imagine what you have been doing to that boy."

"It is all Sylvia," said Aunt Elizabeth.

"Nonsense! It is all Aunt Elizabeth and Annette, who feeds him tremendous meals, and all the girls at the factory. They show him everything they know, and he has picked up their work in quite a wonderful way. You know, Jack," she added, "he has an amazing flair for colour and design, and such clever fingers. I am sure he will be an artist some day."

"Well, I am coming out, next time Jack comes," persisted Peggy, "Eh Jack?"

"Depends on how you behave yourself," said Jack, "and--and on other things too."

"Aunt Elizabeth," said Peggy, "I should like to come to church out here."

"Ask Jack to bring you," said Aunt Elizabeth with a twinkling smile.

"Now indeed, Aunt Elizabeth," said Jack, "your man I confess got me to-night, but to be candid I don't believe in his methods and in many of his ideas."

"Why Jack, you believe," began Peggy.

But Jack interrupted her. "That will be enough from you, young lady. I have all I can handle already in that line in this family."

"You will acknowledge, Jack," said Sylvia earnestly, "that he was quite sound in his industrial theories tonight, wasn't he? Cooperation in industry and all that."

"Yes," said Jack, "I confess his theories seem sound enough, but it is the application of them in this modern world of ours that is the trouble."

"Yes, it is the application of them," said Sylvia, in rather a sad voice. "That is the real problem, I find."

"Yes indeed," said Peggy, "As that wonderful man said: 'What are you going to do about it?' Oh, I'm all worked up inside. But I have no one to talk to about it. Jack is always so busy on old Scaiffe's trail--"

"Peggy!" said Jack sharply.

"Well, they all say so, Tom and everyone," replied Peggy, slightly abashed.

"It is none of your business, Peggy, and you are not to talk about it."

Peggy flashed a queer little look of defiance at him, threw up her head, but apparently thought better of it and remained silent.

"Come out and go to church with us any time you like," said Sylvia. "We shall always be glad to have you."

"Thank you," said Peggy very earnestly. "When I can get our car or Jack's."

"Jack's eh? Not just yet, my girl," replied Jack.

"Never mind, Peggy. Come when you can, and we shall have fine, long talks together," said Sylvia.

"Yes, and I suppose you will convert her to your socialist ways of thinking. I will have to keep an eye upon her," said Jack decisively as he moved toward the door.

"Kiss him, you fool," whispered Peggy. Then in a loud voice, "What in the world have I done with my wrap?"

Aunt Elizabeth had the good sense to assist her in the search for her fur.

"Sylvia," said Jack when they were alone. "You are doing wonderful things for Nickie. You are a dear, dear girl. Can't we forget all these foolish economics and other questions? We love each other and that is enough."

"Oh yes, Jack--oh yes--yes--" Sylvia murmured yielding herself to his arms and to his kisses.

"Let's quit all this foolish discussion, let's forget all these social fads," said Jack in a pleading tone.

"Oh Jack! I can't! I can't. I wish sometimes I could, but you know they are part of my very life. You can see that Jack, can't you?"

"Well, never mind, darling, we'll make out somehow."

"Found it upstairs," cried Peggy coming out to them with a noisy rush. "Good-night you darling Sylvia. A wonderful evening we have had. I shall never forget it."

After they had gone and when Sylvia was in her own bedroom, she said to herself: "Yes, a wonderful night--a wonderful night. I wonder--oh Jack, my darling, I cannot live without you Jack."

CHAPTER XXII

The Christmas season in Montreal and the surrounding district this year was one of hectic hilarity, and indeed of wild dissipation. Business was roaring, the stock market booming, money flowing as never in the history of Montreal. The flood-gates of social festivity let loose upon the city a tide of riotous and reckless gaiety such as had never before been witnessed. The churches of both Protestant and Roman Catholic communions were packed with worshippers. The dance halls, the picture shows, the theatres were all equally packed with their devotees.

Sylvia saw very little of Jack during these gay days. His financial operations were every day expanding, exacting more and more of his time and strength. His social engagements became increasingly enthralling. Two or three times in the week, sometimes accompanied by Peggy, he would rush out for dinner at Hilltop House.

During these wild and hectic days Sylvia became apprehensively conscious of an ever widening gap between the currents of their lives, and consequently carried in her heart a daily ache, that grew at times into an intolerable pain. Well it was for her that her business affairs made ever larger demands upon her time and strength. One such bright spot was the work carried on by Roderick Macdougall in the hardwood camps up the Ottawa. Once every fortnight the young camp boss found it convenient, if not necessary, to run down to Riverside to make personal reports and consult with his chief, or more frequently with her second in command, in regard to the work. Before freeze-up he had been able actually to run a raft of beautiful white oak logs to the Riverside mill. The very sight of these logs, piled high in the mill yards, delighted all the old lumbermen of the district. Chief among these was old Sandy Brodie, who in his younger days had been a master tanner.

"Yon's fine oak bark," he said to Sylvia one day as he met her on the street. "It breaks my heart to think of all the fine and beautiful lambskins and sheepskins that are being burnt or buried in this country."

"Why, Sandy," said Sylvia, "do you think you can do anything with them?"

"I am not so sure," he replied. "But I should like weel to have a crack at the tannin' again."

"Go to it then! Sandy," cried Sylvia eagerly, "I will back you. There are the vats, there is the white oak bark, you have the skins, and you might as well make the attempt. Go to it!"

And Sandy went to it.

It fell upon a morning after the height of the Christmas season's festivities had been passed that Timothy Brady drove up in his splendid car to make a call upon the secretary of the Riverside Mills.

"Here I am!" said Mr. Brady cheerfully, as he walked into the outer office. "I am like that bird that always brings bad weather. What do you call it?"

"Good morning, Mr. Brady," said Frances. "We are always glad to see you. And if I remember right you generally bring good weather with you."

"How is my young lady to-day?" enquired Mr. Brady.

"She's well, and if she were not she wouldn't let on," said Frances.

"And you are right there," Mr. Brady concurred. "But it seemed to me she was worrying about something or someone," he added, with an inquiring glance at Frances' face. But Frances refused to gossip.

"And how is the hard wood doing?" asked Mr. Brady.

"Well, we have brought one raft down," replied Frances.

"The hard wood is perfectly fine, Mr. Brady," said Sally with uplifted eyebrow. "We are all terribly interested in the hard wood and in the camp, not to speak of those who run it."

"So I have heard," said Mr. Brady with a twinkle in his eye, "and it's good luck I wish him. By the way, Miss Sally," he continued, "How is your minister going on with his grand sermons? I hear he is making you all communists and Russian bolsheviks."

"Never you fear, Mr. Brady," replied Sally. "Our minister is a fine man, and he carries a level head. Indeed it would have done you a great deal of good had you heard his sermons."

"They were telling me there was a divil of a row in your church one night."

"Then," said Miss Sally, "they were telling you a lie."

"I know the chap well," said Mr. Brady, "Dave Derring is his name, another of your communists. I hear he gave you all hell."

"Nothing of the sort, Mr. Brady," replied Sally warmly. "He spoke good religion and good business, and our minister backed him up."

"Well, it is a queer business to happen in church. The like of it my priest would not stand for a minute."

"Let me tell you about that," said Sally. "I have it on the best authority that our minister searched that man out and that they have come to be great friends."

"Friends?" echoed Mr. Brady.

"Yes friends!" said Sally emphatically. "Our minister has had him up to tea, and he has visited him in his own home, and has spoken at his club, and all that sort of thing. That's the sort of man our minister is."

At this point Frances, who was becoming a little impatient with Sally and her unbusinesslike flippancy, interposed: "Do you wish to see Miss Sylvia?" she enquired.

"I do," said Mr. Brady, "and will you tell her, please, that I won't keep her more than a minute."

"Good morning, Mr. Brady," said Sylvia as that gentleman walked into her office.

"Good morning, Miss Sylvia, and sorry am I that I'm bringing you trouble."

"At least I am afraid it may be trouble," Mr. Brady continued, "I have heard a rumor that they are talking of closing down this plant almost immediately."

"Closing down Riverside Mills," said Sylvia, dismay in her voice.

"That is what I hear."

"Why Mr. Brady, that is very disturbing news. I know our plant has not been paying. We cannot make sales in any department, except our furniture factory. But of course the winter is not the best time for sales. And the overhead is certainly very heavy."

"That's what it is," said Brady. "There is a heavy overhead all along the line.

There has been rather wild and rash expenditure in plant and the market has almost entirely disappeared. I am afraid times are getting bad for some of the industries in this country. The financial concerns and the stock market, of course, are very grand, and booming to beat the band, but the work--"

"What do you advise, Mr. Brady?" enquired Sylvia anxiously.

"Well, it is to advise you that I came in, and what I say is this. It would be a good thing if you could slip in and have a talk with the president, Mr. Huntington. He tells me that the directors are becoming more and more anxious and impatient. They are having a meeting this week."

"I wish I could meet those directors," said Sylvia. "I'd like to have a talk with them."

"And why not then?" said Mr. Brady. "My! but that would be a grand idea. And now I mustn't keep you."

"Good-bye, Mr. Brady, and thank you for calling."

"Good-bye, Miss Sylvia. If you had only invested that fifty thousand you got from me you would have been a millionaire to-day."

"I don't want to be a millionaire, Mr. Brady. I suppose all your money is invested in this terrible stock boom."

"Every penny," replied Mr. Brady cheerfully.

"Mr. Brady, would you think it rude in a girl like me to offer you advice?"

"Rude, my dear? Indeed it's proud I'd be to get any word of advice out of that clever little head of yours."

"Well then, Mr. Brady, I am going to ask you have you put aside none of the profits from your investments in the stock market?"

"Well," said Mr. Brady, "I have settled my house upon my wife, and she has got that, if she hasn't mortgaged it for the stocks herself."

"I wish you would promise me, Mr. Brady," said Sylvia earnestly, "to put half your money into solid investments, bank stock, or government bonds or something like that."

"I will promise you," said Mr. Brady, "that I will invest fifty thousand dollars this week as you say. And now about that meeting, Miss Sylvia--"

"I was just talking, Mr. Brady," said Sylvia, "I wouldn't dare attend a meeting of the directors."

"Wouldn't you, then? I think it might be a good thing to have a talk with Mr. Huntington about it."

"I will think it over," said Sylvia, as Mr. Brady left the room.

Immediately Sylvia turned to her telephone and called up Mr. Huntington.

"I am surprised and shocked," she said, plunging at once into the business, "to learn that you are thinking of closing us up here."

"Why, dear Miss Sylvia, if I may call you so, I am delighted to hear your voice, and I am sorry that things are not too good. We have a big overhead, sales are bad, and apparently with this infernal stock boom there is no money for legitimate business. Who brought you your bad news?"

"Well, it was Mr. Brady. And do you know Mr. Huntington, he made a rather wild suggestion."

"And what was that pray?"

"That I should ask you whether I might attend the meeting of directors this week."

"Ah! that is an idea," cried Mr. Huntington. "Tomorrow our directors meet at 10:00 A.M. Come right along to my office at 9.45 and I will take you in."

"But Mr. Huntington, I should be terribly frightened. I must confess, though, I am more frightened at this plant closing down. So that if you think I might dare, I will go to it."

"Come along, my dear I will take care of you."

At 9.45 on the day appointed, Sylvia found herself in Mr. Huntington's office. He greeted her with a cheery smile.

"And you look very much too lovely, my dear, to feed to a director's--meeting," he said.

"Mr. Huntington," said Sylvia in a hurried voice, "now that I am here, I am terrified, but I do want to tell them our plans for the coming season."

"Do," said Mr. Huntington. "And tell them about your girls. I will back you, and don't be afraid of them. They will all fall for you at the very first glimpse they get of your face."

It was with an air of possessive pride that Mr. Huntington presented Sylvia to the Board of Directors.

"Gentlemen, this is our secretary at the Riverside Mills, Miss S. Rivers, the most efficient, prompt and business-like official in our whole corporation. I have asked her to come and tell you something about her plans for the coming season. Miss Sylvia, these gentlemen form your board of directors, and I want to assure you that they will be delighted to have you tell them something of the fine work you are doing at Riverside."

With a little touch of colour in her pale, lovely face, Sylvia stood up and in a voice clear, though tremulous, which gained strength as she went on, told her story.

"I heard you were going to close up the Riverside Mills," she began breathlessly rushing in medias res. "I was very grieved and very surprised, for you remember you gave me a two-year contract, and then you promised to give me the chance of buying you out too, besides. But first, I want to tell you about our plans. I know we are not paying our way, but that is because of the big overhead. You see you put in all that new machinery in the sawmill, and one hundred and fifty men up in the camps, getting out hard wood; and they have got quite a lot of it; a raft of beautiful white oak came down the river before freeze-up. And from all that of course there is no return as yet." She paused a moment for breath. "But you see, that is not our fault," she went on more deliberately, "I would not have put in all that new machinery, as we could have got along without it. But in our own factory we are paying our way. We make furniture you know, nursery furniture, the loveliest things, and games and toys and playthings for children, all nicely decorated."

In her excitement Sylvia was still rushing her words as if at any moment her speech might be arrested.

"Take your time," said the vice president, Mr. Selby Manners.

"They are really very lovely," she continued, "and the people are crazy about them. We can't make them fast enough, and we are going to open a showroom in Montreal, at least I am going to ask Mr. Huntington if we may."

At this the board of directors relaxed in a broad smile.

"And we will have the girls of our factory out and they will sing. Nickie will lead them. He is wonderful! Nickie is the late Mr. Roger Tempest's little lame son, he is only ten, but with his violin he leads our girls in their songs and trains them beautifully, too. They sing French-Canadian and Scottish and Irish songs and Negro Spirituals, and a lot of other things. They are quite wonderful I assure you and they are such dear girls. Oh, I just wish you could come out and see them. Oh--I do hope you won't really close us up. You see they have all worked for me since they left school, and their fathers worked for my father, and I would hate to see them shut out from the factory, where they earn their own living and--well--I am sorry to have taken all this time, and I haven't really told you what I want to say."

The big blue eyes looked at them earnestly with anxiety, and there was a suspicion of tears not far away. "I would like to answer questions--I believe that would be better--for you know what I ought to have told you. And oh! I brought you some copies of my last statement. Perhaps that will help you better to understand." She handed the President a number of copies of her last monthly statement, which Mr. Huntington passed round to the members of the board.

"And here are some pictures of the stencilling and decorations that we use in our nursery furniture. People just love them. And I brought also some pictures of our singing and dancing classes and all that, but perhaps you haven't time to look at them." She laid the pictures on the table beside her.

One of the members reached for them and proceeded to turn them over with two members looking over his shoulder. Soon smiles began to broaden into grins and explode into chuckles. From hand to hand the pictures passed round the table and soon the whole board of directors were delightedly commenting on the pictures before them.

"Who did this work?" enquired a member.

"Most of them were done by the girls themselves, some of the best, however, are the work of Nickie Tempest. He has marvellous hands, and is wonderfully clever at his work." No questions were asked as to the condition of the business at Riverside as presented in the statement. A brief glance was sufficient for these men, trained as they were to examine statements of all accounts for weak spots and disturbing gaps.

"This statement, Mr. President," said one of the members, "should be mimeographed, and sent round to every office in our company, to show our secretaries how a monthly statement should be prepared."

"Quite right," replied Mr. Huntington. "It is an excellent statement, terse and complete."

"Thank you, Mr. President," said Sylvia, "for letting me come; thank you all for letting me speak. I am sorry I have taken so much of your time. But I must go. We are really quite busy in our factory."

"Before you go, Miss Sylvia," said Mr. Huntington, rising from his chair, "I will ask Mr. Selby Manners, our vice president, and our most fluent speaker to express our appreciation of your visit."

Nothing loath, Mr. Selby Manners told her what they thought of her in words of beautiful courtesy, "And I believe Miss Sylvia, that I can promise you that the Riverside Mills will be the last plant in our corporation that will be closed."

The President then gave the board a brief account of his visit to Riverside Mills. "I assure you, gentlemen, it was one of the happiest experiences in my life. You would all enjoy a visit."

"Why not go out?" enquired a director.

"Oh, would you?" cried Sylvia. "I could give you tea, and you would understand so much better."

The directors looked at one another in amused silence.

Then the vice president said:

"I have the honor to accept, on behalf of the members, your very kind invitation. We shall be very pleased to visit you any day that you may say."

"Would to-morrow do?" enquired Sylvia eagerly.

A laugh went round the table. "Good business!" said a member. "I should say that to-morrow would be a very appropriate date."

"Oh, thank you very much. You won't expect anything but a simple tea."

"We expect a very happy time," said Mr. Huntington, as he opened the door and showed her out.

The afternoon tea given to the Board of Directors of the Central Canada Lumber and Furniture Corporation at Riverside Mills was an event long cherished in the memories of the members of the Board. They inspected the sawmill and the various departments of the factory. With critical and appraising eyes they noted every sign of careful management, but the charm and grace of the young lady, and the bright and cheery efficiency of her assistants, awakened in the minds of the visiting directors feelings of admiration and appreciation of the quality of work done, and of the spirit and cheerful pride of achievement on the part of all the workers in labour which too often is a dreary and monotonous grind.

But more than all were they delighted with the musical part of the entertainment. Nickie's violin numbers, too, given at Sylvia's request, were received with appreciation. Many of the directors had known the little lad's father, and his pathetic handicap, his beautiful face, the excellence of his musical performance, and his obvious delight and pride in the work of his class, went to all hearts.

When the president and vice president came to take farewell of their hostess, Mr. Huntington said: "This is a new experience for me and for all the directors. This spirit that we have all felt to- day, if present in all our factories, would solve most of our industrial problems."

"Very fine indeed," said the vice president, "and let me assure you, my dear young lady, the last machinery to stop in this organization of ours will be in this room."

"Some girl, eh Manners?" said Huntington, as they walked together toward their car.

"My dear Huntington," replied the vice president, "this is indeed a rare experience. Unfortunately there is much that is sordid and unpleasant in our industrial system. To me the experience of this afternoon is like coming upon an old English garden in the midst of a city slum. What charm, what grace, what sweet dignity, in that young lady, and all combined evidently with rare efficiency and strength."

"Yes," replied Huntington, "and her relations with that little lad and her service to him are quite beautiful. Did you speak to the boy at all?"

"I did," replied Manners, "it was a deeply moving experience, listening to the little chap as he told the story of the new life and light and cheer and hope that this girl has brought to him. I knew Roger Tempest well, a man of high character, though somewhat inaccessible. I fancy that this girl has brought into the lad's life a new interest, a new work to do and a new joy in service to others."

"You have got it exactly," said Huntington. "And my dear Manners, when we close down this place, as I am afraid we shall be forced to do in a few months, we must find some way by which this unit shall be kept intact, and possibly even handed back to its original owner."

"If we can, Huntington, if we can," replied Manners. "But business is a hard and merciless thing. Still, we must do something. This is a rare girl. She has a heart for her people and a head for this kind of business. It is in her blood. She is a Glengarry girl remember."

CHAPTER XXIII

The spring break-up this year was earlier than usual, and soon after Easter the Blackwater River floated down booms of hard wood timber safely to the Riverside Mills. A gay and heartsome sight it was to the old rivermen, carrying them back to days forty years gone.

Sylvia was cheered to have such a lot of good timber safely boomed and landed at her mill before the Company had closed down the Riverside plant. But, as if he had been waiting for the hard wood rafts to appear, almost immediately after their safe arrival Sylvia had a telephone message from the president of the Company announcing the imminence of this fatal event.

"Come in and see me," he said.

And with sickening heart Sylvia went and found Mr. Huntington in deep gloom.

"It is a bitter disappointment to me. This was no merger for stock selling purposes," he explained. "It was a genuine effort to reduce production costs and increase the profits to all engaged in the work. And now, my dear, I am about to make you an offer, the best that can be had from the receivers. The assets under normal conditions would be considerable, but when a collapse like this comes all values are shattered. The receivers, therefore, offer you your whole plant and outfit at a figure a good deal better than the ratio of assets to liabilities. They offer you the plant and outfit at ten percent of the rated value of its assets."

"And what does that mean?" asked Sylvia.

"The figure is five thousand dollars. It is a terrific slaughter in values. But value in a case like this is what is offered you."

"I would gladly give more," said Sylvia. "It is worth much more than that."

"My dear, you will find that under the present circumstances, if put up at auction it would bring a good deal less. This is not a question of value, it is a question of buyers. There are none."

"I am sorry, Mr. Huntington," said Sylvia. "But I will accept your offer. I think we can keep the furniture factory going, and perhaps also can do something with the mill. Mr. Huntington, you have been more than good to me. I wish I could help."

"Miss Sylvia, this is a bitter experience for me, but it is a pleasure, a great pleasure, to be able to offer you such a deal, and I wish you all good luck with it. Goodbye, Miss Sylvia. It is a joy to have known you."

Sylvia left the office with a sad and sinking heart. The future of the plant was exceedingly doubtful. It was very questionable if she could keep the business going at all.

At dinner that night the whole company agreed that Mr. Huntington's offer was quite generous.

"I feel quite mean in taking it," said Sylvia.

Professor Hale, who was spending his Easter holidays in the city replied: "You will find that values will soon be mere shadows."

"Why so?" enquired Jack sharply.

"All the signs in the financial sky say so," replied the Professor.

"The world seems to be full of trouble," said Aunt Elizabeth. "Even poor Mr. Matheson, here, has his share."

"Oh, mine are very slight," said Mr. Matheson with his usual genial smile.

"And what are your special trials?" asked Jack. "Not the market I hope."

"No, not the market," said Mr. Matheson.

"No, it is his Session," said Aunt Elizabeth impatiently. "Fancy, they are opposing the organization of the Young Men into what they wish to call the Canadian Christian Brotherhood. The Session object also to our minister going to address that Club of Mr. Derring's, because it is a Socialist organization. And, worse than all, they wish to dictate to their minister what he should preach."

"Oh please," said Mr. Matheson, "let us not speak of my troubles. I am not worrying."

"All the same it is outrageous," said Professor Hale.

"Yes indeed," said Sylvia.

"Beastly, isn't it, Jack?" said Peggy, who had come out with Jack by special invitation of Sylvia.

But Jack made no reply. He was apparently in no mood for discussion to-night.

"I think I am going to be a Socialist," said Peggy gravely. "They are the only people, I believe, who are thinking about the underdog these days. That Mr. Derring, now, I do think he must be a fine man. Sylvia was telling me about the work he is doing there in the west side of Montreal. He seems to be the right kind of a man."

"Yes indeed," said Sylvia. "Mr. Matheson can tell you about him."

Mr. Matheson's description of Dave Derring set him forth as a strong resolute, utterly sincere man, with a passion for justice, and with a deep sympathy for the unfortunate and oppressed of his fellow men.

"Rather superior type of man, Mr. Matheson," said Jack in a somewhat sarcastic tone.

"In many ways, yes," said Mr. Matheson. "Not without defects of course."

"And yet," said Jack, who appeared to be in an unfortunate mood, "for thirteen years he avoids all churches, he cherishes feelings of contempt, hatred almost, for church people. Do you know to be quite frank he struck me as being a man of colossal egotism, not to say cheek? His attitude on that famous Sunday night, to yourself, sir, and to your people was that of an insufferably conceited, self- righteous man. He makes the mistake common to his sort, especially those of the enthusiastic, socialistic type, namely of imagining that ability to point out vices in others is a proof of the opposing virtues in themselves. I confess," continued Jack, apparently throwing all reserve to the winds, "I am getting a bit fed up with these superior chaps. Most of them are men who because of some defect, or more frequently because of sheer laziness, have made a failure of life, and therefore are filled with envy and hatred of those who by ability, hard work and self-denial have made good. There, that's quite a speech," said Jack with a little laugh. "But I'm not going to apologize."

Jack's attitude was that of a man who had flung his hat into the ring and was ready for all comers.

It was rather unfortunate that the man to accept the challenge should have been Professor Hale, for whom Jack had lost all respect, and for whom he had a feeling of jealousy. It was more unfortunate that it should have been Sylvia who felt called upon to back up the Professor in his position.

The argument waxed warmer and warmer until it approached the verge of acrimony.

Finally Jack, whose nerves were on the ragged edge of a breakdown, threw aside his customary courtesy of manner in reply to a statement of Professor Hale's to the effect that the capitalistic class is largely composed of men, who, because of their wealth, as a rule are overbearing and tyrannical.

"Overbearing?" said Jack. "Ah! take your friend Derring for instance. Of course, Professor Hale does not know what he is talking about. He labours under the disadvantage of knowing neither the circumstances, nor the personalities, round which this argument turns. The rest of you who were present that night, however, will remember the whole attitude of this man. His conceit, his arrogance, his air of superiority, his utter lack of courtesy, his insufferable insolence toward the minister, were all clearly indicated by his classifying the whole congregation composed of respectable and decent people, among them the company at this table, as a lot of damned hypocrites; which meant of course, that he was the only honest and sincere man present. This is the sort of thing that I feel I have the right to resent. I might indeed, have retorted, as of course I would not, that he and those he represents were a lot of damned bounders, to use his own adjective."

"Aunt Elizabeth," said Sylvia with face pale and lips trembling, "will you please excuse me?"

"Sylvia?" said Aunt Elizabeth. "Will you please sit down."

"I cannot sit still while my friends are being insulted."

"Sylvia, you will please sit down," commanded her Aunt. "Perhaps you will allow me to be judge in this matter."

After a moment's hesitation Sylvia resumed her seat.

"Miss Murray," said Jack, rising from his chair, "if I may be permitted."

"Jack, you will please allow me to preside at my own table. At least you can remain until dinner is over."

"As a matter of fact," broke in Mr. Matheson in a cheerfully pleasant voice, as if the discussion had been about the weather, "I am inclined to agree with Jack in much of what he has said."

Sylvia gasped.

"But," continued the minister, including the whole company in a genial smile, "I always find it rather more conducive to cogency and clarity in argument to confine the discussion to the abstract rather than to the personal. It reminds me of a story that one of my professors in Edinburgh used to tell his class annually." The humour of the story the genial countenance of the minister, the calmly reasonable tone of voice enabled the company to recover their equanimity to a certain degree.

Needless to say the discussion was not resumed.

After the dinner was over Jack went to Aunt Elizabeth and asked to be excused. "I have an extra bit of work to prepare for to- morrow," he said. "Besides, I confess I am hardly fit company these days for civilized people. My business is rather distracting. It is an entirely honest business," as he continued his head went back a little, "as was my father's before me. It might be for the present however, that it would be better that I should keep away from those to whom I represent a doubtful element in the community."

"Jack," said Aunt Elizabeth, with an air of quiet dignity, "we shall always be glad to see you."

"Oh Jack," protested Peggy, "I wanted to hear Sylvia sing to-night, some special songs."

"I am not singing to-night," said Sylvia coldly. "Aunt Elizabeth," she continued, "Jack has his opinions and I have mine. We cannot expect him to change his opinions to suit us."

"Sylvia," said Aunt Elizabeth sharply. "What is the matter with you? What do you mean?"

"The meaning is quite obvious, Miss Murray," said Jack quietly. "I am sorry I am not an economist. I have only the theories of my class, I suppose, and I certainly don't propose to give them up, even if they may not agree with economic experts, no matter how distinguished."

"Why Jack, my dear boy," began the minister.

"Pardon me, Mr. Matheson," said Jack bowing very stiffly. "Peggy, do you propose to go home with me?"

"Professor Hale will take you home, Peggy," said Sylvia.

"Certainly, with pleasure," said the Professor.

"And let Jack go home alone?" said Peggy indignantly. "Not much! Wait a minute, Jack, I shall just run up and get my things."

"I am sorry, Peggy" said Sylvia, as they went upstairs together "that you should have to hurry away. Professor Hale would have been glad to drive you home."

"No doubt," said Peggy, "but that is no reason why I should go with him. He'd talk my head off with his economic stuff. That man tires me. Wasn't it terrible of Jack?" continued Peggy, as they reached Sylvia's room.

"Unpardonable," said Sylvia.

"Oh, I don't know about that," said Peggy. "Jack's nerves are in a bad state these days. He blows up for nothing. He is carrying a big load and doing big things. I am told that old Scaiffe wants him for a partner. So I think there is a good deal of excuse for Jack. Besides that Professor is a very opinionated sort of chap."

"Professor Hale is a brilliant scholar," said Sylvia, "and recognized as a sound economist."

"Well," said Peggy, "he is the kind of person that always makes me mad, and just now I think Jack needs someone just to kind of cuddle him, you know."

"Why not do it then, Peggy," said Sylvia, with a little laugh.

"Wouldn't I love to. That is what he needs all right, and it is a shame he can't get it."

"Oh, he's not a baby," said Sylvia.

"Well, I don't know. He is a kind of baby. All men are at times," said the worldly-wise Peggy. "Why do you argue so much with him, Sylvia? Jack is in this business of his and can't get out, and you are all against him here. Poor Jack!" The tenderly maternal tone irritated Sylvia. "Yes," continued Peggy, "Jack needs someone to cuddle him, as I said before. And if he were mine I'd give him all he wanted, I can tell you, and Jack could take a lot."

"How do you know, Peggy?" asked Sylvia rather sharply.

"Well, I can tell. There are some boys, you know, that need a lot of it and are the better for it."

"Peggy, what are you talking about?" said Sylvia. "Rather disgusting, I call it."

"Oh, Sylvia, you don't know you're alive. I bet you never kissed a boy till you kissed Jack."

"Of course not," said Sylvia indignantly.

"There you are," said Peggy triumphantly. "You don't know boys."

"Peggy, I am ashamed of you. A young girl like you. It is positively disgusting."

"There you go again," said Peggy. "You are engaged to Jack. I bet you never kissed him till he couldn't breathe."

"Peggy, you are positively insufferable," said Sylvia.

"Well, that is what he needs," said Peggy, "and if he doesn't get it from you, he will get it from somebody else."

"Peggy, you are perfectly dreadful. You speak as if you were an animal. Surely we have minds and souls."

"Oh, rats!" said Peggy. "You don't kiss a man with your soul, but with your lips."

"Stop this talk, Peggy. You are almost coarse."

"No," said Peggy, "only modern. All this hold-off stuff was all right for our grandmothers."

Suddenly Peggy became very serious.

"Sylvia," she said, her words coming out in a perfect torrent, "I have been talking like a fool, but it is all true, and if you don't watch out you will lose Jack. For God's sake, don't you want him?"

"Peggy, you are a silly little school-girl," said Sylvia. "I am sick of your talk. You are all animal. Your mind is asleep. Of course I love Jack. But surely love is not an unintelligent tickling of your nerve centres. Love is a noble thing, but love is not everything. There is such a thing as conscience."

"Conscience?" cried Peggy. "What has conscience got to do with loving a man. It is right to love him, and it is right to show him you love him. What has conscience got to do with it? You talk to me about animal passions. Don't they belong to us. What is love? The greatest thing in the world, the Bible says so. Animal passions! Come on down. But listen to me," here she turned suddenly and fiercely upon Sylvia, and with sobs choking her utterance she continued. "Listen to me. That boy wants you. He wants your love, and you talk economics. You don't deserve him and you will lose him if you don't hold him by your love. He wants to feel your body in his arms, your lips on his lips. Economics? Damn economics! There! You made me swear, and I promised mother I would never swear without telling her. But if it's got to be love or economics--I am going to say it again--damn economics!"

"Peggy, you are a silly girl, I think we had better stop talking about this," said Sylvia, and led the way downstairs.

"My dear Peggy," said Jack, "have you the very least idea of time."

"Yes, if it is a good time, Jack. Poor Jack he is tired and worried," she said to Aunt Elizabeth, "but I will look after him, smooth out his wrinkles, kiss away his scowls and put him to bed a sweet and dimpled baby. Come along Jack, darling."

In spite of his wrath, Jack grinned at her.

"I know well what you want, Peggy."

"What?" said Peggy with a daring look in her eyes. "So do I! I am going to drive and Jack can go to sleep if he wants to very much, eh Jack?"

Aunt Elizabeth could not forbear a look at Sylvia's face. What she saw there startled her. Cold as ice it seemed, but behind the ice a gleam of fire.

"I think I shall go right up to my room, Aunt Elizabeth," said Sylvia. "I have some papers to look over. Say good-night to Mr. Matheson and Professor Hale for me."

"Very well, Sylvia," said her Aunt, looking as if she longed to take her in her arms but dared not. She met the Professor in the hall and gave him Sylvia's message.

"Good-night, Miss Murray, I quite understand," he replied.

"Love is a terrible thing," said Aunt Elizabeth going into the room. "Terrible yes, but after all the greatest thing. Yes! but a terrible thing. Look at these two young people for instance."

"The trouble is not their love," said the minister, "but the denial of love, the thwarting of love," he added with a voice of infinite sadness.

"Yes, you are right. Oh! you are very right," said Aunt Elizabeth. "It is the thwarting of love. Pride will do it, or ambition more frequently, or anger, or jealousy. Oh! I know it well."

The minister sat with his eyes quietly resting on her face.

"May I tell you?" said Aunt Elizabeth in a low voice.

"It might be good," he said.

"I loved her father, we quarrelled. I thought it was for conscience' sake. I know now it was pride and self-will, and with it all a foolish jealousy. He married my sister, my only dear, dear sister who loved him. There, that is the story of my life, a common story," she said with an attempt at a laugh. "But if it was my fault, and it was, oh yes, all my fault, I have paid the price in full."

"But love was yours, the greatest joy is in loving. No matter what comes of it--nothing--nobody can ever deprive you of that. That is my experience," said the minister.

Together they sat in silence.

"You have told me," he said. "May I tell you?"

Aunt Elizabeth nodded.

"Twenty years ago I thought I loved. It was merely a thing of the eye. She was a girl of rare beauty, and sweetness and grace. It was before I entered college. We couldn't wait. We were married, I twenty, she seventeen."

"She died," said Aunt Elizabeth.

"No," said the minister, a deep pain in his voice. "For eighteen years she has been in a home for the incurably insane."

"Alive?" cried Aunt Elizabeth, sitting sharply erect. "Your wife!" Then her hands went suddenly to her face. "Oh! My God! My God! have pity."

"Do not grieve for us," said the minister. "We both found out very soon that we had never known real love. We remained good friends and good comrades for two years. She lost her first baby. She never recovered."

Aunt Elizabeth sat, her face tortured with pain. "Oh, why didn't you tell me-- long ago?" she said. The hopeless agony in her voice startled the minister. "You should have told me long ago," she said.

He made no pretence at understanding her. "We may still have love, Elizabeth," he said taking her hand in his.

She looked up quickly into his eyes and read their message.

"Oh, Mr. Matheson--Malcolm," she cried giving him both her hands, "is it indeed true, and can it be right that we should love?"

"Right? Love is never wrong. Even if it must endure all things. Love suffereth long."

Long they sat at the fire talking over the wonder and the gladness of the thing that had come into their lives.

"What shall we do, Malcolm?" she said at last.

"We shall just love each other in the meantime. This to me is so wonderful that it is joy enough to go on with."

"Not for me, Malcolm," whispered Aunt Elizabeth, and her arms went up about his neck. "Oh, I am a foolish old woman, but my heart has been starved for love all these years. I want you, Malcolm, I want to see you every day and all day long. I want to feel that it is right for you to hold me in your arms. Oh! I am a fierce and terrible lover, I warn you."

"It is the only love that is worth while," said the minister. "A love that gives all and demands all. But in the meantime Elizabeth, we shall be patient till we see the way a little more clearly. I had never dreamed of this joy coming to me, hence I have never thought of the possibilities. But something we shall work out. In the meantime we must be patient."

"Oh Malcolm, I am ashamed to say it, but it must not be too long."

"Ashamed?" said the minister. "We are both at the best time in our lives. We love each other. There is no shame in that. I promise you we are not going to miss any of the joy of loving for the rest of our time together. In the meantime, like the soldiers in the trenches, we must just 'carry on.'"

CHAPTER XXIV

Sylvia slept little that night. Gentle as was her disposition, she had much of her father's stubborn will and with it his sensitive Puritan conscience. All night she fought a desperate battle against conscience. Her two years' experience of industrial life and business affairs had made questions of economics, not mere theories, but life itself, and that life not only her own, but of all those for whom she could not escape responsibility. With her hereditary instincts and her life-long training, there never was any doubt as to the issue of the conflict. Her principles she could not surrender, though her heart might break.

In all this struggle she was quite fair to Jack. She could not escape the feeling that she had been unreasonably impatient and harsh with him at dinner. But she could not escape, either, the clear conviction that Jack's attitude was not, as she had once thought, a thing of mere temperament, but a habit and a principle of his very life. She could not ask him to surrender his principles any more than she could bring herself to surrender hers. They were both tied to the wheel of fate, from which there was no escape.

During the days that followed life was to her one bitter and unceasing conflict. She was too proud to fly any flag of distress. Fortunately the days were filled with business interests and grave problems connected with the very existence of the plant. The negotiations for the transfer of the Riverside Mills to herself took up every spare moment of her working hours, and indeed of her rest hours as well. Her nights, however, were her own.

Throughout this period of heart struggle and business anxiety the presence of Professor Hale was to her a great source of comfort and strength, and with his aid the details of the transfer were in due time completed in early summer. The lumber camps were closed up and the men paid off, with a month's pay for very worker. Roderick Macdougall was retained for service in the sawmill which must be kept going until the hard wood logs were turned into lumber. But her old love for her work seemed to have evaporated. She longed to be free from the responsibility and from the toil of the whole business. But it would be like running away from the front line on the eve of battle, for she could not avoid accepting Professor Hale's opinion that a period of industrial depression was steadily drawing near. From her experience of the past six months she could see no prospect of a market for the products of the plant. The furniture factory, it was just possible, might be able to carry on, and work in the tannery, strange to say, under old Sandy Brodie's care seemed to be meeting with distinct success.

For the past few months all communication with Jack had ceased. True, he drove out once a week, sometimes alone, often with Peggy, who apparently was always eager to accompany him in these trips, to visit Nickie.

Jack had suggested that the people of Hilltop House should be relieved of the responsibility of Nickie's care. But both Aunt Elizabeth and Sylvia pleaded that no change be made, not only for their sakes, but for the sake of the boy's health and enjoyment.

"Why take him away from us?" said Aunt Elizabeth. "He is no trouble to us. He is like sunlight in the house and you can see that he is growing stronger every day; and he is quite happy."

"But it is not fair," said Jack, "that my brother should be a care to you. I know that he is growing stronger every day. What you are doing for him I don't know, but you are making him over inside and out."

It was Nickie himself, however, who settled the matter.

"I am going to stay with Sylvia," he said in a voice of definite decision. "I like Sylvia and I think she likes me too."

"Nickie, darling," cried Sylvia, "you know I love you."

"Well that seems to settle it," said Jack. "Love after all should settle things. Besides I can see quite well it would be a rotten change for him to come home with me. It is like a cemetery there now. If Aunt Arabella and Peggy had been at home it would have been different. Indeed they both were anxious he should come to them, but they are doing Paris at the moment." The sadness in his voice, and in his eyes awoke in Sylvia's heart an intolerable pain. It took all her fortitude to refrain from throwing her principles to the winds and herself into his arms.

Jack's next words, however, steadied her.

"Then too," Jack continued, "the financial situation in the city is perfectly appalling, the pace is tremendous. I am driven day and night. What is coming God only knows. One can hardly keep sane. Meantime it is a great joy to me to know that Nickie is with you here. And I wish you both to feel that you have the whole gratitude of my heart for what you are doing for the lad. Well good-bye--you lucky, lucky boy. Be sure now you obey Aunt Elizabeth."

"I do what Sylvia says," said Nickie stoutly.

"Oh yes, he is Sylvia's boy," said Aunt Elizabeth.

After he had gone, Sylvia went upstairs to her room to fight once more the bitter fight. "Oh," she groaned, "is it worth while after all?" But there was her terrible conscience. And besides every day was bringing fresh proof that a great and terrible crisis in the financial world was rapidly approaching.

During these days Sylvia made frantic, but vain efforts to get into touch with Jack. His firm though badly shaken was still able to weather the storm, but as to his private speculations no one seemed to have much knowledge. Tom Foster's firm, Chamberlain, Jessop and Foster, came down to utter ruin with a crash. A cable brought his mother and sister hurrying home from Europe.

One morning, the latter part of July, Mr. Timothy Brady drove up to the door of Riverside Mills, and entered the outer office. He still carried his jaunty air, his Corona cigar still hung in the corner of his mouth, his hat had still its gay tilt over the left ear.

"Ah, good morning, young ladies," was his salutation. "Nice quiet corner you have here."

"Oh, Mr. Brady," cried Sally springing excitedly from her desk. "How is International Nickel?"

"Say, didn't you unload when I told you, young lady?"

"Oh, I was just going to, but--"

"Listen to me," cried Mr. Brady. "That telephone book. Who is your agent?"

"Well--well--Bartie Bingle used to look after my business, but recently Mr.--Mr. McGarrick has been--"

"Get him--get him at once! Here let me have that telephone book. What's his number?"

Mr. Brady took hold of the telephone, got his man and began to speak. "Mr. McGarrick, I'm speaking for Miss Sally Long. Yes, she's right here. I am acting for her. Brady is speaking, you know me. She wants to sell International Nickel. Do you get me-- no, no. Now look here young man, can you take an order or not? Yes! She's right here. All right speak to her."

Covering the phone with his hand Mr. Brady spoke in a low, almost savage tone to the girl. "Tell him not to wait one minute, every minute is a point--Don't argue with him--order him to sell."

As the result of an excited and somewhat heated conversation Miss Sally was relieved of her holdings of International Nickel.

"You got anything, Miss Frances?" asked Mr. Brady.

"I am in Imperial Oil," said Frances faintly.

"Sell!" said Mr. Brady. "Don't wait a minute or you'll be sorry."

In a few minutes Frances too had got rid of her holdings in Imperial Oil at what was considered that day ruinous figures, but which two days later proved to be an exceedingly fortunate sale.

"Now," said Mr. Brady, "can I get to the Lady?"

In a moment he was in Sylvia's office.

"Good morning," said Sylvia, rising from her desk and turning anxious blue eyes upon him. "Have you got any word of Jack?"

"Steady on, my dear, steady on!" said Mr. Brady in a quiet voice. "Jack is all right. I saw him yesterday. I gave him your message. He is a dandy that boy, cool as a frigidaire ice pan."

"How was he looking, Mr. Brady?"

"Well not as fit and rosy as one would like, but his hand is as steady as a crook's on the butt of a gun, so don't you worry about him."

Sylvia sat down without a word.

"Say, Miss Sylvia, you want a drink. I have got a flask right here. What about a nip, eh? First aid you know. No? All right."

"How about you, Mr. Brady? Has the market hit you?"

"As you see, Miss Sylvia, clean as a baby."

"Everything gone? Surely not everything?" asked Sylvia.

"Every--little--thing," said Mr. Brady with a cheery smile.

"Mrs. Brady will have her house," said Sylvia anxiously.

"She had, but she put it into Canada Breweries. She's got the froth now."

"Oh, Mr. Brady, how terrible. What are you going to do?"

"Sell fanning mills for you, if you will let me," replied Mr. Brady gaily.

"Mr. Brady," said Sylvia in a hesitating voice, "you bought my stock. I knew you were paying too much. I'd like--oh--won't you let me give you some of it back," she concluded rushing her words eagerly.

Mr. Brady turned his face away, rose, walked slowly to the window, stood studying the landscape a few moments, coughed, walked slowly back to the desk, sat down and leaned forward with his hands on his knees, tears quietly running down his cheeks.

"Say, Miss Sylvia, I am nervous these days, I haven't been used to the kind of thing you're giving me." He pulled out a silk handkerchief of a delicate shade of green and wiped his eyes. "Miss Sylvia, them's tears. Did you notice 'em? Do you know, I'd like to kneel down and kiss those little shoes of yours?"

Sylvia too, was wiping her own tears away.

Mr. Brady continued, "I have been fighting bulls, bears and wildcats the last two months. I took my mauling, and none of them ever heard a whimper out of Tim Brady."

"I am sure that is true," said Sylvia, "I know you are a brave, good man."

"My dear, my dear," said Mr. Brady hurriedly, "stop it! I bought your stock at $52,500.00 and sold it for $65,000.00 within a month, and I guess he made something out of it."

"But I would like to do something," said Sylvia with pleading eyes.

"I say," said Mr. Brady throwing up his hands. "Will you drive me out av this office? But thank the Blessed Mother Mary that there's women like yourself left in the world. I can go out and meet the divil himself now with a smile, and so I can."

There followed a silence of a few moments, then Mr. Brady proceeded once more.

"Miss Sylvia, it is a bold thing I am doing now and you will forgive if it is too bold. It is about that boy of yours. You need not shake your head at me. He has cleaned up a lot of money. He is a clever lad, you hear me. But the consequence is that there are lots don't like him and some would do him harm, real deadly harm. I told him about it. I wanted him to get away for a few weeks. He could go quite easy until the first heat is over, but he laughed at me. Now couldn't you or that young kid he's playing around with, get him out of town for a few weeks, that's all? I wouldn't have told you if I didn't know what I was talking about. It is terrible times we are in anyway."

When Mr. Brady had taken his departure, Sylvia sat with her head in her hands. It was indeed a terrible time. Ruined men with vengeance in their hearts were on the trail of those who had been their undoing. She had heard rumors of Jack's successes. All successful men in these days had their enemies, sometimes rightly so. After long pondering she took up her telephone and called Peggy Foster. Peggy was resourceful, and Peggy was going about with Jack everywhere these days.

Peggy did not take her message lightly.

"Things are surely awful just now in the city," she said. "Every man is carrying a gun. Jack has one in his car in a pocket right before him. And I have heard that there are men following his trail. He knows it too, but he laughs at them."

"Well Peggy, I was desperate so I thought I'd call you. I don't see Jack much nowadays."

"More fool you," interrupted Peggy crossly.

"And you are going about with him a good deal," continued Sylvia.

"Every chance I get, you may just bet. If you don't want him, I do!"

"Please Peggy, not over the phone."

"Oh, I can't stand your silly nonsense," Peggy said angrily.

"But Peggy," Sylvia went on, "I hear you have brought a grand man from overseas with you."

"So I have, and he is a dandy. But my Lord! if Jack would only--"

"Oh Peggy please--"

"Oh go to blazes!" snapped Peggy and slammed down the telephone.

In half an hour Jack called Sylvia on the phone.

"Peggy has just been telling me some fool stuff, which she said she had from you. She made me promise to call you up about it, and get what particulars you might have."

"Oh, she made you promise?"

"Well, you don't think I would take it so seriously as all that on my own."

Sylvia repeated to him Timothy Brady's message.

"Oh--oh Tim has it all right, I know all about that. I am not worrying."

"But do take care, Jack," begged Sylvia.

"What difference does it make to you, particularly?" enquired Jack.

Sylvia made him no answer.

"Hello--hello--" came over the phone.

"You should not hurt me more than you must, Jack."

"Hurt you! Of course I can't hurt you very much. I saw Professor Hale the other day and I gather things are going very nicely. May I not congratulate him and you."

"Good-bye," said Sylvia, and shut off.

It was true that only the previous night Reggie Hale had told her that his engagement with Pearl had been broken off, and had asked her if there was any hope for him.

"I am afraid not, Reggie," she had said, but with some hesitation. Which answer, to her surprise, had apparently somehow cheered him.

Within ten minutes after her conversation with Jack, Peggy was on the telephone again.

"Just to say, Sylvia," she said in a bitter tone, "that you are a heartless fool, and it would serve you darned well right if you married that economic blizzard, Reggie Hale. That's all!" The telephone was banged to her ear.

It was still early in the afternoon, but Sylvia had received so many shocks during the day that she closed her office and went home, weary in body and mind and sick at heart. She let herself quietly in and opened the door of her Aunt's room. With a gasp she stood paralyzed. As she entered, her Aunt Elizabeth sprang from the lounge from beside the minister, her hair dishevelled, her cheeks aflame, and on her face a look of dismay.

The minister rose slowly and calmly looked at Sylvia.

"You might as well know now as later," he said, "we made up our minds indeed to tell you to-night: your Aunt Elizabeth has done me the great honour of consenting to be my wife."

"Your wife? Aunt Elizabeth?"

"Are you very sorry, Sylvia, dear?" Aunt Elizabeth murmured.

"Sorry?" shouted Sylvia. "Why I never imagined--"

"I know--it seems silly for old people like me," said Aunt Elizabeth twisting her fingers like a child caught in the preserve closet.

"Old people?" exclaimed Sylvia. "What nonsense! You are the youngest thing in this house. Why you darling, it is perfectly glorious!" And Sylvia rushed at her Aunt and catching her in her arms kissed her again and again.

"What about an old fellow like me?" asked Mr. Matheson humbly.

"Old fellow? Old fiddlesticks! Why it is the jolliest thing I ever heard of in my life." Sylvia ran to him and gave him her hands. The minister drew her into his arms.

"It is awfully good of you to be so glad," he said and kissed her.

"Why, Uncle Malcolm," she cried with a little rapturous giggle, "it is perfectly, gloriously splendid. Isn't it just?"

"Gloriously splendid," said the minister, "at least for me."

"And for Aunt Elizabeth, and for me too. Oh, I am so happy about it dear, dear Auntie. Now then," continued Sylvia, "we'll have the biggest and bestest dinner ever. What a shock to poor St. Paul's and to all the old maids and widows." She danced delightedly about the room. "Well I must say," she continued, "I sometimes thought of it as possible, and even wished for it, but never imagined it could really come off."

"Why Sylvia, you never guessed it?" Aunt Elizabeth appeared horrified at such a possibility.

"Well, not exactly guessed. But lately I had my suspicions. I caught a look in your eyes now and then."

"Never! My eyes? You never did. Oh, how dreadful!"

"Yes, and in the minister's too," said Sylvia. "Though he was more guarded. But do tell me how it happened."

"Sit down Sylvia, please," said the minister. And he proceeded to tell the story of his marriage and of the calamity that had befallen his girl wife some twenty years ago. "And," he added, "I was on the point of arranging for a legal separation when only yesterday a letter came bringing news of my poor wife's death, a happy release after twenty years of misery."

After a few minutes' silence Aunt Elizabeth said: "And Sylvia, there is something more to tell. There is a little congregation on the West side of Montreal of working people, you know, where Mr. Derring's friends are, and they want Malcolm to be their minister. Malcolm is thinking about it. It might be good to get away from St. Paul's."

"Of course, it would," cried Sylvia. "I am sick of St. Paul's."

"There, I told you, Elizabeth," said the minister, "that Sylvia would like it."

"Now for our announcement dinner," cried Sylvia. "Come Auntie, let's get it going. Just ourselves, eh?"

"Well, perhaps Professor Hale," suggested Aunt Elizabeth timidly. "He is an old friend, and really he is a fine man and doing so well. Malcolm has seen his new book and he says it is very well done."

"No!" said Sylvia sharply. "Just our own selves."

After some minutes of quiet thought in her room, however, Sylvia said to herself. "Why not? It is their party, not mine, poor dears. Aunt Elizabeth would like to have Professor Hale." She caught up her private telephone and called a number. "Professor Hale can you come over to-night for a quiet little dinner. It is Aunt Elizabeth's special invitation. Oh, I have a great bit of news for you. Can you come?"

The Professor could certainly come.

"Now," said Sylvia to herself, "what about Peggy? No, she couldn't come alone. No--oh no--that would never do."

With a little moan she threw herself face down on the bed. "Oh, I am dead tired of it all," she groaned. "I must get away for awhile, I can't stand much more of this."

It was a glorious dinner. Aunt Elizabeth and the Professor kept up a continuous stream of gay chatter. The minister was in his best form full of humorous tales and clever conversation. Sylvia took the opportunity of laying before them what she had long pondered and recently discussed with her staff and some of her workers. It was a plan for transforming the Riverside Mills Company into a co- operative concern. The main features of the Company would be (1) Control should go with all factors of the organization, capital, management, labour and the consuming public. (2) All profits should be equitably distributed among all four factors. (3) The insurance of life, health and work should be borne by the company. She had talked over this plan with her staff and the workers, and almost all of them were eager to try the experiment.

After the dinner Professor Hale, acting as secretary for the dinner party, set down in the logical sequence the outline of the constitution.

After the company had all gone, the old weariness came back upon Sylvia with redoubled force, the old heartache, the old despair. "They say," she said to herself, "that time cures all heartache, but look at Aunt Elizabeth. She has carried her sorrow for twenty years." The prospect almost drove Sylvia to despair, till from sheer weariness she fell asleep.

CHAPTER XXV

The extreme gravity of the situation in the financial world made Sylvia hesitate to launch her new scheme of a cooperative company. By Professor Hale's advice she determined to postpone final action.

"These crashing securities do not represent only paper losses," said Professor Hale. "Money which has been flowing in little rills into the stock market has mounted to the enormous figure of two hundred and twenty million dollars. This, mind you, is new money which has come from working people, from washwomen, day laborers, shop girls and clerks, as well as from the professional class, merchants and manufacturers. All this means an enormous reduction of purchasing power in the country. Then, too, the heavy losses of stock holders in great financial concerns will further reduce this purchasing power. For instance, I understand the stockholders in International Nickel lost over six hundred million dollars, in Imperial Oil five hundred and fifty millions, in Brazilian two hundred and sixty millions, in International Petroleum two hundred millions, and so on. No wonder that manufacturers can find no market for their products. I think it would be wiser for you to wait a little while, and meantime you might have a talk with your own working people. See what the rank and filers think."

Sylvia took his advice and decided first to visit Sandy Brodie.

She found him busy at the vats in the tannery. "I'll just come out and talk to ye," said Sandy. "It's no that refreshin' in here."

"What a lot of skins you have, Sandy," exclaimed Sylvia, as they entered the storeroom, "and what lovely leather. You surely will have no difficulty in selling these."

"Ay! it is sound leather, none better for a' their chemicals and new fangled methods, indeed none as good. Give us time and we'll get our market with those that know."

"Well, I do hope so, Sandy," said Sylvia, "because I am thinking of making a change in our organization here. You remember I spoke to you about it some time ago."

"Ay, I remember," replied Sandy.

Thereupon Sylvia laid the details of her plan before him to which Sandy listened with keen and intelligent interest.

"What do you think of that now, Sandy?" she asked.

Without an instant's hesitation Sandy made answer.

"Ay, it is a gran' scheme, Miss Sylvia. But like a' things that have life there is one thing that is important."

"And what is that, Sandy?"

"The heid. Gin yersel' were at the heid the plan micht be a gran' success, but the question is can ye git a heid, a manager?"

"Well," said Sylvia, "I was thinking of James Macdonald."

"Ay, Jimmy's a fine honest hard workin' lad, but will he put the hairt into it? Can he handle yon singin' lassies? Will he haud Mac your engineer back from the drink? Ye ken weel Mac stays sober because his manager visits his sick wife. Will Jimmy do it? And will a' the lot of them haud together when Miss Sylvia is no here at the heid?"

"But, Sandy, surely we can get a good man as manager."

"Lassie, lassie, there's many a guid manager with a fine heid for figures and gran' organizing powers, but to haud him fast to this kind o' wark, that's the question. The passion for siller, ye ken, is gone from this concern. What ye need is a man wi' a passion for the people, as in yersel', Miss Sylvia. That will do it. But where will ye get that passion in a man?"

"And can no man be got with a passion for the people, Sandy?" asked Sylvia.

"Ay, that is the question ye'll need to find an answer for."

With a sinking heart Sylvia next called on James Macdonald.

"It seems a fairly reasonable scheme," replied James Macdonald, when Sylvia had placed the details before him. James was sitting at the desk opposite her, the papers in his hand. Suddenly he laid the papers down and looked at her, a burning light in his eyes.

"Where would you be in this scheme?" he asked.

"I propose to retire," she said. "I might be president of the company or something like that, but I am rather tired just now, and I thought--"

"Count me out," said James Macdonald.

Sylvia looked at him in amazement and dismay.

"Why, James, you believe in the co-operative idea?"

"I do, no matter about that. Count me out!" said James emphatically.

"I thought," said Sylvia faintly, "you might be our manager."

"Your manager, and you out of it." A grey pallor crept over his face. "Why do you think I have stuck to this plant these three years? I have had plenty of offers. Why did I stick here? Because you were in it. The whole plant could have gone to blazes but for you, Sylvia. It was you--oh---I know I'm a crazy fool--I know it is a bit of ghastly presumption, but there it is. Until that young stock gambler came along I had a faint hope, but since then that hope has gone. Even then I could not tear myself away. The chance to see you every day, to hear your voice now and then through the plant, to catch a glimpse of you going in and out, that held me--that held me here."

He rose quickly to his feet, a fierce hungry light in his black eyes.

Sylvia rose in terror for what he might do next.

"No! Don't be afraid," he said slowly, with a pitiful smile. "I could easily die for you, but never could I harm a hair of your head. Now I am going."

"Where, James?" she said in a trembling voice. "Oh, James, you have been so good to me--so good to me."

"Good?" he laughed bitterly. "Good? No, selfish. It was the breath of life to be near you. Good-bye."

"Where are you going, James?"

"Where? I have not thought. As far away as the world will let me."

And without another look at her he walked out from the office and from her life.

In a kind of blank despair, and with an overwhelming sense of defeat, Sylvia went to her minister and told him her trouble.

"Take a little more time, Sylvia, my dear. Sandy Brodie is right. The key to success in the co-operative movement is a driving passion, in the man responsible for its direction, for service to the people. Never fear, your man will come. There are such men, but you will need to be patient."

"Oh, I am weary of it all," said Sylvia. "I am weary of everything."

"You must just wait," said the minister. "Meantime I would like you to drive me out to the west side to-night. I have a lecture on The Substitute in Modern Industry for the Profit Motive, and your Aunt Elizabeth would like to come along."

"Oh, all right," said Sylvia, "I will drive you and I will chaperon you and Aunt Elizabeth."

"Professor Hale assured me he could find a man," continued Sylvia. "But I'm not so sure. Professor Hale is a dear. He is very clever, but I am not so certain that he quite understands men."

"Yes, Professor Hale is a fine man, and an able man," said Mr. Matheson. "And he is eager to serve you."

"He would like to," said Sylvia in a very low voice. "He would like to," she repeated, "and perhaps it might be as well."

"Again, Sylvia, I would say--wait! wait until you are very very sure. Twenty years of suffering are at the back of my very earnest prayer that you wait," said the minister in a tone of grave solemnity.

And Sylvia resolved that so far as Reggie Hale was concerned she would wait till she was much surer than she was now.

CHAPTER XXVI

The following morning Sylvia was late in appearing at her office, and soon after her arrival she was surprised to see a large and very handsome Rolls-Royce drive up to her office door, and more surprised to see Peggy spring from the front seat and come into her office.

Without a word of greeting Peggy cried:

"Oh, Sylvia! There is the most awful trouble!"

"Why, Peggy, what is the matter?"

"Jack is nowhere to be found. He is not at his office--not at home-- he has been out all night--He drove me home last night at nine o'clock--no one has seen him since--I'm sure they've got him at last. Last night we had--oh--a perfectly lovely time--Jack was so awfully good to me--just treated me, not like a little girl, but as if I were quite grown up--oh--he was perfectly darling--and I was sure he was going to come right across."

"Right across?" echoed Sylvia.

"Yes, you idiot--with your darned economic stuff you've lost him anyway--and I was sure he was going to--well, settle it right there-- And I did my level best to--I just--oh, you don't understand-- you'd be shocked--and I guess Jack was too--I certainly made him breathe quick. I thought it might be my last chance-- and he has been so lovely to me these last days--you know--no, you don't know-- what do you know about it? You economic frost. But Jack knows, all right, so I just went right out after him. Perhaps I hit him too hard. Oh, it was sickening--after he got his breath again he looked at me with that funny smile he can give you--as if I were a nice, but naughty little baby--Well, he looked at me with that smile--I could have smacked him--and what do you think he said?--I don't care what you think--he said: 'Say, kiddie! Your technique is very smooth, but I suggest you change your lipstick'--Oh--oh--I could have slowly strangled him to death just to see that horrid little smile fade off his face. He took all my kisses like a baby taking candy--but he wasn't giving me anything-- he was thinking lipstick. Why do I tell you all this now? I'll tell you--I want to hurt you. He's gone! He's gone because you didn't care a darn whether he lived or not. And you sit smiling there--I suppose you have been freezing up to that economic iceberg of yours. Well I hope to God you freeze together--And you smiling there--And nobody knows where Jack is."

"Well, you see, I'm very happy, Peggy," said Sylvia.

"Happy," cried Peggy--"and Jack--but you don't care for Jack-- What's all the glee about, anyway? Engaged, I suppose!"

"Yes, I'm engaged. And I'm very, very happy--" said Sylvia joyously.

"Ugh, I am wasting my time--Here I've come on the chance you might know where Jack was. Well, I've kept poor Alistair out there long enough. Good-bye--" said Peggy turning toward the door.

"Come up to the house, Peggy. You haven't seen Aunt Elizabeth since--"

Peggy paused. "Oh--yes--Aunt Eliz--lovely isn't it? It is good some love affairs go right. Yes, I will go with you--I'll drive you up--Alistair is really a very nice boy."

Alistair, when he saw Sylvia, sprang from the car and greeted her with a bow, and an expansive smile. During the drive to Hilltop House he could do no more than remark that it was a lovely day-- that this was his first visit to Canada--that the St. Lawrence was a very noble river--that he did not know how long he would stay-- which, with appropriate intervals for breath took up the time till they were at Hilltop House.

While the young ladies rushed into the house, Alistair preferred to remain in the car. "He's awfully shy," said Peggy, "but we'll teach him a few things, I guess."

Aunt Elizabeth met them with smiles and blushes.

"Look at the young thing," said Peggy, "with her blushes. Say, she's knocked off twenty years. Well, you darling Auntie," she said, folding her in a maternal embrace. "You clever kid. You could give us all pointers. There must be something in the atmosphere of this home--ministers and professors. Well--I don't know--As to professors everyone to her taste. I confess I can't get terribly het up about that."

"Peggy ran out to tell us," said Sylvia, "that Jack is not to be found. He is not at home--"

"No," interjected Peggy, excitedly, "and you know we were warned that they were going to get him."

"And they very nearly did," said Aunt Elizabeth. "Poor Jack. If it hadn't been for Sylvia and Malcolm."

"And Aunt Elizabeth," cried Sylvia. "Oh, she was funny!"

"Funny? Jack? Are you all crazy?" said Peggy. "Do you know where Jack is?" she demanded of Sylvia with a look of dawning suspicion.

"Not exactly," said Sylvia, "but we had word from him, and he is all right--Well not quite all right--They nearly got him--but he is recovering," said Sylvia giggling.

Peggy looked from one to the other. "Well, I'll be darned. I believe he is in the house. Say!" she shrieked at Sylvia--"it's him and not your darned old iceberg after all. Oh, you little devil--you certainly took me for a ride--I'll shake the liver out of you." She caught Sylvia by her arms and shook her till she could not get her breath.

A door opened quietly upstairs.

"Well," Peggy continued, "since Jack is all right, I am going. The altitude is too high for me here."

"You won't see Jack?" said Aunt Elizabeth.

A hot blush came to Peggy's face. "No!" she cried decidedly. "Certainly not!"

A genial smiling face beamed at them over the balustrade upstairs.

"Run up and see your Uncle Malcolm," said Sylvia, still convulsed with giggles.

"You bet I will," said Peggy running up the stairs two at a time followed more slowly by Sylvia and Aunt Elizabeth.

The minister came to meet her at the head of the stairs.

"Well," exclaimed Peggy, when the minister had let her go. "You certainly are the quick thing--or you've had a mighty good instructor."

At this point the bedroom door opened. "Oh, I say!" said a voice. "Can't I get in on this?"

Peggy made a dash for the stairs, but Sylvia was too quick for her.

"Come, Peggy, you must see Jack," she said.

"All right," said Peggy. "Go on."

They all trooped into Jack's bedroom. Peggy took one look at him and went into a scream of hysterical laughter. And small wonder. An ample dressing gown of grey lamb's wool of the minister's enveloped his form, but shyly peeping out at breast and neck were the pink frills of one of Aunt Elizabeth's nighties. About his head was a bandage with ominous stains showing in spots.

Peggy's hysterical laughter subsided at the sight of the stains.

"Oh, you poor boy," she said in broken tones, as she came slowly toward him. "They very nearly got you--They might have got you."

Jack drew her toward him, and kissed her.

"Yes, Peggy," he said quietly and kissed her again.

For a single moment she lay upon his breast struggling to regain her control. Then she flung herself from him.

"Tell me," she said.

"Well, it was Sylvia," began Jack.

"Nonsense, it was Mr. Matheson--Uncle Malcolm," said Sylvia.

"Not at all," said the minister, "it was Sylvia and Aunt Elizabeth."

"You are all mad," said Peggy angrily. "Will someone please give me some coherent account of what happened?"

"Well," said Jack, "I'll tell you what happened. I had been visiting Nickie. I knew he was to be alone."

"We were down at the west side at a lecture that Uncle Malcolm was giving to his socialist friends," explained Sylvia.

"And," continued Jack, "I was just getting out of the town on the highway, when a car came honking behind me, and in passing crowded me into the ditch.

I was properly mad. Two men jumped out and came running. I had opened my door to meet them when one of them dealt me a blow on the head--a black jack--it turned out to be. I fell back into my car. The other reached for me trying to drag me out, but I caught him a kick that sent him back. The other came on and struck me again--and after that I don't know much of what happened."

"Now, it is my turn," said the minister. "We were driving along the highway at a moderate pace--Sylvia driving--when I saw two cars on the road side, and two men moving about them. 'That's Jack's car,' cried Sylvia, throwing on the brakes, 'and they are at Jack.' She was out of the car like a streak, her aunt shrieking at her to come back, and tearing open the door of Jack's car, disappeared inside. I thought I'd better see what she was doing."

"My turn," said Aunt Elizabeth. "When Sylvia dashed out in that reckless way-- What could a girl do with two men?--Malcolm was out like a--like a--like a--"

"A thunderbolt," said Jack.

"Exactly; and rushed like a crazy man right at the fellow. I heard a shot, a crash of splintering glass, and a cry from the car, so I rushed out. There was Malcolm and one of the men struggling on the ground. I heard another bang--I thought they were shooting at him, so I just jumped in and caught the man on top round the neck and pulled him back with all my might."

"It was me!" said the minister chuckling. "She nearly strangled me. Now it's Sylvia's turn."

"Well, as soon as I saw Jack's car I at once remembered what Tim Brady had told me, you know, Peggy."

"Yes, he told me too," said Peggy.

"So I sprang into Jack's car at the far side. The man was trying to pull Jack out by the legs, and Jack kicking feebly. All at once I thought of what you said, Peggy, about Jack's gun in the case. I looked, and sure enough, there was the case. I snatched the gun and pulled the trigger--there was a crash and a cry--I guess my aim wasn't very good."

"Thank Heaven," said Jack.

"So I just pulled again," continued Sylvia. "The man who was attacking Jack fell back. Once more I pulled, and both men started to run away."

"And she just kept pulling the trigger," said the minister, "so I dragged Elizabeth down beside me and lay as flat as possible to the ground."

"Yes," said Aunt Elizabeth, "with his arm around my neck, almost choking me."

"Yes," said the minister, "and she crying in my ear, 'They are killing her! Let me go!' Then there was silence, and looking up I saw the car moving off down the road with Sylvia still firing at it. Fortunately her ammunition, by this time, was soon spent, and we were safe. Jack was a horrid sight--a mass of blood-- and that's all."

"And about enough too," said Peggy, who with pale face and quick breath had listened to the tale, which, punctuated with shouts of wild laughter had come in turn from each member of the party. "Well, you may laugh," Peggy continued, "but I can't see the joke myself. Only I wish to God I had had that gun."

"Thank God you hadn't," said Jack. "There would have been at least two dead, but highly respectable gangsters on the highway, and an awful mess in the papers next morning."

"Well, I'm blowed!" exclaimed Peggy. "And what about your old conscience and the stock market game?"

"The stock market game? I have decided that I have all I can do to look after my own conscience without taking care of Jack's. Jack will look after his own, I guess," said Sylvia smiling at Jack.

"The stock game?" said Jack. "Well, they have cleaned me out all right. I'm an engineer now."

"And where are you wounded, Jack?" asked Peggy.

"Oh, it is nothing very serious," answered Jack.

"A deep cut in the head that took six stitches," said Aunt Elizabeth, "and an arm dislocated and bruises all over his body. Ah! it was God's mercy that we were not all killed."

"And are you suffering much?" asked Peggy.

"Well, there are some slight pangs, I confess," replied Jack. "But after all it was worth it."

"Worth it?" exclaimed Peggy.

"Yes, Peggy, it was worth it--and worth a lot more. You see I have got Sylvia again."

THE END

www.ingramcontent.com/pod-product-compliance
Lightning Source LLC
Chambersburg PA
CBHW060452290526
45791CB00001B/77